REINVENTING ARCHITECTURE AND INTERIORS:
A SOCIO-POLITICAL VIEW ON BUILDING ADAPTATION

REINVENTING ARCHITECTURE AND INTERIORS:
A SOCIO-POLITICAL VIEW ON BUILDING ADAPTATION

First published in 2013 by Libri Publishing

Copyright © Libri Publishing Ltd.

Authors retain the rights to individual chapters.

ISBN 978 1 907471 73 5

The right of Graham Cairns to be identified as the editor of this work has been asserted in accordance with the Copyright, Designs and Patents Act, 1988. All rights reserved. No part of this publication may be reproduced, stored in any retrieval system or transmitted in any form or by any means, electronic, mechanical, photocopying, recording or otherwise, without the prior written permission of the copyright holder for which application should be addressed in the first instance to the publishers. No liability shall be attached to the author, the copyright holder or the publishers for loss or damage of any nature suffered as a result of reliance on the reproduction of any of the contents of this publication or any errors or omissions in its contents.

A CIP catalogue record for this book is available from The British Library

Book and cover design by Carnegie Publishing

Printed in the UK by Short Run Press

Libri Publishing
Brunel House
Volunteer Way
Faringdon
Oxfordshire
SN7 7YR

Tel: +44 (0)845 873 3837

www.libripublishing.co.uk

CONTENTS

INTRODUCTION 1
Layton REID and Graham CAIRNS

REINVENTION: AN OVERVIEW OF AIMS 3
Graham CAIRNS

1 **ADAPTIVE RE-USE AS AN EMERGING DISCIPLINE:
AN HISTORIC SURVEY** 13
Bie PLEVOETS and Koenraad VAN CLEEMPOEL

2 **WASTESPACE** 33
Graeme BROOKER

3 **REMEDIATING SHOPPING CENTRES FOR SUSTAINABILITY** 53
Kirsty MÁTÉ

4 **ON HUMAN ACTIVITY AND DESIGN – TOWARDS MORE
SUSTAINABLE DEVELOPMENT** 77
Marc FURNIVAL

5 **RE-PRESENTING THE *TITANIC*** 95
Nuala ROONEY

6 **SOUTH AFRICAN PUBLIC INTERIORS:
REDRESSING THE PAST, CRAFTING THE PRESENT** 119
Monica DI RUVO and Amanda BREYTENBACH

7 **FOOTPRINTS FROM THE PAST IN THE WORK OF
MEXICAN ARCHITECT MANUEL PARRA MERCADO** 141
Jaime F. GÓMEZ GÓMEZ and Cinita A. PAEZ RUIZ

8 **AN ARCHITECTURAL GLEANING** 157
Tonia CARLESS

9 **NO LONGER AND NOT YET** 177
Edward HOLLIS

CONCLUSION 195
Graham CAIRNS

CONTRIBUTOR BIOGRAPHIES 197

Layton REID
Ravensbourne

Graham CAIRNS
Architecture_MPS

INTRODUCTION

The design of an interior space is often something done before a building has been built, the designer working with the architect on the realisation of the new project. That said, it is also a discipline inseparable from the re-use of existing spaces, buildings and structures. Whether designed before or after construction, however, the 'interior' exists within a context that is already given and, as such, many of the design issues inevitably overlap. It is our assumption – and indeed, a premise of this conference – that in both cases the interior should be considered as 'an extension to the body'; the body in this case being the physical building that houses it.

As an extension to the body, it opens up the possibility of being defined as a sort of clothing; a wrap or a surface. It can of course be much more than that, involving considerable and fundamental alterations to the body: surgical interventions akin to adding or taking away a limb or plugging in a prosthetic. In this sense, the interior contrasts significantly with the exterior which, by nature, is more fixed, static and controlled. The 'body' analogy, then, also opens up space for us to consider the building and its interior, the shell and its innards, as separated and divorced.

This is ever more the case when the question of building scale becomes an issue, when a large, sometimes enormous, exterior building instigates an inevitable disconnect between the environment outside the shell of the structure and the interior intimacies on the inside. These intimacies may be so physically distant from the building shell as to exist in another world altogether. The developer-led projects that normally instigate this definitive scale-based fragmentation between interior and exterior are, perhaps, most common at the moment in Asia, a place where the economic context for development is very different to the current one in Europe or North America.

Despite this geographical disparity, many smaller European and North American new-build projects share with their super-scaled Asian counterparts a similar disconnection between the interior and the exterior. For many years, the clip-on interior has been part and parcel of commercial developments; today, however, the clip-on exterior is also a common feature. The Ravensbourne building in London, designed by FOA architects and the site of the 2012 IE conference, is one such example. This approach can be seen as recyclable architecture or, equally, as disposable architecture. It has certainly been instigated in an economic climate in which people seek to maximise profit through quick and adaptable construction techniques.

The clip-on exterior, then, is an approach to architecture that raises interesting questions that coalesce around the themes of the conference. Beyond the socio-economic issues it raises, however, a building such as this also points out another question that was considered by delegates: the status of the architect and of the interior designer. Clip-on exteriors present an approach to building that blurs the technical differences between interior and exterior and this, in turn, parallels a potential blurring between the role of the architect and that of the interior designer – something seen as inherent in the adaption of existing buildings. In the case of clip-on exteriors, the architect is appropriating some of the tools traditionally employed by the interior designer whilst, in the case of adaptations, the interior designer is appropriating the materials and forms left by the architect. In both scenarios, an interesting amalgamation of concepts and practices emerges.

Thus, as reflected in our chosen title, *Reinventing Architecture and Interiors*, we would like to suggest that this volume's focus on the re-use of existing structures does not limit its potential relevance to the traditionally, and incorrectly, defined limits of interior design, on the one hand, and architecture, on the other. On the contrary, in the realm of re-use and possibly even new build, these definitions have been blurring for years. Thus, what this book represents is not just a collection of essays from an isolated discipline; these essays represent examinations of the changing nature of the built environment and built-environment practice in a complex and ever-changing socio-cultural, and practical, context.

Graham CAIRNS
Architecture_MPS

REINVENTION: AN OVERVIEW OF AIMS

The history of design has traditionally been a story of new ideas, new theories and, above all, new construction. However, today, the developed world is on the cusp of a new era. The financial crisis, the sustainability movement and the conservation agenda are all leading to ever more alterations of existing buildings and ever fewer new-build projects. This new condition will have major consequences for all those involved in the design of the built environment, both now and in the future.

In one regard, simple economics is bringing into question the need, indeed the desirability, of constructing from scratch. Numerous small- and medium-scale businesses across Europe are seeing the option of extending existing premises as a preferable alternative to new build. At the level of housing, various studies across Europe have revealed the same tendency, as potential 'second- or third-time buyers' alter their existing houses as a cheaper alternative to moving home. The potential long-term consequences for the building industry are significant.

From a sustainable perspective, the same picture can be seen to be forming, at least in certain contexts. The material resources involved in new build make it an ecologically detrimental and damaging option when compared with renovation. This does not mean that every building alteration leaves a minimal carbon footprint or that alteration is necessarily a better environmental option than some of the more advanced 'green' approaches to new construction. Indeed, major adaptations to existing structures can be equally as demanding of resources as new constructions. Nevertheless, if one takes the standard construction templates used for new build across the developed world, the re-use option normally comes out on top in the argument about environmental impact.

All of this sits alongside a now deep-rooted heritage agenda in Europe and, increasingly, in the Americas, Africa and Asia. Invariably, the arguments put forward from this perspective discourage new build when it involves the destruction of existing valued building stock. Even when proposed developments do not mean the complete elimination of existing infrastructures, what we may call 'the heritage lobby' is a significant factor in controlling the adaptations permissible to the buildings that make up our present towns, cities and regions. It is not only a powerful lobby in terms of architecture and design, however: its agendas can and do affect issues of economic development, environmental impact and our sense of 'place'.

The process of adaptive re-use does not, of course, always involve the adaptation of 'old' buildings; buildings that would fall into the traditional heritage category. It can involve the adaptation of relatively recent buildings. This is indeed ever more common as the pace of socio-economic change increasingly leaves all but the most adaptable of our buildings obsolete in one aspect or another, in ever shorter time spans. The lives of our buildings may well be extended through re-use but their original forms are having increasingly shortened effective lifespans.

This specific conundrum is the subject of the opening and closing chapters of this book, which take on the idea of adaptation, preservation, conservation or re-use (call it what you will) from two very different but surprisingly similar perspectives. In our opening chapter, Bie Plevoets and Koenraad Van Cleempoel begin our investigations into re-use with a historical overview of the phenomenon and its theoretical arguments. They begin by identifying a classic division in thought that would plague the practice of building adaption for centuries: the dichotomy between the ideas of Viollet-le-Duc in France and those of John Ruskin in England.

Setting out Viollet-le-Duc's approach to 'restoration' as one that allowed, indeed encouraged, the adaption of existing buildings to the needs of the present generation, Plevoets and Van Cleempoel lay bare the premise of all building renovations. This they place alongside the 'conservationist' approach of Ruskin, for whom old buildings were sacrosanct and should be allowed to exist in wonderful abandonment or isolation from the world around them. The fact that such an approach may lead to 'dead' architecture, in terms of buildings that actually function and contribute to anything other than the heritage and tourist industries, becomes self-evident when mirrored by Viollet-le-Duc's uncompromising, if stylistically straightjacketed, approach.

On the basis of this outline, Plevoets and Van Cleempoel run through almost two centuries worth of debates that either oscillate between these positions or, more commonly, seek some middle ground. In doing this, they introduce the ideas of Alois Riegl and Camillo Boito from the late nineteenth and early twentieth centuries, then move on to discuss the more contemporary arguments of Sherban Cantacuzino and Radolfo Machado from the 1970s. In Machado they suggest we see the beginnings of a theory on re-use that stands on its own and defines itself as distinct from architecture, on the one hand, and conservation on the other; as a practice worthy of recognition on its own terms and, more importantly for them, one that begins to show a sensibility of approach that may offer an indication for the designers of today and tomorrow.

Building on the ideas of Machado, Plevoets and Van Cleempoel end with an overview of contemporary practices which, whilst self-confident and clear in their definition of re-use as an independent practice, lack a subtlety of approach. This renders many contemporary interventions or renovations somewhat sterile or obsessed with function and the technicalities of their own construction. They thus use their historical overview to build an argument for those involved in the adaptation of buildings to draw on the skills and sensibilities of the interior designer. These attributes, defined as 'soft values', are seen as key attributes in sensitive renovation – renovations capable of capturing and developing what they term the 'genus loci of the building'.

Having set out a vision of what building adaptation may be, and having laid out a historical framework that the rest of this book will use as conceptual bedrock, the work of these authors passes over to that of Graeme Brooker, a teacher and author who has been involved in the field for a number of years. In his contribution, Brooker takes on the question of sustainability, albeit from a very particular perspective: that of wastespace. Brooker begins with the premise that we live in a society of over consumption, a society continually producing waste and one that continues to be engrossed with the 'freedom' of the throw-away. Far from submitting to this constant wave of material use and dis-use, however, he identifies numerous examples in contemporary and historical societies of reactions against it.

From the still-legal activity of mud-larking on the banks of the River Thames to the practice of 'spolia' in ancient Rome, he identifies examples of people, individuals and collectives involved in reusing 'what they find' to create anew. In proposing this as a way forward for contemporary designers involved in constructing and re-constructing our built environment, he introduces a number of issues that potentially have fundamental consequences for design as we know it. In this context, the designer, the creator of space or the builder of the monument, must relinquish exclusive rights to ownership: copyright becomes a question for designers as the materials, motifs and features they incorporate into their designs are actually the product of somebody else's labour and imagination.

In proposing a celebration of wastespace, the use of waste in the construction of our environment, he suggests that the 'superfluous landscapes' of our towns and cities can be remade and reimagined. They become sites for design 'hackers' that reconstitute building (and other) elements that allow meanings to carry over from one structure or social sphere to another. He uses the example of the Dutch studio *Superuse* as indicative of this potentially new direction which, he hints, could be applicable to interior design architecture and, by extension, urban designers as well. With the notion of wastespace, he suggests that the designer involved in adapting existing buildings, already a 'waste-spacer' of sorts, could be the epitome of a trend that has begun to establish itself and may even become one of the defining ideas of our generation.

The potential social implications latent in these ideas are picked up in the following chapter by Kirsty Máté who takes on one of the most devouring consumerist beasts in the recent history of commercial architecture: the shopping mall. Places for the production of waste par excellence, these palaces of consumption are examined in the light of recent socio-economic trends that, in the context of the United States at least, have seen them threatened with the possibility of long-term extinction. As Máté points out, they are currently closing faster than they are opening and, as consumer's become ever more environmentally active, their reputation and kudos is only likely to fall even further.

Máté does not exactly celebrate this trend: she doesn't see it as the consequence of the end of the capitalist model of economic production and consumption, but she does see it as representative of a change. This change may not yet materialise and, as she underlines by starting her contribution with the 'shopping malls of ancient Greece', it has been long in coming. One of the things she achieves by retracing the steps of these places of consumption, however, is to underline their importance and their central place in modern Western culture – something that may explain her insistence on examining a possible anti-consumerist future for these buildings in the context of our existing economic model.

In the light of their horrific carbon footprint, both in construction and daily use, and in the context of the current economic conditions in the United States, Máté questions whether these 'spaces of consumption' may not be turned around and converted into 'places of production'. Is it possible, she muses, to adapt the energy-absorbing infrastructure of these buildings and turn them into self-sufficient energy users – possibly even producers? Could, she asks, the tendency of massive chains such as Wal-Mart, Whole Foods, Tesco and others to address the environmental and social consciousness of their products be turned and directed at their buildings?

In asking such questions, Máté raises the possibility of converting the massive parking spaces of these buildings into gardens for the production of crops sold at the point of cultivation; asks whether their massive roofs could be used for water storage and collection; and queries whether their interiors could be designed to be carbon neutral. The application of the most avant-garde technologies of ecological design, together with the major reconsideration of the use of these buildings that she proposes, is presented as much as a utopian polemic as a practical and fully detailed plan. However, the adaptation envisaged here of these existing buildings takes spaces that both produce waste and are in danger of becoming waste and questions how they may be radically reconsidered in the light of current socio-economic circumstances. She asks how they may be made sustainable.

Sustainability also plays a central role in the arguments put forward by the urban designer Marc Furnival. He outlines a project that envisages the renovation of a small existing barn in a semi-rural town as a key element in a much broader sustainable tapestry. Indeed, Furnival's principal argument is that the renovation of buildings should never be considered as separate from that broader tapestry – one that, as an urban designer, he engages with on a daily basis. He thus brings an outsider's perspective to the adaption of existing buildings which insists that the interior designer or the restoration architect has to look beyond the walls of the building they physically operate within.

Furnival describes a proposal for the use of the creative industries as economic and cultural drivers in an attempt to help rebuild the economy and sense of community lost in a region of Spain that has seen constant emigration over the past five decades. The area he deals with, Cabrales, is a former farming region which, after decades of decline, has been left with unspoilt natural scenery and a raft of derelict farm buildings scattered around the region. His proposal, which is currently seeking funding, is to adapt a number of these buildings into artists' residences and studios with the aim of re-using the region's existing infrastructure in very new ways.

He begins his piece with the examination of his own attempts to renovate such a building and thus starts at what, for him, is the smallest possible detail: the single building. After taking the reader through the process of renovation and eventual reconstruction, he employs some of the principles applied at this level of the project to explain the larger proposal within which the building renovation actually sits. This then gives way to more generalised and conceptual comments on how such an apparently alien project in a former farming area may help to rebuild a sense of community, long since lost after generations of people leaving what was once 'a home for life'.

In these final comments, however, Furnival not only calls for interior designers and interior architects to consider more than the building as an 'object' when they engage in renovation: he proposes the necessity of reconsidering the nature of community itself. Just as buildings have to adapt to the changing socio-cultural and economic factors around them, so too do some of our more conceptual notions of living and working that are bound up with them. Thus, he suggests, a project that envisages the re-use of an existing derelict barn can become a key component in something much bigger and, in a sense, much more important: a project that helps rebuild a community.

Furnival's emphasis on the role a single building can play in the economic regeneration of an area, and a sense of community, is taken up by Nuala Rooney, who examines a very different building typology and a very different geographical place. With Rooney, we move from small-scale interventions in semi-rural areas to large-scale and high-profile museum projects in a definitely urban industrial context: the city of Belfast. Rooney examines the recently opened Titanic Belfast, an £100-million museum and tourist attraction opened near the site of the *Titanic*'s construction.

In particular, she questions the role of its major design feature, an interior inside an interior: the reconstructed 'grand staircase' of the *Titanic*. This has been reproduced in full scale and in all its original detail as the museum's principal attraction. Considering this simulacrum first in the context of the arguments of Debord, Baudrillard and Eco, she identifies our tendency to see it as a consumerist folly, a kitsch and tawdry attempt to create (or re-use) the 'real thing' in a world of consumer spectacle. However, she also points out that this feature could be central to the financial success of the project. Thus the possibility that the simulacrum may have a social utility is brought into debate.

Beyond the purely practical question of economics and design's potential to facilitate its growth, however, Rooney's examination of the Titanic Belfast's principal interior attraction raises more conceptual questions about the human need to empathise and our ability to do this through physical objects – even ones that may seem crass to the eyes of a 'cultured designer'. Developing the ideas put forward by William Neill in his examination of the project, *The Debasing of Myth*, she hints at the potential of this (re-used and re-created) interior feature to connect the visitor with deeper emotions.

Despite being an apparently superficial way of memorialising a tragedy and despite its commercial tourism context, the 'grand staircase' seems capable, she suggests, of prompting significant contemplation, one may even say pathos. Thus, Rooney suggests that this twenty-first-century museum premised on the commercial exploitation of an early-twentieth-century disaster may not so easily be explained away by automatically defining it as hyperreal, simulacrum or spectacle. It may well have the power to operate on more significant levels – the practical and economical but also the emotional and humane.

In her explanation of a contemporary project that incorporates visual references to the past, with the aim of boosting the economy on the one hand and creating a new image for its region on the other, Rooney's essay again overlaps with our following one. In this case, this latter is a text whose geographical focus is on a completely different continent. Monica Di Ruvo and Amanda Breytenbach examine the South African government's attempts in the 1990s to use architecture and interior design to kick start the South African economy and help create a sense of a unified and recuperated identity. In doing so, they offer socio-political interpretations centred on three government buildings: the Mpumalanga Provincial Legislature, the Northern Cape Provincial Legislature and the Constitutional Court.

They begin, however, by pointing out that the period of transitional government in South Africa coincided with a time of raised awareness amongst designers of the environmental implications of their work. As such, they begin by underlining the role these projects played in tabling these issues in the South African context. More specifically, they identify how these buildings were intended to showcase South African arts and crafts as part of a drive to promote a new creative economy in the country that would move it away from low-mark-up agricultural production to high-mark-up designed and manufactured goods.

Promoting the sale of these goods was seen as potentially providing a source of work for the vast numbers of unemployed people in the rural and semi-rural areas of the country, and these buildings were expected to facilitate the achievement of those ends. Furthermore, they were intended to operate alongside community projects for the training of local people in these and other fields. Consequently, Di Ruvo and Breytenbach examine the rich decorative interiors of these buildings as elements in a national-level economic policy that clearly placed interior design within the broader tapestry of socio-economic factors underlined as important by Furnival.

Beyond the purely economic, however, Di Ruvo and Breytenbach argue that these buildings were expected to create a particularly South African 'sense of place' that was at once modern and traditional, in equal measure. They were thus seen as symbols of the South African majority regaining power and were intended to present an image that celebrated liberation but which also celebrated the recuperation of the past. In examining this political, economic and symbolic context, they draw on the work of cultural theorists and historians and, inevitably, take on some ideas from the realm of post-colonial studies.

Di Ruvo and Breytenbach, then, present us with projects that attempt to incorporate traditional interior elements in predominantly modern architectural shells for what we call symbolic and political ends. Much the same can be said of the essay written by Jaime Goméz Gomez and Cintia Paez Ruiz, who examine the work of the post-revolutionary Mexican architect Manuel Parra Mercado in similar terms. Here, we are presented with a political interpretation of the work of an architect and interior designer whose projects are generally considered apolitical idiosyncrasies operating within the context of state-sponsored modernism in the years after the Mexican Revolution.

Starting off by laying out the history of that revolution and the shift to the political left it instigated, Goméz and Paez identify the dominant design ethos of the period as one of a modernist ilk and argue that, whilst not banned, to operate outside it was potentially problematic. It is for this reason that the projects of Parra that they outline are all domestic, being private residences commissioned by individuals rather than the state. As a designer who wished to incorporate a richer, more historic symbolism into his work, Parra's opportunities to build the large-scale and attention-grabbing projects of his contemporaries were simply non-existent.

What Goméz and Paez do is describe a designer who, principally through the interior of the individual house, made a sort of political anti-statement: one that celebrated the individual, the historic and the traditional; one that sought to invest the home with what Bachelard called the 'poetics of space'. In drawing on Bachelard to examine the interiors of Parra, they clearly attempt to identify the gulf that existed between Parra's work and that of his contemporaries, modernists working on large-state projects.

In place of a homogenised, industrial aesthetic that celebrated the modernity of the state, they argue that Parra gave us intimate and historically laced spaces of intuition. Despite their emphasis on Bachelard, however, what Goméz and Paez primarily underline is the deliberate re-use of historic elements, symbols and materials in Parra's works. They call these historical references 'footprints' and stress their antithetical position when compared with the architectural preferences of the government of the time.

These 'footprints' often involved salvaging materials and elements from old sites, buildings that had been left to decay and ruin because they lay outside the then-accepted aesthetic canon. They are not just symbols of a personal (and thus political) stance, then: they also open up the work of Parra to a progressive ecological interpretation which the authors acknowledge through the writings of the Mexican architect and critic Carlos Mijares Bracho. In this regard, they identify that Parra – nicknamed 'the thief' for his preference for reusing found materials – was in certain ways a pioneer for the Mexican architects and interior designers of the next generation; architects and designers inspired by his eclectic re-use of elements and his political insistence on the importance of the individual.

Goméz and Paez then frame their arguments about Parra in three ways: the personal, the political and the ecological. In this regard, the ecological is seen as the re-use of found objects and this principal, also identified as a modern trait by Brooker, is the explicit subject of our penultimate text by Tonia Carless. Carless takes on the notion of 'gleaning', the activity of searching through debris to find things that can be re-used and incorporated into anything new – in her case, primarily architectural renovations. Her starting point is somewhat different to those of the other authors in this volume, in that it begins with a film, *The Gleaners and I* by Agnes Varda.

Varda's documentary film is the focus of her introduction to the theme and notion of gleaning and she uses it as a metaphor for the design projects she later examines. Picking up again on some of the theorists already mentioned, Baudrillard in particular, Carless attempts to define gleaning, and architectural practice when seen as operative within its context, in the terms of Marx and Lefebvre. She thus clearly positions her interpretation and promotion of 'an architecture of gleaning' within a political framework. That framework is intended to question the nature of capitalism as a consumer-led economy, on the one hand, and to open up the possibility of seeing design as a work of activism, on the other.

This she primarily does in the second half of her text, in which she presents a number of design proposals carried out by students working within the intellectual framework of gleaning and Varda's film. These experimental projects cover a whole range of scenarios and the author takes us through their initial conceptual exercises before leading us onto the projects themselves. These projects include: a 'city factory and construction library' off Commercial Street in East London; a 'high-level urban pier' in an existing, squatted and re-used building, re-named Non-Commercial House Free Shop; and a 'menagerie and manufacturing laboratory' for spider silk, all in the same area of London.

Each of these projects is premised on the idea of re-using found elements, objects and building sites so as to redevelop areas seen as waste, as useless. In this sense, they represent literal manifestations of the idea of 'gleaning'. However, many of the ideas contained in these projects are far from literal or obvious and include the notion of re-using the sounds of the city in vibrating architectural skins. The projects Carless describes clearly function to reveal avenues for further development that the author seeks to follow by putting the notion of 'architectural gleaning' into practice.

In many ways then, Carless brings us back to some of the ideas marked out early in this volume: the notion of wastespace and adaptive re-use as discussed by our first contributors. In the final chapter of this book, Ed Hollis completes this circle and brings us right back to our first chapter. He reintroduces the ideas of Viollet-le-Duc and John Ruskin with which Plevoets and Van Cleempoel began but also picks up where they left off in another sense. Whereas our first authors suggested the practice of adaptive re-use was in need of a reorientation that would incorporate the interior designer's sensibilities, what they called 'soft values', what Hollis suggests is very different. He suggests that the best option is to do nothing.

In a way, this proposition may be seen as echoing that of John Ruskin and his concern with allowing old buildings to remain in their current state through a careful process of 'conservation'. Hollis's ideas, however, have to be considered in the very specific context within which he works: the debates about the possible re-uses to be given to a very specific building on the outskirts of Glasgow, St Peter's Seminary, designed and built in the 1970s but, by 1987, left as a ruin.

Hollis charts the debates that have surrounded this building and the attempts by local residents either to vandalise it or to have it demolished. However, he also charts the attempts of developers to re-use the building and give it a new commercial life. Both have failed. On the one hand, Hollis identifies how the building's concrete form makes it a difficult building to demolish through vandalism or redevelop through glossy renovation schemes. On the other hand, however, he also argues that it is such a programmatically specific building that attempts at re-use are thwarted by a second issue: its planning.

With regard to new build, he suggests that there is a clear lesson: design a building programmatically and you'll end up with a ruin. With regard to adaptation, he suggests that there may be another approach (or at least, one applicable in certain contexts): do nothing; allow ideas to emerge; act tentatively; work slowly. His essay documents the implementation of this approach through the work of the Glasgow arts charity, NVA (Nationale Vitae Activa). NVA is a collaborative group of designers, artists, activists and authors that has, to all intents and purposes, taken over the development of St Peter's and is planning on doing nothing – or at least, very little.

Their argument is that a designer-led project is likely to lead to the imposition of a one-dimensional, perhaps one-generational, project; a project that may respond to some specific need of the moment and may well make money for the developer behind it, but that is unlikely to produce a long-term solution for the building. This, they suggest, should be allowed to evolve and emerge more naturally, as local people come to terms with the building, come up with multiple innovative uses for it and, importantly, experiment with its inhabitation. Such an approach to 'design' cannot be architect- or interior-designer led and cannot immediately serve financial ends. It has to be allowed to grow and change.

This final essay, then, represents a proposal that inverts the position laid out at the beginning the book and serves as a suitably challenging conclusion that seeks to consider the re-use of buildings from a socio-political standpoint. This is a book that does not see design as an isolated activity or the building as an isolated object, but rather envisages design as an extension, or microcosm, of the cultural context that surrounds, moulds, forms and cajoles it. As we indicated at the beginning of this piece, that context is one in which the traditional emphasis on new build in the design and construction industries may well be under threat; a context in which financial, ecological and cultural limitations are placed on the amount and type of new construction we engage with.

It is a context in which re-use, adaptation, renovation and remodelling all come to the fore. It is a context in which the interiors of buildings may well become more important than their skins and in which distinctions blur between the interior designer, the interior architect, the architect and, as some of the authors here stress, the urban designer and the planner as well. In this scenario, it is not only the nature of the design of our built environment that may evolve; it is the nature of our professions and the definitions we apply to them.

Bie PLEVOETS and
Koenraad VAN CLEEMPOEL

PHL University College & Hasselt University

ADAPTIVE RE-USE AS AN EMERGING DISCIPLINE: AN HISTORIC SURVEY

Plevoets and Van Cleempoel begin by identifying a classic division in thought that would plague the practice of building adaption for centuries: the dichotomy between the ideas of Viollet-le-Duc in France and those of John Ruskin in England. ...

They... use their historical overview to build an argument for those involved in the adaptation of buildings to draw on the skills and sensibilities of the interior designer. These attributes, defined as 'soft values', are seen as key attributes in sensitive renovation – renovations capable of capturing and developing what they term the 'genus loci of the building'.

1. Introduction: the Tension between Architecture and Heritage Conservation

Working with existing buildings so as to repair and restore them for continued use has become increasingly important in contemporary architectural practice today. The reasons for this are multiple and include the contemporary world's understanding of the need for sustainable development patterns, the current economic climate's need for less costly physical architectures and an ever increasing awareness of the benefits of retaining our architectural heritage. All of this adds to the importance of what can be called 'adaptive re-use'. This term, although not fully established in the minds of people involved in the design and construction industries, is useful and is premised most obviously on changing the function of buildings as the needs of the economies and societies that originally gave them birth evolve.[1]

Figure 1: Facade of a housing block, Siena, 2010

The phenomenon it describes, however, is far from new. During the Renaissance, for example, monuments from ancient times were often transformed for new uses and materials from one building used in the construction of another. During the French Revolution of the eighteenth century, religious buildings[2] were, after having been confiscated and sold, polemically adapted for industrial functions and military uses.[3] These generally 'pragmatic' interventions tended to occur outside any notion of what we may call today 'heritage preservation'.[4] The driving force behind them tended to be purely functional and financial.[5]

The beginning of more theoretical discussions on adaptive re-use, as a way to preserve historic monuments, only really started in the nineteenth century when it quickly became a debate split between two opposing perspectives. One orthodoxy can be described as the 'restoration movement' led by Eugène Emmanuel Viollet-le-Duc (1814–79) in France; whilst the other may be defined as the 'conservation movement' led by John Ruskin (1819–1900) and his pupil William Morris (1834–96) in England. This debate has morphed over the last century and a half, however, as different theorists, conservationists and designers have sought to define the best approach to dealing with existing buildings.

Today, the approaches and opinions on what 'adaptive re-use' actually is are more multifarious than in the time of Viollet-le-Duc and Ruskin. Indeed, it now represents a field of intellectual and practical activity that operates at the interface of architecture, interior design, conservation and planning. It is a phenomenon that is both challenged and propelled by economic, ecologic, cultural, social and political concerns, but also a phenomenon whose terms of debate are still evolving. A shared and accepted vocabulary and definition of what adaptive re-use is, and what it involves, remain unclear. As a result, many other terms are used interchangeably: 'remodelling', 'retrofitting', 'conversion', 'adaptation', 'reworking', 'rehabilitation', 'refurbishment' and so forth.[6]

In what follows, we will sketch out this terrain and the historical developments that led up to it with the intention of defining some of its terminology so as to offer a fresh theoretical understanding of the discipline as it stands today. We suggest that this understanding has moved on, or at least should move on, from the often-circular arguments on 'restoration versus conservation' that characterised the Viollet-le-Duc and Ruskin debate. The first indications that this debate would move on came through the ideas of Alois Riegl (1858–1905) and Camillo Boito (1836–1914); and their evolved ideas were further developed by more contemporary thinkers and designers such as Sherban Cantacuzino and Radolfo Machado, both of whom made a significant contribution to our understanding of adaptive re-use today. By recapping on the ideas introduced by these and other figures, we hope not only to understand the scene today but also to propose a clearer definition of what it should entail, how it could operate and what directions it may take.

1.1 Viollet-le-Duc and John Ruskin: Re-use and Heritage Preservation

The French Revolution (1789–99) was an important turning point in the history of building conservation. In this period of radical social and political upheaval, the absolute monarchy that had ruled France for centuries collapsed and traditional ideas about monarchy, aristocracy and religious authority were abruptly overthrown. In the place of these long-established notions, the Enlightenment put forward a completely new set of principles upon which to base the seemingly new society that was on the horizon. In an attempt to address the state's financial problems, the National Assembly declared, on 2 November 1789, that all property of the Church – buildings, lands and works of art – were to be confiscated. Soon, they started selling the confiscated properties but also kept many important buildings as state property. In 1790, in the middle of the maelstrom, the *Commission des Monuments* was founded in order to set up an inventory of all national properties seen as 'useful for the public education, of the nation'; manuscripts, books, movable objects and monuments in general. Many of the confiscated buildings that were kept as state property came under the responsibility of this commission which, after the revolutionary dust had settled in 1837, was divided to allow for the establishment of a separate commission responsible for historic monuments. The first chief inspector of the nineteenth-century *Commission des Monument Historiques* was Eugène Emmanuel Viollet-le-Duc.[7]

In the position of architect and chief inspector, Viollet-le-Duc was to be involved in numerous restoration works, many of which were Gothic buildings including icons such as the Cathedral of Notre Dame in Paris, the castle of Pierrefonds and the citadel of Carcassonne. The interventions he proposed in dealing with the task of 'restoration' were often far-reaching and, in some instances, involved adding completely 'new parts' to the building, albeit 'in the style of the original'.[8] This approach was rooted in the nationalist zeitgeist which saw historic buildings as national monuments that were to be restored so as to illustrate the 'achievements of the nation'. Despite being a national movement and one that generally focused on a strict stylistic preference for the Gothic, the influence of the restoration movement as understood and practised by Viollet-le-Duc was not limited to France. Influential architects such as George Gilbert Scott (1811–78) in England and Pierre Cuypers (1827–1921) in the Netherlands were also followers of this type of restoration approach. A clear indication of what it involved and why it still resonates today is evident in both Viollet-le-Duc's work and his writings. Concerning re-use of historic buildings, he claims:

> 'the best of all ways of preserving a building is to find a use for it, and then to satisfy so well the needs dictated by that use that there will never be any further need to make any further changes in the building. … In such circumstances, the best thing to do is to try to put oneself in the place of the original architect and try to imagine what he would do if he returned to earth and was handed the same kind of programs as have been given to us. Now, this sort of proceeding requires that the restorer be in possession of all the same resources as the original master – and that he proceeds as the original master did.'[9]

Here, Viollet-le-Duc clearly gives a mandate for contemporary architects to alter the original building for re-use in clear, direct and practical ways. However, it not only resonates today because it serves as a historical precedent for contemporary physical adaptations of old buildings. In a sense, it resonates with Fred Scott's concept of *sympathy* as developed in his 2008 publication *On Altering Architecture*, in which he compares restoration with the translation of poetry; an act that also requires 'sympathy':

> 'Translation in poetry is akin to the work of bringing a building from a past existence into the present. This carrying over of meaning in poetry is recognized as a work requiring inspiration equivalent to that of the original author and so similarly, one might come to view restoration as an art equivalent to any other related to building.'[10]

Despite its international and historically long-term influence, however, the work and theories of Viollet-le-Duc were not, and are not, free from criticism. Both contemporaries and descendants have been totally against the approach he promoted, with John Ruskin, for example, describing this kind of restoration as 'a destruction accompanied with false description of the thing destroyed'.[11] Elsewhere, he called it 'the most total destruction which a building can suffer'.[12] According to Ruskin:

> 'It is impossible, as impossible as to raise the dead, to restore anything that has ever been great or beautiful in architecture… Do not let us talk then of restoration. The thing

is a Lie from beginning to end... Take proper care of your monuments, and you will not need to restore them.'[13]

In these words, Ruskin lays out his pure conservationist philosophy which is premised on the rejection of the destructive aspects of Viollet-le-Duc's 'restorations' and a preference for the protection, conservation and maintenance of monuments. Ruskin's pupil, William Morris, founded the Society for the Protection of Ancient Buildings (SPAB) in 1877 in the context of the 'Romantic back-to-nature' philosophy of his own circle. The SPAB saw historic buildings as unique creations by an artist in a specific historic context. For them, age in itself contributed to the beauty of a building and, as a result, the marks of age were seen as an essential element to an object or a building. As such they should not be removed or restored but rather retained; much less should a building's function be changed.[14] In their manifesto they state:

> *'It is for all these buildings, therefore, of all times and styles, that we plead, and call upon those who have to deal with them, to put Protection in the place of Restoration, to stave off decay by daily care, to prop a perilous wall or mend a leaky roof by such means as are obviously meant for support or covering, and show no pretence of other art, and otherwise to resist all tampering with either the fabric or ornament of the building as it stands; if it has become inconvenient for its present use, to raise another building rather than alter or enlarge the old one; in fine to treat our ancient buildings as monuments of a bygone art, created by bygone manners, that modern art cannot meddle with without destroying.'15*

For the anti-restoration movement, then, the building should be allowed to exist on its own terms and display its own history. It should be conserved. The differences between these two approaches were to remain a point of debate throughout the nineteenth and into the twentieth centuries.

1.2 Riegl and Boito: Use-value and Rule Books

The polemics of this situation were reframed in the first decades of the twentieth century by the Austrian art historian Alois Riegl who, in 1903, was appointed General Conservator of the Central Commission of Austria. In his essay *'Der Moderne Denkmalkultus: Sein Wesen und seine Entstehun'* from the following decade, he ascribed the prevailing theoretical conflict to the different value system that underlay their views on monuments. [16] Riegl distinguished different types of values which he grouped as *commemorative values* – including age-value, historical-value and intentional-commemorative-value – on the one hand, and *present-day values* – including use-value and art-value (newness-value, relative art-value) – on the other.

For Riegl, the supporters of the restoration movement strived for the combination of newness-value (unity of style) with historic value (originality of style); they aimed to remove all traces of natural decay and to restore every fragment of the work to create a historic entity. By contrast, he suggested that supporters of the anti-restoration movement appreciated monuments exclusively for their age-value and that, for this

Figure 2: Portrait of Alois Riegl, c. 1890

grouping, the incompleteness of an artefact should be preserved as traces of natural decay that testify to the fact that a monument was not created recently but at some point in the past. He described the scenario thus:

> 'the entire nineteenth-century practice of preservation rested essentially on the traditional notion of a complete amalgamation of newness-value and historic value: the aim was to remove every trace of natural decay, to restore every fragment to achieve the appearance of an integral whole. The restoration of a monument back to its original condition was the openly accepted and eagerly propagated purpose of all rational preservation in the nineteenth century.

> 'The rise of age-value in the late nineteenth century generated opposition and conflicts which are apparent wherever monuments are to be preserved today. The contradiction between newness-value and age-value is at the centre of the controversy which rages over the treatment of monuments. ... Where a monument has ceased to have use-value, the consideration of age-value has begun to prevail in its preservation. The situation is more complicated where the use-value comes into play; most would prefer to regard a building in use as something sturdy rather than as something ag[ing] and decaying.'[17]

He points to the innumerable monuments that are still in use or that have received a new use in the course of history and states that:

> 'Material life is a prerequisite for psychic existence, and indeed is more important because there is no psychic life without physiological basis. It follows then that an old building still in use must be maintained in such a condition that it can accommodate people without endangering life or health – any hole or leak must be repaired immediately. In general, we may state that use-value is indifferent to the treatment of a monument so long as the monument's existence is not affected and no concessions whatsoever are made to age-value. Only in cases where use-value is fraught with newness-value must consideration of age-value be even more tightly restricted. [As such] practical considerations allow age-value only in a few exceptional cases.'[18]

What we see in these arguments is that, while Riegl understood both sides of this argument, his inclination, in the final analysis, was to support a form of adaptive re-use: a restorative approach. It was an approach that would be of fundamental importance for Austrian conservation policy but which was rather limited in effect internationally, the abstractness and complexity of his writings making them difficult to translate.[19] 'Der Moderne Denkmalkultus: Sein Wesen und seine Entstehung' was only translated into English in its entirety in 1982, since when his ideas of 'value assessment'[20] and 'conservation theory[21] have been cited with regularity.

Whilst Riegl's approach towards the restoration and adaptation of monuments was rather theoretical, there was another author who took up the polemic previously set out by Viollet-le-Duc and Ruskin in more partial terms: Camillo Boito. Boito presented his paper 'Questioni pratiche di belle arti, restauri, concorsi, legislazione, professione, insegnamento' at around the same time Riegl published his essay on monuments but, for the first time in the history of the debate, proposed concrete and practical guidelines for the restoration of historic buildings.[22] Just as Riegl had done, he compared Viollet-le-Duc and Ruskin and was critical of both. In Viollet-le-Duc's approach he saw a loss of the *material authenticity* of the building; whilst in Ruskin's thinking he found a concept of advocating decay, a notion he rejected as impractical.[23]

Searching for a path between these two arguments, Boito proposed that the restoration method employed for any given project should depend on the individual circumstances of the building or monument in question. In doing so, he distinguished between three methodologies, which he called 'archaeological restoration' (for Antique monuments), 'picturesque restoration' (for Medieval monuments) and 'architectural restoration' (for Renaissance and other monuments). Moreover, he proposed eight methods that designers/restorers could use to allow them to adapt buildings without producing any confusion as to what was old and what was new. These, he suggested, should be applied depending on the nature of the specific project. They included:

> 'Differentiating between the style of the new and the old;
>
> Differentiating between construction materials;

Suppressing of profiles or decorations;

Exhibiting removed old pieces which could be installed next to the monument;

Inscribing the date of restoration (or other conventional sign) in each restored piece;

Using a descriptive epigraph carved on the monument;

Describing and photographing the different phases of the work and placing the documentation within the building or nearby;

Underlining notoriety.'[24]

Although Boito focuses on monuments rather than buildings, his ideas are directly applicable to both situations and indicate another early theory that sought to overcome the two extremes of the conventional wisdom of the time.

1.3 World War and its Effects on Restoration Theory

The influence of Boito on Italian and international conservation practice was to prove fundamental and was a key factor in the adoption of the Athens Charter in 1931, the first international document to promote modern conservation policy.[25] The Charter was the work of the International Museum Office which had been established after World War I to analyse problems related to heritage conservation and, more specifically, the restoration of buildings and even whole towns destroyed or damaged during that war. In general, the charter denounces 'stylistic restorations' and promotes what may be defined as regular and permanent maintenance. It states that:

> *'the Conference recommends that the occupation of buildings, which ensures the continuity of their life, should be encouraged but that these buildings should be used for a purpose which respects their historic or artistic character.'*[26]

Conversely, however, the destruction of the war also created an opportunity for modernist architects to apply their own ideas, not only at the level of individual buildings but also at an urban scale. Nowhere was this more evident, or more forcefully promoted, than in the fourth CIAM congress, 1933. The congress analysed the problems of thirty-three cities and proposed a set of 'statements' for the creation of the ideal modern city. Their analyses led to the now-famous proposal for the division of the ideal modern city into four main functions: dwelling, recreation, work and transportation. [27] The CIAM conclusions on how to deal with historic parts of cities, however, are less well documented. They state that:

> *'Historic objects (separate monuments or sectors of the city) must be retained:*
>
> *- When its existence is not bought at the price of bad living conditions for the population that is compelled to live in it.*
>
> *- When the opportunity is afforded to remove its restricting influence on development by the diversion of traffic round it or the shifting of the focal point.'*

It also states that:

> 'An aesthetic adaptation of new parts of the city to the historic area has a catastrophic effect on the development of a city and is in no way to be desired...'

and furthermore that:

> 'By the demolition of slum dwellings surrounding the historic monuments, green areas can be created, which improve the hygienic conditions in those areas.'[28]

According to the ideas of the CIAM as set out in 1933, then, historic buildings should only be preserved under certain quite specific conditions and were to be seen as 'isolated monuments' in the modern urban fabric. As a result, a clear split emerged between conservation and restoration on the one hand, and modern architecture on the other. Whilst conservationists and renovators dealt with issues of 'scientific restoration' (cf. Boito) and 'value-assessment' (cf. Riegl) with the aim of conserving the remaining historic fabric of the post-war-period and adapting it to the needs of the modern world, modern architecture's belligerent belief in the future and new techniques led it to dismiss existing architecture and see it is a barrier to development and advancement.

In many ways, the clarity of this division was a complete inversion of the situation that had persisted for almost a century: Viollet-le-Duc and Morris, for example, both played major roles in conservation as well as practising as contemporary architects and designers (albeit working in a predominantly neo-gothic style). By the 1960s, however, this oppositional perspective was being challenged and architecture and conservation began to move closer together as a number of important architects and design theorists began to show increasing interest in working with historic buildings.

This shift in the thinking of architects was paralleled by a shift in ideas coming from the field of conservation. Until the nineteenth century, the notion of heritage was limited to antique and medieval buildings but, as a result of the destructions of the two world wars, there was also an increasing awareness regarding the value of buildings from other historical periods, as well as an increasing interest in different typologies as worthy of preservation. Vernacular architecture, industrial buildings and even complete historic cities were now considered as falling within the remit of the conservationist. [29] The increased number of buildings that would potentially need 'conserving' in this new and expanded context was enormous. Inevitably, a reconsideration of the notion of conservation emerged and was reflected in the 1964 Venice Charter which points to the importance of 'adaptive re-use' as a form of 'conservation' practice. It states:

> 'the conservation of monuments is always facilitated by making use of them for some socially useful purpose'.[30]

Thus, the ideas of architects and conservations can, in a sense, be seen as coalescing in the context of the 1960s and '70s.[31] This was to be evident in the work of a number of important architects who began to work with historic buildings as a matter of course and, indeed, as a speciality. Amongst these were Carlo Scarpa (1906–78) in Italy, Raphaël Moneo (b. 1937) in Spain and Sverre Fhen (1924–2009) in Norway. Inevitably, this was to be reflected in both the theory of conservation and restoration and its publication. In May 1972, the *Architectural Review* published a special issue titled 'New Uses for Old Buildings' that dedicated itself to building re-use.[32] It was also evident in two international symposia held in 1977, in Glasgow and Washington DC respectively: 'Old into New' and 'Old and New Architecture: Design Relationship'. Both conferences led to book publications in the years that followed and set the foundations for the emergence of a new discipline in its own right.[33]

An early exponent and beneficiary of this new open theoretical context was Radolfo Machado who published a moment-defining text in 1976: 'Architecture as Palimpsest'.[34] In this text, Machado transcended the 'internal conflict' between the restoration and the anti-restoration movements, on the one hand, and the external debate about whether architectural design has to be based on a tabula rasa, on the other. He did so through the use of the palimpsest as a metaphor which he describes thus:

> 'A term referring to any inscribed surface from which one text has been removed so that the space could be used again for another. In antiquity the word was applied loosely to any writing material that had been cleared and re-used. ... In late classical and medieval times the scarcity and costliness of vellum were so great that it was quite frequently salvaged after the text, which had been inscribed thereon, fell into neglect. ... Some architectural drawings could be regarded as the equivalent of a palimpsest. ... but also the remodelled architectural work itself [can likewise be regarded as the equivalent of a palimpsest], since it can be seen as a text of a special kind that is characterized by the juxtaposition and co-presence of other texts. If an original building is considered as a first discourse that conditions future formal discourses to be inscribed upon it, then remodelling can be conceived of as rewriting.'[35]

Here Machado employs the term 'remodelling' to refer to adaptive re-use and draws an analogy with writing which allows him to consider the overlaying of formal interventions within an existing form (i.e. adaptive re-use) as a creative act in and of itself. It was one that did not destroy the existing context but which was not completely restricted by it either. It would prove to be an indication of what the future of adaptive re-use would conceive itself to be in the coming decades.

2. Adaptive Re-use and a Multitude of Approaches

The 1970s, then, can be seen as the historical moment in which the notion of 'adaptive re-use' came to establish itself as a creative discipline in its own right with a philosophy or a theory behind it. This does not mean, however, that there was, or is, only one approach or theory of contemporary re-use. On the contrary, even then, but especially since then, various approaches have coexisted, each of which offers its own insights and identifies its own salient issues. In this part of our text, we will outline what can be considered to be the four main strategies currently in play, beginning with what we call the 'typological'[36], before proposing a framework for what it could, and possibly should, become.

2.1 The Typological Approach

One pioneering researcher into adaptive re-use during the period of the 1970s was Sherban Cantacuzino, author of *New Uses for Old Buildings* (1975), a book based on the special issue of the *Architectural Review* which he had edited three years earlier.[37] The introductory essay to this book is a history of adaptive re-use and its role in current conservation practice, and is followed by a selection of international examples organised according to the typology of the host space. Cantacuzino discusses eleven different typologies for which he formulates new possible functions: (1) churches and chapels, (2) monastic and religious establishments, (3) fortifications, gates and barracks, (4) town houses, country houses, outhouses and other ancillary buildings, (5) schools, (6) corn exchanges, (7) barns and granaries, (8) mills, (9) maltings and breweries, (10) warehouses and other industrial buildings, and (11) pumping stations.

Cantacuzino followed up this ground-breaking text in 1989 with a second book that had a very similar structure, but which focused on only six typologies that he subdivided into several building types. In this publication, his typologies included: public buildings, private buildings, commercial buildings, industrial buildings, ecclesiastical buildings and rural buildings. Following Cantacuzino's documentary- or category-based approach, several authors including Derek Latham, as recently as 2000, have studied adaptive re-use by analysing case studies through the typology of the host space and have developed ideas not dissimilar to those of Cantacuzino.[38] James Douglas[39] is another author who has also organised part of his extensive work on building adaptation according to the typology of the host space and, although the variety of building types he discusses is limited in comparison to Cantacuzino, he also proposes a number of possible new uses for each typology he discusses. Furthermore, Douglas backs this up by focusing on the reason for the redundancy of the specific building and its typology in the first place.

Numerous other studies have emerged under the umbrella of this genre and investigate the re-use possibilities and appropriate approaches for specific building types, including religious buildings, industrial buildings and housing. Authors and works worthy of mention in this regard are: Alavedra, *Converted Churches*; Morisset, *Quel avenir pour quelles églises? [What future for which churches?]*; Bordage, *The factories – Conversions for urban culture*; Stratton, *Industrial Buildings Conservation and Regeneration*; and Henehan, *Building Change-of-Use – Renovation, Adapting, and Altering Comercial, Institutional, and Industrial Properties*. All are useful in that they offer a practical understanding of the relationship between a typology, its form and the range of activities it is capable of housing; a useful guide, if not a deeply rooted theory like that of Ruskin or Machado.

2.2 The Technical Approach

In contrast to Cantacuzino and the other authors mentioned here, some writers have approached building adaptation as primarily a technical question and, in a sense, have become even less theoretical in their thinking. In this vein, there exist a number

Figure 3: Castelvecchio Museum, Verona, Carlo Scarpa

of 'guidebooks' focused on how to adapt a building so as to ensure it can best accommodate a new function. The first, and best-known, book of this type is perhaps Highfield's *The Rehabilitation and Re-use of Old Buildings* (1987). Here, Highfield makes a distinction between domestic and non-domestic buildings and then goes on to develop a technical chapter in which he discusses the improvements necessary to adapted buildings in terms of fire resistance, thermal performance, acoustic properties, prevention of damp, condensation and timber decay. To back up these specific questions, he also presents a series of technical studies of specific buildings.[40] This reference text has been followed up by numerous other editions in which he has expanded the number and range of technical issues to be considered by the designer adapting existing structures to include issues of sustainable redevelopment.

These issues have inevitably come to the fore in the theory and practice of re-use in recent years as ecological imperatives have imposed ever more complex technical challenges on the designers of these newly adapted spaces.[41] Throughout the literature dedicated to these questions, there is an emphasis on the fact that reusing existing buildings is, in principal, a sustainable practice in itself; the amount of resources needed for re-use being generally far less than those necessary for new constructions. However, all the authors dealing with these purely technical strategies

Figure 4: Interior of the Prado Museum Extension, Madrid (Architect: Raphael Moneo)

of re-use also identify that historic buildings often perform poorly in terms of energy efficiency and, as such, are not invariably beneficial in ecological terms.

One consequence of the increased concern across the design world with issues of environmental importance is, naturally enough, an explosion in the theories and investigations into the issue. Authors worthy of note in this regard are: Giebeler, *Refurbishment Manual: Maintenance, Conversions, Extensions*; Rabun, *Building Evaluation for Adaptive Reuse and Preservation*; Greenan, *Adaptive Reuse of Chimney Flues in Historic Buildings*; Carroon, *Sustainable Preservation – Greening Existing Buildings*;Gelfand, *Sustainable Renovation – Strategies for Commercial Building Systems and Envelope*. The issues and the approaches to adaptive re-use raised by those concerned with the technical side of re-use tend to treat the host space merely as a container that can be adapted for functional, financial and technical ends. Although of fundamental importance for the present and the future of adaptive re-use, there is little scope within the confines of either this or the typological approach for the consideration of conservation and heritage or what we may call the *genius loci* of the host building.

Figure 5: Selexyz Dominicanen, Maastricht (Architects: Merkx+Girod Architecten)

2.3 The Programmatic Approach

A third approach to re-use that has yet to be fully examined in theoretical treatises but which has been applied in reality for some time is the programmatic strategy. This approach involves selecting as a starting point a specific function or program and then subsequently adapting the host building so as to accommodate it. In the studies that have been made into this strategy there tends to be an emphasis on contemporary architecture and interventions into relatively new buildings rather than ones that require the special attention afforded to buildings of heritage value.[42] Given the huge building stock of post World War II architecture across Europe and North America, this is perhaps not surprising, with developers looking to squeeze as much profit out of their building stock as possible.

Nevertheless, it is important that this approach should re-orientate its view to accommodate older structures as well – in particular, given that historic buildings are continually and increasingly being adapted for a whole range of commercial functions: retail, leisure, sport, care or domestic. In each of these cases, the developers behind the projects often specifically look for historic buildings because of their 'authentic character'. In the case of the retail sector, for example, this may be to help in brand differentiation or, more prosaically, because the buildings that occupy our city-centre shopping areas are often old.[43]

The early investigations that exist into the programmatic approach to re-use need to address these and other issues if, as some of its proponents claim, it can help solve not just practical and functional issues but also help alleviate social ills. Being able to adapt buildings to different programmes is essential, they suggest, if issues such as housing for an aging demographic is to be fully developed within our existing building stock. Although the programmatic approach differs from the previous two in that there is less emphasis on physical structures and more focus on the social (and hence on the less tangible), it still does not address the poetic potential of adaptive re-use. This, however, is more evident in what we can call the strategic approach.

Figure 6: Caixa Forum, Madrid (Architects: Herzog & de Meuron)

2.4 The Strategic Approach

In 'Architecture as Palimpsest', Machado considers a series of metaphors to suggest different possible ways of thinking about the remodelling of buildings. He argues that the act of remodelling should not be limited to the production of 'form' (or indeed function, as in the cases discussed thus far) but rather that the 'meaning' of the past and the way the architect or designer deals with it should be considered as essential. He states that:

> 'In the process of remodelling, the past takes on a greater significance because it, itself, is the material to be altered and reshaped. The past provides the already-written, the marked "canvas" on which each successive remodelling will find its own place. Thus, the past becomes a "package of sense", of built-up meaning to be accepted (maintained), transformed, or supressed (refused).'[44]

Although these more 'poetic' ideas did not initially receive much consideration, by 1989 they had been taken up by Robert who recalled the metaphor of the palimpsest to explain the concept of conversion.[45] Robert presents seven 'concepts of conversion' that he identifies as existent in a number of historical and contemporary examples: (1) building within, (2) building over, (3) building around, (4) building alongside, (5) recycling materials or vestiges, (6) adapting to a new function and (7) building in the style of. Each of these concepts refers to a specific physical intervention but contains traces, albeit less forceful ones, of Machado's more poetic palimpsest ideas.

More recently, these ideas have emerged in the writings of Brooker and Stone who, as with Robert, define different design strategies for building re-use by looking at exemplary case studies. They identify three strategies: (1) intervention, (2) insertion and (3) installation. Their approach also starts from physical intervention but their focus is on the 'affective' aspect of each adaptation: by applying one of the proposed strategies, they suggest, the meaning of the building can be either accepted, transformed or supressed. In *Context + Environment*, they explain:

> 'It is through an understanding and interpretation of the spirit of place and the particular contextual setting within which a building exists that the designer or architect can heighten, change and reactivate a space. An existing structure is bound to its setting; it has certain qualities that are unique only to that particular situation. The designer can analyse and use these found qualities as the starting point or basis for the next layer of construction.'[46]

Their use of categories and latent concern for a sense of place is also evident in the work of Jäger who uses three types of classification: (1) additions, (2) transformations and (3) conversions. Cramer and Breitling[47] develop these ideas in a slightly different way through a distinction between 'design strategies' and 'architectonic expressions'. Common to them all is an approach that is not only practical but also acknowledges a more poetic understanding of adaptive re-use more akin to the ideas of Machado than any of the other strategies we have mentioned.

3. Conclusion – The Future of Adaptive Re-use and the Role of Interior Architecture

In this discussion, our focus has been on the notion of re-use and the various theories, designers and concepts that have developed around it. As we have seen, the arguments have evolved over time and become ever more nuanced, complex and, possibly, contradictory. We have suggested that in today's context, there are four discernible schools of thought, each one of which emphasises a different key issue. Some of these are clearly practical in nature and, as issues of sustainability become ever more pressing, will only grow in importance. Others are concerned with the role the adaptation of our buildings may be able to play in the adaptation of society at large to the issues it will face in the coming years. Others, by contrast, begin to focus on a more 'poetic' understanding of adaptation and draw on the ideas of Machado and the notion of the palimpsest.

Although each of these strategies is different in nature and tone, there is one thing they all seem to have in common: the people behind their conception, development and promotion have tended to be architects. This is perhaps one of the reasons why the more ethereal and intangible ideas of the palimpsest have not been fully explored. This has been the case historically, with Ruskin, Viollet-le-Duc, Alois Riegl, Camillo Boito, Sherban Cantacuzino and Radolfo Machado all coming from an architectural background. In recent years, however, there has been a sea change, with more writings on the subject of re-use emanating from the pens of interior architects and designers. One case in point is Brooker and Stone; another is Klingenberg. In *What is Interior Design?*, Brooker and Stone state that:

> 'Interior architecture, interior design, interior decoration, and building reuse are very closely linked subjects, all of which deal, in varying degrees, with the transformation of a given space, whether that is the crumbling ruin of an ancient building or the drawn parameters of a new building proposal.'[48]

This identification and the increase in publications by interior designers are to be welcomed. It is perhaps by introducing the sensibilities of the 'interior thinker' into the equation on adaptive re-use that another imbalance can be addressed: the focuses on practical questions evident in the strategies we have outlined. Such a shift could, we propose, give way to the emergence of a fifth contemporary approach which we argue is necessary. That approach would draw more on the 'soft values' of the interior designer. It would be able to draw the parallel between alteration and poetry identified by Fred Scott[49] and introduce notions of empathy and generosity in our response to existing buildings and their adaption to the needs and sensibilities of new users.

It could be an approach that combines the typological, technical, programmatic and strategic concerns we have discussed, but one that does so with more sensitivity; that does so in what we may call a 'designerly approach'. We propose this as an attempt to draw attention to the need for an understanding of 'the poetics of the space when adapted'. Hints at the possibility of applying intangible aspects or 'soft values' to adaptation are found in the writings of Scott and of Brooker and Stone[50] and also exist in work of Klingenberg. Some of these authors have stressed the importance of retaining a sense of the historic interior in adaptations; not just aesthetically, however, but also through the notion of the building's own *genius loci* – what Klingenberg calls its 'cultural experience value' and we may choose to call 'the spirit of its interior'. Perhaps then, the next stage in the development of adaptive re-use theory lies here, in an understanding of interiors – and its concomitant understanding of 'soft values'.

Acknowledgements

The authors would like to thank the reviewer for the constructive comments on our paper. This research was funded by a PhD grant of the Institute for the Promotion of Innovation through Science and Technology in Flanders (IWT-Vlaanderen).

Notes

[1] Brooker, G. and Stone, S. (2004) *Re-readings: Interior Architecture and the Design Principles of Remodelling Existing Buildings*, London: RIBA Enterprises, p.11.
[2] Cunnington, P. (1988) *Change of Use: the Conversion of Old Buildings*, London: Alpha Books.
[3] Dubois, M. (1998) Hergebruik van gebouwen in Europees perspectief, *Kunsttijdschrift Vlaanderen. Het hergebruik van gebouwen* 27/13, pp.121–7.
[4] Pérez de Arce, R. (1978) Urban Transformations & the Architecture of Additions, *Architectural Design* 4, pp.237–66.
[5] Powell, K. (1999) *Architecture Reborn: Converting Old Buildings for New Uses*, New York: Rizzoli International Publications, Inc.
[6] See: Machado, R. (1976) Old buildings as palimpsest: Towards a theory of remodeling, *Progressive Architecture* 11, pp.46–9; Markus, T. (1979) *Building Conversion and Rehabilitation*, London: Butterworth; Giebeler, G. (2009) Definitions, in Liese, J. (ed.) *Refurbishment Manual: Maintenance, Conversions, Extensions*, Basel, Boston, Berlin: Birkenhauser, pp.10–15.
[7] Jokilehto, J. (1999) *A History of Architectural Conservation*, Oxford: Elsevier.
[8] Vaccaro, A. (1996) Restoration and Anti-Restoration, in Price, N., Talley, M. and Vaccaro, A. (eds) *Historical and Philisophical Issues in the Conservation of Cultural Heritage*, Los Angeles: The Getty Conservation Institute, pp.308–13.
[9] Viollet-le-Duc, E. (1990 [1854]) *The Foundations of Architecture: Selections from the Dictionnaire Raisonné*, B. Bergdoll (ed.), New York: George Braziller, pp.222–3.
[10] Scott, F. (2008) *On Altering Architecture*, London: Routledge, p.80.
[11] Ruskin, J. (1849) *The Seven Lamps of Architecture*, London: Smith, Elder, p.148.
[12] Ibid., p.184
[13] Ibid., pp.184–6
[14] Jokilehto, 1999, op. cit.
[15] Morris, W. (1977) Manifesto of the Society for the Protection of Ancient Buildings, in

Price, N., Talley, M. and Vaccaro, A. (eds) *Historical and Philosophical Issues in the Conservation of Cultural Heritage*, Los Angeles: The Getty Conservation Institute, pp.319–21.
[16] Riegl, A. (1928 [1903]) Der Moderne Denkmalkultus: Sein Wesen und seine Entstehung, *Gesammelte Aufsätze*, Augsburg-Wien: Dr. Benno Filser Verlag, pp.144–93.
[17] Riegl, A. (1982 [1903]) The Modern Cult of Monuments: Its Character and Its Origin, *Oppositions* 25/Fall, p.44.
[18] Ibid., p.39
[19] Jokilehto, 1999, op. cit.
[20] See: Bell, D. (2009) The Naming of Parts, in Stanley-Price, N., and King, J. (eds) *Conserving the Authentic: Essays in Honour of Jukka Jokilehto*, Rome: ICCROM, pp.55–62; Mason, R. (2002) Assessing Values in Conservation Planning: Methodological Issues and Choices, in de la Torre, M. (ed.) *Assesing the Values of Cultural Heritage*, Los Angeles: Getty Conservation Institute, pp.5–30; Tomaszewski, A. (ed.) (2007) *Values and Critera in Heritage Conservation: Proceedings of the International Conference of ICOMOS, ICCROM, Fondazione Romualdo Del Bianco*, Florence: Edizione Polistampa.
[21] Boito, C. (1893) *Questioni pratiche di belle arti, restauri, concorsi, legislazione, professione, insegnamento*, Milan: Ulrico Hoepli.
[22] Ibid.
[23] Jokilehto, 1999, op. cit.
[24] Boito, C. (2009 [1893]) Restoration in Architecture: First Dialogue, *Future Anterior* 61, p.76.
[25] Jokilehto, 1999, op. cit.
[26] International Museum Office, *The Athens Charter for the Restoration of Historic Monuments*, in Destrée, J. (ed.) (1931) Adopted at the First International Congress of Architects and Technicians of Historic Monuments, Athens, Article 1.
[27] Van der Woud, A. (1983) Het Nieuwe Bouwen International: Housing Townplanning, Delft: Delfts University Press & Rijksmuseum Kröller-Müller.
[28] CIAM (1933) Statements of the Athens Congress, in Van der Woud, 1983, op.cit., pp.163–7.
[29] Choay, F. (2007) *L'allégorie du patrimoine*, Paris: Seuil.
[30] ICOMOS (1964) *The Venice Charter: International charter for the conservation and restoration of monuments and sites*, Venice: ICOMOS, Article 5.
[31] Cantacuzino, S. (1975) *New Uses for Old Buildings*, London: Architectural Press.
[32] Cantacuzino, S. (1972) New Uses for Old Buildings, *Architectural Review*, CLI/903: pp.262–324.
[33] Markus, T. (1979) *Building Conversion and Rehabilitation*, London: Butterworth, p.30.
[34] Machado, R. (1976) Old Buildings as Palimpsest: Towards a Theory of Remodeling, *Progressive Architecture* 11, pp.46–9.
[35] Ibid., p.46
[36] Plevoets, B. and Van Cleempoel, K. (2011) Adaptive Reuse as a Strategy towards Conservation of Cultural Heritage: a Literature Review, in Brebbia, C., and Binda, L. (eds) *Structural Studies, Repairs and Maintenance of Heritage Architecture XII*, Chianciano Terme, Italy: WITpress, pp.155–64.

[37] Cantacuzino, 1975, op. cit.
[38] See: Cunnington, P. (1988) *Change of Use: the Conversion of Old Buildings*, London: Alpha Books; Latham, D. (2000) *Creative Re-use of Buildings*, Shaftesbury: Donhead.
[39] Douglas, J. (2006) *Building Adaptation*, Oxford: Elsevier.
[40] Highfield, D. (1987) *The Rehabilitation and Re-use of Old Buildings,* London & New York: Spon Press.
[41] Carswell, A. (2011) Adaptive Reuse, in Cohen, N., and Robbins, P. (eds) *Green Cities: An A-to-Z Guide*, Los Angeles, Londen, Nes Delhi, Singapore & Washington DC: Sage, pp.4–7.
[42] See: Powell, 1999, op. cit.; Fisher, A. (1992) *New Life in Old Buildings*, Stuttgart & Zurich: Verlag.
[43] See: Plevoets, B., Petermans, A. and Van Cleempoel, K. (2010) Developing a theoretical framework for understanding (staged) authentic retail concepts in relation to the current experience economy, in *DRS2010, 7–9 July 2010*, Montreal;   Plevoets, B., and Van Cleempoel, K. (2012) Creating sustainable retail interiors through reuse of historic buildings*, Interiors: design, architecture, culture* 3/3.
[44] Gelfand, L., and Duncan, C. (2012) *Sustainable Renovation: Strategies for Commercial Building Systems and Envelope*, Hoboken, New Jersey: John Wiley & Sons, p.4.
[45] Robert, P. (1989) *Adaptations: New Uses for Old Buildings*, Paris: Editions du Moniteur.
[46] Brooker, G., and Stone, S. (2008) *Context + Environment*, Lausanne: ava publishings sa, p.22.
[47] Cramer, J., and Breitling, S. (2007) *Architecture in Existing Fabric*, Berlin: Birkhäuser.
[48] Brooker, G., and Stone, S. (2010) *What is Interior Design?*, Mies: Rotovision, p.6
[49] Scott, F. (2008) *On Altering Architecture*, London: Routledge.
[50] Brooker, G. (2009) Infected Interiors: Remodelling Contaminated Buildings, in *Living in the Past: Histories, Heritage and the Interior*, 6th Modern Interiors Research Centre Conference, 14 & 15 May 2009, Kingston University, London.

Graeme BROOKER

Middlesex University, London

WASTESPACE

Having set out a vision of what building adaptation may be, and having laid out a historical framework that the rest of this book will use as conceptual bedrock, the work of these authors passes over to that of Graeme Brooker, a teacher and author who has been involved in the field for a number of years...

Far from submitting to this constant wave of material use and dis-use, however, he identifies numerous examples in contemporary and historical societies of reactions against it. He proposes the celebration and embracing of wastespace...

* * *

'Civilization did not rise and flourish as men hammered out hunting scenes on bronze gates and whispered philosophy under the stars, with garbage as a noisesome offshoot, swept away and forgotten. No, garbage rose first, inciting people to build a civilization in response, in self-defense.'[1]

Recently, I realised that I have been doing a lot of thinking about, and working with, waste. This realisation was partially prompted by two recent projects undertaken at the University of Brighton and at the Artesis University College in Antwerp. In Brighton, the project involved running a unit for undergraduate interior architecture students titled 'The Wunderkammer'. This was a project based upon understanding the processes of mudlarking, an eighteenth-century occupation that involved foraging on the banks of the River Thames in London for items of value that could be cleaned up and resold. Today, mudlarking is still a lawful occupation, though regulated, and involves the extraction of discarded artefacts from the archaeologically diverse and anaerobically rich mud of the banks of the Thames. These finds are then passed to the Museum of

Figure 1: Wunderkammer Unit: section through museum with artefacts by Lizzie Munro

London to be valued and, if it is deemed necessary, put on display. The students in the Wunderkammer unit were asked to design a display space, a 'cabinet of wonders' that would house the discarded detritus of the city that had found its way into the river. They were to make a space for the debris that was considered to be valuable, yet they needed to take into account that these objects were once deemed to be throwaway. Waste and the values of waste were a central theme of the project.

This interest re-emerged in a week-long workshop in Antwerp in 2012 called Nonuments. This project was based upon the re-use of a discarded plinth located in a quiet courtyard of the school (Figure 2). The statue that once stood on the plinth, a cast of a figure of the founder of the Academy of Fine Arts in Antwerp, David Teniers the Younger (1610–90), had long been removed and placed in a more prominent location in The Meir, one of the main streets of Antwerp. The plinth had never been reoccupied and was considered useless, redundant and of no value: it had become a waste of space. Nonuments involved the rehabilitation of the plinth, resuscitating it through new occupation. The project that was eventually constructed upon the plinth was designed by the students to provoke reflections upon the school and its relationship to them. It took the form of a challenge: to mount the plinth and slide down a chute from its considerable height into the courtyard. For a moment, the user of the installation had ascended the plinth and had been monumentalised, as though a statue, before they came back down to earth. The plinth was rehabilitated for just the one week of the workshop and introduced back into the daily life of the school (Figure 3).

Both of these projects prompted reflections upon, and thoughts about, the loss of value in spaces and objects and their journey towards the condition of becoming 'waste'. Each object excavated from the banks of the River Thames could be considered to be a thing of transience, an item that had, through time, journeyed through a series of judgments about its worth. The plinth had lost its meaning when the statue was removed and placed elsewhere: its 'value' had been diminished and subsequently its role within the courtyard, and the school, had been lost. Both projects were formulated

Figure 2: Empty plinth

Figure 3: The proposal by the students to occupy the plinth

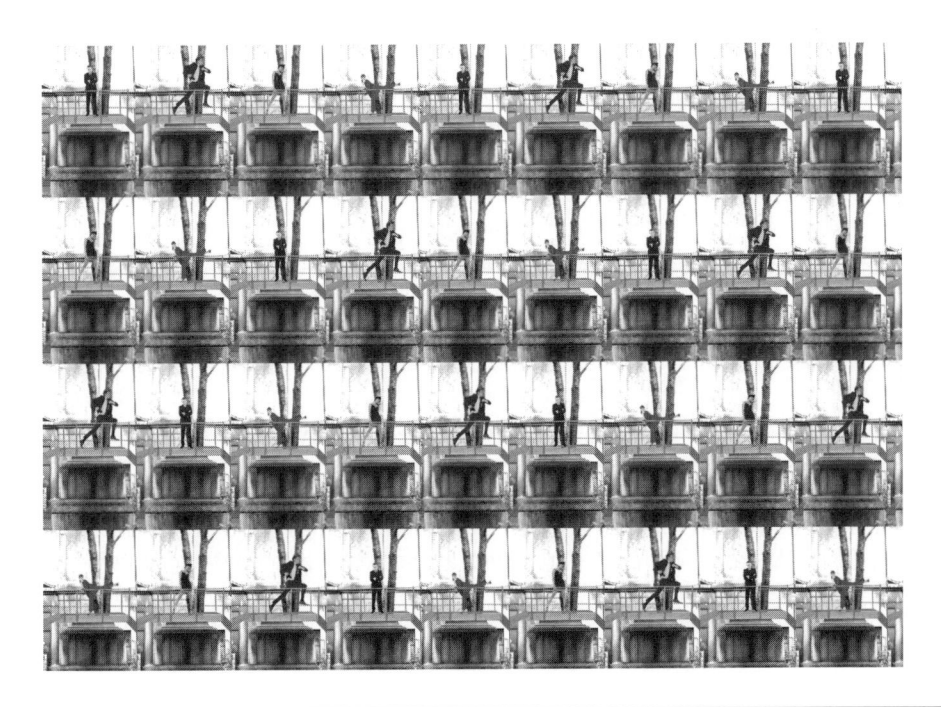

WASTESPACE 35

in order to ask students to consider the ephemeral and yet durable qualities of objects and spaces, where loss of meaning and worth could be considered to be a momentary or transitory condition, one based on fluid opinions and sets of values that altered throughout time.

The Interior as Waste

'Rubbish is temporally, socially, politically and economically dynamic'.[2]

This paper is titled 'Wastespace' and is a speculation upon ideas regarding redundancy and waste in the creation of the interior. It comes from the realisation that not only is waste an important theme but that, to some extent, it has been present in previous research, writing and teaching I have been engaged with about the broader implications of waste – especially in relation to the re-use of existing buildings. In particular, it is based on the notion that the production of an interior, in an existing building, could be described as a process reliant on the result of the loss of value, an erosion of worth and the redundancy of usefulness: a space created from the processes of wasting. Normal descriptions of waste depict the detritus that is often considered to be rubbish: packaging, litter, broken consumables, disposable or short-life materials and so on. It is considered to be anything that appears to be no longer of value and has therefore been discarded. More importantly, alongside the traditional understanding of 'rubbish', this text would like to consider the term 'waste' to be applicable to redundant or discarded urban spaces and buildings. If rubbish is the accrual of the discarded excesses of society, redundant spaces and buildings are the decayed and eroded garbage of the city. Their abandonment may happen for a number of reasons: they become outdated and no longer fit-for-purpose; they are vacant through loss of ownership, economic decline and so on. Buildings perish because of their location, their loss of relevance and their insignificance. Whatever the cause of wasting, over time buildings become surplus to requirements and, unless action is undertaken to arrest the decline, their redundancy initiates a slow slide into dereliction. Wasted spaces are the detritus of the city; they are site-specific urban *land fill*.

These processes of decay and decline are not always the end of a life cycle of an object, space or building. Obsolescence in objects, ruin and redundancy in buildings, can provoke reflections upon their recycling and their value in order to consider them for the transformation into a new use. In urban space and buildings, this process of rehabilitation breathes new life back into wasted spaces. Traditionally, methods of building rehabilitation take the form of adapting the redundant shell for a new use. These might result in new leisure spaces such as restaurants, hotels, bars and shops, workspaces with modern office environments, or the development of new homes. Each new adaptation transforms the derelict site and rehabilitates the building by bringing it back into the daily cycle of everyday use. Sometimes in this process, the previous life of the building is retained and immortalised. This aide memoire often consists of elements that have been retained in order to counterpoint the bright new interior space of the rehabilitation. Often their role is to act as a petrified reminder of the turbulent past of the space.[3] This dynamic cycle of rehabilitation recoups what may once have been use-less and accords it commodity status once again. This re-commodification of once-redundant things creates a cycle of waste and reappropriation, and is part of the requirements of sustaining a vibrant economy. As O'Brien states in 'Rubbish Power: Towards a Sociology of a Rubbish Society', waste is a dynamic entity, contradicting the thought that it is devoid of value. Instead rubbish and waste are valuable, lucrative even, especially when part of a cycle of re-use, reappropriation and then ultimately re-consumption; a sequence of decomposition and recomposition where the ecology of all matter has an uneven trajectory of value and worth.

In the book *Rubbish Theory: The Creation and Destruction of Value*, Thompson ascribes three categories of value to objects. He argues that some items – and thus, by extension for this paper, urban matter such as buildings – can be described as 'transient', 'durable' or 'rubbish'.[4] Transient items possess a finite use-value that depreciates over a period of time. For instance, transient goods, such as a fridge or a car, will decrease in value as they get older. The value of a durable item remains the same or even increases over time. A painting or a sculpture is a good example of a durable item that can increase in value over time, especially if it's importance, and thus worth, is developed by dealers and auctioneers in the marketplace. Different to these two categories of worth are things with zero value: rubbish and waste.

It is Thompson's suggestion that at some point in the life cycle of all objects and spaces they will be assigned zero value and considered to be rubbish. That which is deemed valuable will at some point be, or have been, discarded as worthless. Thompson argues that the dynamic processes through which objects and spaces journey reassigns them into the differing categories of transient, durable and rubbish. During its lifetime, each item will oscillate between these conditions. Thompson accepts that this framework of value can be rendered ambiguous by shifts in wider cultural and generational values, where forces such as fashion and politics impact upon societal ideals and principles. As well as this, processes such as recycling, particularly in land-fill sites and rubbish heaps in the developing world where detritus is salvaged and re-used to become commodities or consumable goods, further polarise cycles of value and worth. The fundamental point is that obsolescence is a fluid condition and is a status that changes throughout the life cycle of things. Tim Edensor also points this out in *Industrial Ruins: Space, Aesthetics and Materiality*, suggesting that obsolescent objects, spaces and buildings contain the conditions of change within them:

> 'The commodity, as well as other objects, appears as an entity which possesses a fixed meaning and use-value, and when these are exhausted or irrelevant, the subsequent loss of exchange value turns it into waste.'[5]

Like objects, buildings and urban matter constantly undergo these changes in their assigned value and therefore can never be described as stable entities. The meaning and value of wastespaces is forever changing. They can be considered as dynamic entities from which meaning and hence new ways of living can be fabricated. As Edensor states:

> 'Ruins contain excess, waste with which people can construct meaning, stories and practices...'

This paper does not explicitly address environmental issues or overtly position itself as a call to arms with regard to an ethical approach to waste. Instead, the intention is to establish a relationship between waste space and its role as an active and dynamic force in the creation of the interior. Waste is both a provocative concept and a challenging entity. It is fair to say that, in the last decade, the relationship between society and its waste has changed dramatically. The political dimension of waste, its systems of governance, its framework of policies, its environmental considerations and the impact they have all had on everyday lives have significantly increased. Commentators such as Gay Hawkins have noted:

> 'There is no doubt that over the last thirty years, in the face of escalating amounts of waste, the rules surrounding putting out the garbage in late capitalist countries have changed. Waste has become problematised, it has become a domain of life in which our taken for granted practices have been subjected to scrutiny and [shown to be] in need of attention and care. In problematising what we should do with our waste, these campaigns (such as reduce, reuse, recycle) have also subjected who we are and how we should be in the world.'[7]

Others such as John Frow have suggested that:

> 'Waste is the degree zero of value, or it is the opposite of value, or it is whatever stands in excess of value systems grounded in use. Yet waste is at the same time constitutive of the structure of value: on the one hand it is residually a commodity, something from which money can be made. On the other hand the category of waste underpins any system of social distinction, as the principle of uselessness that establishes a non-utilitarian symbolic order.'[8]

In the UK alone, the British Environment Act of 1995 sets out a national waste strategy in which it identifies sixteen different types of waste, much of which can be recycled and/or reassigned as valuable, thus becoming lucrative sources of income.[9] As Hawkins and Frow suggest, the complexities and contradictions just in the recent history of waste are numerous and overlap with issues of consumption, possession, status and identity; as well as ethical issues and personal responsibility.

So why wastespace? As stated earlier, reflections prompted by student projects led to the realisation of the power embedded in the narrative of waste. Waste, and in particular waste space, is an important component in the understanding of creating the interior – particularly when using redundant buildings. On a simple level, this paper positions the idea that the interior, and hence building re-use, is a sustainable built-environment process. Moreover, examining waste is an opportunity to consider deeper issues of the subject of the interior and speculate upon core aspects relative to the discipline. 'Wastespace' is a term devised for this paper because it can be used to describe the reworking of existing buildings considered to have become waste or 'rubbish' as they have, for whatever reason, reached a condition of redundancy or have fallen out of use.

Wastespace explores how reusing waste questions normative patterns of consumption and abandonment, disposal and casting off; and how ideas such as salvage, re-use, recycling, up-cycling, rehabilitation, remodelling and 'vintage' conflate the normative processes of the design of the interior. Interior architects and designers are particularly predisposed to working with 'waste'. Common language in the field includes 'making do', 're-use', 'rehabilitation', 'gleaning', 'adaptation' and so on. To this glossary of the subject, we can add words such as 'waste', 'garbage', 'litter', 'rubbish' and 'leftovers'. It's a discourse that is particularly pertinent to interiors and in particular the re-use of extant material. It is also relevant to interiors in that it describes economies and ecologies of the re-use of particular materials. This discourse includes the words 'off-cuts', 'throw-aways', 'junk', 'discards' and 'detritus', each of which describe unwanted or useless things. These things or spaces that no longer have a use can be reworked and revalued and, in turn, inserted back into the life cycle of things. Waste consists of things that are full of potential.

If, as suggested here, waste is important, it creates a number of distinct issues. Firstly, it puts interiors, re-use and adaptation at odds with modernism and modernity, one of the dominant paradigms of the twentieth century. Secondly, notions of 'originality' and the enduring concept of the perfect and unborrowed, the new, are rendered ambiguous. Thirdly, waste and its re-use has a political dimension, one from which reprocessing could be regarded as a political act and one that could be construed, as Hawkin stated earlier, *to be an action that has the capacity to challenge traditional patterns of consumption*. The processes of adapting and reusing waste short circuit the cycle of obsolescence and then consumption; they form a course of action that can in some way vaporise commodification. Reusing waste could be considered to be a form of resistance to this cycle – an idea the next part of this paper will examine in more detail.

Modernity and Waste

> *'In a functionalist model, all works of architecture stand in danger of being considered at some time or other, by some agency or other, as a waste of space'.*[10]

Sustainability is one of the main areas of research in the field of the re-use of waste. The systems of both the Building Research Establishment Environmental Assessment Method (BREEAM) and Leadership in Energy and Environmental Design (LEED) consist of rating and analysing the design, construction and operational credentials of urban matter. These measures are often reflected in contemporary debate through the use of terms such as 'retro-fit' and 'refurbishment'. This is a language that describes the re-use of waste space and material in unsatisfying terms. 'Retrofit' conjures up images of a style that is out-of-date, whilst 'refurbishment' implies a surface condition: to 'furbish' anything is to brighten something by rubbing or scouring it – for example, the polishing of a surface. This unfortunate use of language is exasperated by the architectural media's tendency to assign little merit or importance to the re-use of waste; an issue that was taken up by a recent editorial in a national publication: 'Architectural values are often assigned little importance in retrofit'.[11]

Other sources of commentary on waste also appear negatively inclined toward leftovers. In 'Junkspace', Rem Koolhaas examines current tropes of contemporary buildings:

> 'Junkspace is the body double of space, a territory of impaired vision, limited expectation, reduced earnestness. Junkspace is a Bermuda Triangle of concepts, an abandoned Petri dish: it cancels distinctions, undermines resolve, confuses intention with realization. It replaces hierarchy with accumulation, composition with addition. More and more, more is more. Junkspace is overripe and undernourishing at the same time, a colossal security blanket that covers the earth in a stranglehold of seduction... Junkspace is like being condemned to a perpetual Jacuzzi with millions of your best friends'.[12]

Koolhaas's essay is a treatise on the paucity of thought in the creation of many contemporary buildings. In particular, he suggests that junkspace is a seamless, bloated type of space that is characterised by environments such as shopping centres and airports. These are often tenuously held together by phalanxes of air-conditioning, circulation routes and sprinkler systems. 'Junk' is used as a derogatory term and waste is viewed as an undynamic entity.

Modernism and modernity have always struggled with notions of waste. Redundancy and decay, entropy and ruins have always troubled modernism's imperatives of functionalism and purity. Redundancy, the state of being no longer in use or 'out of use', is anathema to modernist functionalist doctrines. The tabula rasa has always haunted modernity and its relationship to buildings that are no longer of use. Apart from wholesale demolition, modernism has no meaningful answer to the problematic and complex idea of a building considered to be 'waste'.

Ironically, whilst ruined modernity is often more beautiful than ever (Figure 4), once function and use are lost and entropy, decay and ruin set in, functionalism no longer has authority: redundancy prevails. Rigidly deterministic functionalist approaches to making space have never suited the re-use and adaptation of the existing. Form cannot follow function when use has been rendered redundant. Re-use and adaptation of the existing doesn't require form to follow function. Instead, the properties of the wastespace are the starting points for re-evaluation.

In his seminal essay, 'Old Buildings as Palimpsest', written over 30 years ago and still relevant today, Rodolfo Machado states that the issues involved in reworking waste spaces ensures that redundant buildings, as opposed to new build, require different strategies in order to make them work again:

> 'If an original building is considered as a first discourse that conditions future formal discourses to be inscribed upon it, then remodelling can be conceived of as rewriting... [I]n remodelling, the past takes on a value far greater from that in the usual design process where form is generated from 'scratch'.[13]

As well as the redundancy of functionalism in remodelling, Machado talks of the 'estrangement' of form. He suggests that the conventions of 'type' and 'typology',

Figure 4: St Peters Seminary, Cardross, by Gillespie, Kidd & Coia
Completed in 1966, this modernist building has been empty since the 1990s.

along with design 'languages', are ruptured when entropy sets in. He suggests that 'estrangement' is a condition that concerns the act of the rupture or fissure between use and shape, form and function. Estrangement is the condition in which use is lost; and when it disappears, a building becomes waste, its value is diminished.

> 'The juxtaposition of different formal vocabularies in a remodelled building produces a natural "estrangement" that can enormously facilitate the criticism, the exposure, of architectural languages as cultural conventions. It can also facilitate the manifestation of a designer's own critical intentions'.[14]

The re-use of a wastespace allows critical judgment to be delivered or exercised via the new intervention on, or within, an existing building. Critical judgment leads to 'value' and a decision regarding 'worth'. These are difficult questions and ones that maybe only designers of interventions and historians of space can truly answer. Machado states that this judgment of values is an important tool in the armoury of the remodeller: 'This could be the most critical function remodelling could offer'.[15]

In any wastespace project, the choice of site, function and material is a critical judgment on its worth. In London in 2010, a group of architects, designers and interested friends utilised a discarded former petrol station and transformed it into a temporary cinema. Primarily constructed using donated and found materials, the Cineroleum (Figure 5)

Figure 5: The Cineroleum

was organised under the sheltering roof of a redundant petrol garage forecourt. It was enclosed by an ornate shiny silver curtain that hung from the roof – a nod to the golden days of cinema spaces. The curtain was fashioned from recycled DuPont Air guard, essentially a damp-proof membrane. The screen was rescued from a skip outside the National Theatre and the chairs and main structure were built from cheap scrap-board that would otherwise have been thrown away. The seating was salvaged from skips and arranged as a tiered bank of temporary terraces. The silver curtain framed the tiered theatre within and managed to protect the audience from the rain and wind, as well as the occasional loud noises and smelly exhaust fumes from the traffic on the adjacent and busy Clerkenwell Road. At the end of each performance, the curtains were pulled up to reveal the packed, hidden theatre to the street beyond; much to the bemusement of unsuspecting passer-bys (Figure 6). The cinema was:

> 'Primarily constructed using donated and found materials; The Cineroleum will be an improvisation of the decadent interiors that greeted audiences during cinema's golden age. Popcorn, paper tickets, elaborate signage and flip-down seats will collectively recreate the familiar excitement of cinema going'.[16]

The Cineroleum was a critique of the re-use of redundant space. The adaptation of the garage was a critical intervention into an urban context. It provoked debate on the re-use of disused garages, of which there are thousands across the UK. The project also demonstrated how changes in value and worth during the adaptation of discarded spaces could be the central element of changes in the re-use of waste. As well as

Figure 6: The Cineroleum with the curtain down

this, the transformation of this wastespace collapsed classifications with regards to originality and origin. Huge bodies of law have grown up around this possessiveness – IP rights, conventions, patents and property rights – all occasionally ruptured by plagiarism and the infringement of copyright. The re-use, recycling and general rehabilitation of waste plunges issues of origin and originality into murky waters. Notions of borrowing, copying, reproducing or recontextualising existing objects, personified by Duchamp's 'readymades', throw doubts upon the authority and sole rights of the author. Originality is no longer important or of interest where the re-use of material, particularly something which was considered worthless, is the most important element in the means of production. The rearrangement and re-editing of existing work is described by commentators such as Nicolas Bourriaud as the dominant mode of current cultural production. In *Postproduction: Culture as Screenplay: How Art Reprograms the World* and in the catalogue *Altermodern* (the book accompanying the exhibition of the same name at Tate Britain), he described how dominant forms of production are akin to the final editing of a film:

> 'It is no longer a matter of starting with "blank slate" or creating meaning on the basis of virgin material but of finding a means of insertion into the innumerable flows of production...'[17]

In postproduction, narrative, scenery, spaces and dialogue are spliced together, sometimes with special effects, in order to finish the film off. Much like the collaging together of a space, postproduction involves the re-contextualising of existing fragments in order to make a new and coherent narrative. This is nothing new. Spolia is the ancient archaeological equivalent of postproduction. It involves the creation of objects, spaces and buildings using off-cuts and waste.

> 'The subject denoted by spolia is materials or artifacts in reuse... [I]nitially spolia were re-used bits of ancient Rome...'[18]

Spolia is an act of gathering and reconfiguring salvage into new elements, buildings and cities. In archaeology, analysing and understanding spolia is a method used to determine periods of history articulated by the adaptation of fragments of waste. The history of the Roman Empire can be mapped not just in relation to periods of prosperity, expansion and wealth, but also in recessionary times when new monuments and buildings were formed, not from material plundered from conquests, but instead from local bits of buildings and spaces that were viewed as redundant and subsequently repurposed. The Arch of Constantine, Rome, makes extensive use of spolia and was continually updated and encrusted with new additions throughout the time of the empire.[19]

As well as monuments, smaller objects have been constructed from spolia. The pulpit of Torcello in Venice was formed from carved friezes stolen from Constantinople. The friezes of the pulpit were carved with images of Kairos and Chronos, Greek myths that personified two types of time. In antiquity, Kairos, the portent of a window of opportunity, personified the concept of 'occasio': the description of a transient time or a moment of opportunity. Another frieze used on the pulpit contained the central figure of *Ixion*, King of Thessaly. With figures of night and day by his sides, the frieze symbolised the punishment that awaits the one who seizes the wrong opportunity. In other words, it symbolised a fatal choice or moment of time frozen in eternity. Together, the two allegories encompass the two major concepts of time in antiquity: *Kairos*, temporal or opportunistic, a window of opportunity; and *Chronos*, eternal and ongoing chronological time. The assemblers of the spoliated pulpit wanted to tell a story. This is as much a contemporary trope as it is historical.

More contemporary forms of the re-use of waste involve the practice of superuse.

> 'Superuse is not simply another word for reuse. Indeed it occasionally may involve the application of new products or parts that have never been used for anything but have simply fallen victim to the whims of over production. Superuse is rather a way of creating architecture by shortcutting the flows of products and elements from their state of maximum added value to the stage at which value has been dissipated...'[20]

Developed by the Dutch architects 2012Architecten as part of the Recyclicity Foundation,[21] the processes of superuse are in many ways a contemporary formulation of spolia. Superuse involves the rehabilitation of leftovers and discarded objects, some waste, some not, and the finding of meaningful ways of reintegrating them back into flows of production. 2012Architecten even describe the locating and establishing of these materials as a new profession, describing the role as that of 'superuse scout'.

Corresponding with Thompson's framing of the values of waste, and paralleling notions of the dynamism of waste, 2012Architecten argue that there are three types, or flows, of superuse materials:

> 'As in recycling the seemingly most straightforward (material flow) is production waste… the second kind consists of materials that can be withdrawn from the traditional recycling flow in various stages… the third category consists of the same kind of products that have reached the last "end of use" state of the lifecycle'.[22]

A fourth category is that of 'dead stock' supplies, parts or elements of production systems that have been created but are no longer called for. They are redundant. The designers intervene into the 'flow' of materials in order to appropriate the waste and use it for a particular use. Projects that incorporate superuse do not use conventional architectural materials. Instead they are characterised by the repurposing of unusual and exotic elements: car parts such as tyres, doors, windscreens; packaging materials such as cardboard, paper, pallets and crates; domestic waste such as carpet tiles, bins, food tins and stacked paper. These have become shelters, walls, lights, furniture and so on. Like spoliated elements, superused materials quite often carry their meaning over to inform their new use. This has ensured that notions of function and form, originality and innovation are rendered entirely ambiguous.

The Interior as Excess

> 'The overlooked can only survive so long as authority is lax. When authority goes looking for the overlooked, the game is up – as it is today in the Lea Valley in East London. The entirely despicable, entirely pointless 2012 Olympics – a festival of energy – squandering architectural bling worthy of vain, third-world dictatorship, a payday for the construction industry – occupies a site far more valuable as it was. It was probably the most extensive terrain vague of any European capital city. The English word 'wasteland' is pejorative, lazy and more or less states that the place has no merit – so why not cover it in expressions of vanity?'[23]

Normative cycles of waste and re-use position objects and buildings within particular cycles of consumption. As we have seen, extreme examples such as spolia and superuse may transcend conventional notions of originality and function, rendering them obsolete as meaningful terms of reference. Methods of repurposing such as superuse and spolia suggest that there is an infinite number of ways in which any discarded object, space or building has the potential to be rehabilitated. There are some forms of waste, and in particular waste spaces, that are difficult or problematic to re-use. Issues of ownership, contamination and/or odious histories can resist the usual functions of rehabilitation noted above. Some things are just too difficult or tricky to rehabilitate and, instead, are re-used in less formal or normative ways. Sometimes these projects may take the form of a kind of re-use that is deliberately provocative and undertaken in order to disturb and challenge normative patterns of legitimacy, function and occupation. They may be used in order to challenge and resist commodification.

Occasionally, there is a political dimension to reusing these wasted objects, spaces and buildings. Wastespace may include urban matter that can be used as a statement and, in the last part of this paper, we will turn our attention to these types of projects.

In 'The Return of the Excessive: Superfluous Landscapes', Tom Nielsen explores the residual spaces of the city, spaces that are leftovers from the growth of urban centres. He suggests that these leftovers, or 'backsides' of cities, emerge in direct contrast to the increasingly controlled main public spaces of the city and are used and reappropriated by people as an alternative. He describes these spaces as superfluous; as spaces that may be considered by city planners to be unnecessary. Yet he argues that their very existence is integral to the well being of the city as they act as commentary on the more controlled and bland city centre environment. Superfluous landscapes are constantly evolving and they change as they move through the various categories of value – much like the objects spaces and buildings described here.

> 'In such a context, not only the superfluous landscapes but also the urban field as such can be understood as an interconnected series of processes of wasting, reappropriation, and consumption of urban matter and space.'[24]

Nielsen goes on to say:

> 'Between the enclaves and their infrastructure, areas left over from the planning and building of the city emerge. Areas that are not useable, not yet used, or already and later abandoned. These superfluous landscapes have been left over by planning because they are situated outside what the planning institutions traditionally have been able to include and understand as their field of action.'[25]

The superfluous landscape is not a stable entity and its transformation, either by its users or when it is finally engulfed or swallowed by new developments, is an inbuilt part of its transience. Superfluous landscapes are part of an ongoing process of transformation. Users of these spaces are often urbanites who themselves may not want to conform to normative patterns of behaviour. Terms such as 'placehackers', 'urban explorers' and 'edgeworkers' are used describes the reoccupation of wasted sites by people who seek out derelict and disused spaces.

'Edgework' is used to describe the appropriation of these types of landscape and can be defined as a method of reclaiming space through occupation, albeit quite often for a short period of time. It usually results in extraordinary photographs and films – often in difficult and dangerous locations and often with the aim of achieving the pursuit of entering and exploring a dangerous spaces. Cultural geographers and sociologists such as Tim Edensor, as well as protagonists such as Bradley Garret, align edgework and placehacking with other spatial reinterpretative and performative arts such as parkour and skateboarding. They are depicted as pursuits in which normative patterns of urban behaviour are redefined. Waste spaces, as in the derelict or the out of use, are reappropriated for pleasure seeking and the thrill of illicit entry. Edensor describes placehacking as a transgressive practice encompassing the reworking of derelict and ruined spaces. He considers ruins as 'waste spaces' that can be categorised as trash, useless, worn out and with no value, whilst the transgressor nevertheless finds pleasure in their use:

> 'Ruins may become spaces for leisure, adventure, cultivation, acquisition, shelter and creativity. And as spaces that have been identified as waste, as well as dangerous and unsightly, ruins also provide spaces where forms of alternative public life may occur, activities characterised by an active and improvisional creativity, a casting off of the self-consciousness conditioned by the prying gaze of CCTV cameras and fellow citizens, and by the pursuit of illicit and frowned upon practices'.[26]

The appropriation or 'hacking' of superfluous landscapes is, Machado suggests, an intervention that is a comment on the 'value' of the place – whether for deviation and illicit purposes or just the spectacular craving of the excitement of transgression. 'Hacking' a place, hijacking its qualities, repurposing or transforming it, even for a fleeting moment or through photography or film, is akin to reworking and remodelling existing buildings – albeit in a hypertrophied and extremely temporal manner. Hacking contrasts with the formalised norms of socially and aesthetically regulated spaces and often allows different and alternative forms of occupation upon neglected sites – ones that are usually found on the outer edges of cities or inner-city brownfields.

As well as fleeting moments of transgression, the hacking or edgeworking of space can provide a deeper commentary on the cultural and political issues surrounding a particular site. One of the largest building projects in Europe, the 2012 London Olympic Park, was built upon a swathe of derelict land in the Lea River Valley in East London. As Jonathan Meades suggests, the development of the largest park to be built in London for 150 years created some deeply felt responses. The Olympic Park involved the clearance of the area around the River Lea, an area that for many years was in steep decline and yet had a vigour that was appealing to its many users and occupiers:

> 'A site of richness and multiple textures which feeds curiosity. It is obviously decaying. But decay, as anyone who has watched meat rot knows, possesses a vitality of its own. Such vitality is infinitely preferable to sterility and stadia'.[27]

From the thirteenth century onwards, the area was home to a number of abattoirs that supplied meat to the city and its occupants. The by-products of this industry such as bones and hide were used for chemicals, fertiliser, china, glue and soap, all polluting the area and contaminating the soil. A derelict factory, existing on the edge of the site and on the river, was left extant during the cleansing of the land and was left in-situ during the building of the park. Musician and artist Nick Franglen clandestinely occupied the building in order to house an installation that he titled 'Legacy'.

> 'I've always liked the Olympics, but when you've got Jeremy Hunt saying we've decided not to have an austerity Olympics, we mustn't hold back, when we're cutting the School Sports Initiative, that's an interesting conundrum. Legacy is a ghastly word. Politicians talk about the legacy of the games to east London and I think what they're concerned about is what their legacy will be. Does east London benefit from all this regeneration or is it negative to have this completely alien infrastructure dropped into it and its heritage

Figure 7: 'Legacy 1'
Nick Franglen and the allotment

stripped out? I was trying to ask a question: what sort of Olympics do we really want? Why does it have to be like this?'[28]

The ruined building on the site was in a dangerous state of dereliction. Entering the building involved the careful bypassing of security patrols and the negotiation of a series of climbs through holes and fences. Inside, the decayed condition of the interior had resulted in a series of rotted and collapsed floors that had dropped onto each another. This meant that a foot in the wrong place could lead to a drop through the numerous levels of the building to the basement. In a series of silent nocturnal shifts, Franglen set up three installations on the upper floors of the building: 'Legacy 1', 'Legacy 2' and 'Legacy 3', his own response to the neighbouring behemoth of the Olympic Park. 'Legacy 1' is on the seventh floor of the building and is a garden (Figure 7). The interior landscape allotment contains rows of radishes and lettuces, watered by rain seeping through the roof.

> 'Over several weeks in early spring 2012 I carried 250 kg of compost into the building and up to the seventh floor, where I spread it out on a raised area to create a small allotment. I sowed the allotment with seeds of radishes, spring onions, chilli, spinach, onions, endive, salad leaves and chives. Fed by light from the large industrial windows in the room and water dripping through the broken ceiling, against all odds the seeds have now grown into plants'.[29]

Figure 8: 'Legacy 3'
The Olympic Games in Athens

All the plants were grown from seeds from a friend's allotment that was demolished to make way for the park. 'Legacy 3', on the same floor, consists of a television showing a continuous loop of the opening ceremony of the Athens Olympics (Figure 8). (Twenty-one of the twenty-two buildings built for Athens are now derelict and closed: a direct comment on the legacy of those games.)

The flat roof of the building used for this installation no longer distributes rain into the blocked and broken guttering that surrounds it and has become a small pond. 'Legacy 2' is situated in this shallow pool of water and consists of 205 solar-light-powered rowing toys: one for each nation competing in the games (Figure 9). During the day, a silent competition takes place, with no spectators, as each boat vies for first place as they row up and down the miniature lake until the sun sets and, one by one, they slow down as their power fades away.

> 'From this beautiful vantage point you can see much of the City and East London up to the Olympic Park. I acquired 200 solar powered toy rowing boats, carried them up to the roof and launched them on the pool. When the sun shines the boats, one for each country competing at the games, will row with each other around the pool'.[30]

The high levels of security surrounding this leftover space, marooned amid the luminescence of the Olympic Park, have meant that the installation has only ever had four visitors: Franglen, a journalist from the *Guardian* newspaper and two friends.

Figure 9: 'Legacy 2'
The Olympic rowers

Instead, 'Legacy' existed as an idea, the use of a leftover space, which is a comment on its gigantic and illustrious neighbour.

The adaptation of waste can be a provocative statement and one that can be undertaken in a particular way so as to provoke reflection on the nature of redundancy and re-use. Waste is a condition that is a process in the life of any material, object and space and, when analysed, is a condition that can be used to challenge and provoke value and differing forms of occupation. It is the assumption of this paper that any material, object or space has a trajectory. This is a journey that all materials and spaces will undertake in their life cycle and something that ensures that they accrue multiple regimes of value in their lifetime. Waste and rubbish have an important role to play in that cycle.

We started with a quote from Don Delillo's *Underworld*, a novel about destruction, particularly in relation to the twin towers, and a book in which waste features prominently. Some of its key characters are involved in waste disposal and analysing its value, not just in terms of resale but also as an indicator of the social habits of the modern city – the contemporary archaeology of life being constructed in land-fill sites which, in this case, takes place in front the main protagonist's eyes. Waste forms a highly visual literary metaphor in the novel, a symbolic stage set and metaphorical device for the analysis of contemporary society.

> 'I'll tell you what I see here Sims. The scenery of the future. Eventually the only scenery left. The more toxic the waste, the greater the effort and expense a tourist will be willing

to tolerate in order to visit the site. Only I don't think you ought to be isolating these sites. Isolate the most toxic waste Okay. This makes it grander, more ominous and magical. But basic household waste ought to be placed in the cities that produce it. Bring garbage into the open. Let people see it and respect it. Don't hide your waste facilities. Make an architecture of waste. Design gorgeous buildings to recycle waste and invite people to collect their own garbage and bring it with them to the press rams and conveyors. Get to know your garbage. And the hot stuff, the chemical waste, the nuclear waste, this becomes the remote landscape of nostalgia. Bus tours and postcards, I guarantee it'.[31]

Notes

[1]   Delillo, D. (1997) *Underworld*, Simon & Schuster, p.287.
[2]   O'Brien, M. (1999) Rubbish Power – Towards a Sociology of the Rubbish Society, in Hearn, J. and Roseneil, S. (eds) *Consuming Cultures: Power and Resistance*, Macmillan.
[3]   See Brooker and Stone (2004), Scott (2008), Hollis (2009), Littlefield and Lewis (2007), Cramer and Breitling (2007)
[4]   Thompson, M. (1979) *Rubbish Theory: The Creation and Destruction of Value*, Oxford University Press.
[5]   Edensor, T. (2005) *Industrial Ruins: Space, Aesthetics and Materiality*, BERG, p.104.
[6]   Ibid., p.108
[7]   Hawkins, G. (2006) *The Ethics of Waste: How We Relate to Rubbish*, Rowman & Littlefield, p.5.
[8]   Frow, J. (2003) Invidious Distinction: Waste, Difference, and Classy Stuff, in Hawkins, G., and Muecke, S., (eds) *Culture and Waste: The Creation and Destruction of Value*, Rowman & Littlefield, p.26.
[9]   Edensor, op. cit., p.107
[10] Scott, F. (2008) *On Altering Architecture*, Routledge, p.5.
[11] Editorial Leader, *Building Design Magazine*, Friday 23 March 2012.
[12] Koolhaas, R., Junkspace, *October* Vol. 100, Spring 2002, MIT Press, p.176.
[13] Machado, R., Old Buildings as Palimpsest: Towards a Theory of Remodelling, *Progressive Architecture*, November 1976, pp.46 and 48.
[14] Ibid., p.49
[15] Ibid.
[16] http://www.cineroleum.co.uk/info/index.html
[17] Bourriaud, N. (2002) *Postproduction: Culture as Screenplay: How Art Reprograms the World*, Lukas & Sternberg, p.13.
[18] Kinney, D. (2010) The Concept of Spolia, in Rudolph, C., *A Companion to Medieval Art*, Wiley-Blackwell, p.233.
[19] Ibid., p.234
[20] Van Hinte, E. (2007) *Superuse: Constructing New Architecture by Shortcutting Material Flows*, 010 Publishers, p.5.
[21] http://2012architecten.nl/
[22] Van Hinte, op. cit., p.16

[23] Meades, J. (2012) Ugly Truths, *Guardian*, 19 September 2012, p.16.
[24] Nielson, T., The Return of the Excessive: Superfluous Landscapes, *Space and Culture*, February 2002, p.56.
[25] Ibid., p.54
[26] Edensor, op. cit., p.21
[27] Meades, op. cit., p.17
[28] Lynskey, D., London 2012: The Hidden Olympic Legacy, *Guardian*, 30 July 2012, available at: http://www.guardian.co.uk/artanddesign/2012/jul/30/london-2012-hidden-olympic-legacy
[29] Franglin, N., http://www.franglen.net/legacy.html
[30] Ibid.
[31] Delillo, op. cit., p.286.

Bibliography

Bourriaud, N. (2002) *Postproduction: Culture as Screenplay: How Art Reprograms the World*, Lukas & Sternberg.
Brooker, G., and Stone, S. (2004) *Rereadings: Interior Architecture & The Principles of Remodelling Buildings*, RIBA Enterprises.
Cramer, S., and Breitling, J. (2007) *Architecture in Existing Fabric*, Birkhauser.
Delillo, D. (1997) *Underworld*, Simon & Schuster.
Edensor, T. (2005) *Industrial Ruins: Space, Aesthetics and Materiality*, BERG.
Hawkins, G. (2006) *The Ethics of Waste: How We Relate to Rubbish*, Rowman & Littlefield.
Hawkins, G., and Muecke, S. (eds) (2003) *Culture and Waste: The Creation and Destruction of Value*, Rowman & Littlefield.
Hearn, J., and Roseneil, S. (eds) (1999) *Consuming Cultures: Power and Resistance*, Macmillan.
Hollis, E. (2009) *The Secret Lives of Buildings*, Portobello Books.
Koolhaas, R. (2002, Spring) Junkspace, *October* Vol. 100, MIT Press, pp.175–190.
Littlefield, D., and Lewis, S. (2007) *Architectural Voices: Listening to Old Buildings*, Wiley-Academy.
Lynskey, D. (2012, July) *London 2012: The Hidden Olympic Legacy*, Guardian.
Machado, R. (1976, November) Old Buildings as Palimpsest: Towards A Theory of Remodelling, *Progressive Architecture*.
Meades, J. (2012 September) Ugly Truths, *Guardian*.
Nielson, T. (2006, February) The Return of the Excessive: Superfluous Landscapes, *Space and Culture*.
Rudolph, C. (2010) *A Companion to Medieval Art*, Wiley-Blackwell.
Scott, F. (2008) *On Altering Architecture*, Routledge.
Thompson, M. (1979) *Rubbish Theory: The Creation and Destruction of Value*, Oxford University Press.
Van Hinte, E. (2007) *Superuse: Constructing New Architecture by Shortcutting Material Flows*, 010 Publishers.
Woodman, E. (2012, March) Editorial Leader, *Building Design Magazine*.

Kirsty MÁTÉ

University of Tasmania, School of Architecture & Design

REMEDIATING SHOPPING CENTRES FOR SUSTAINABILITY

The potential social implications latent in these ideas are picked up in the following chapter by Kirsty Máté who takes on one of the most devouring consumerist beasts in the recent history of commercial architecture: the shopping mall. Places for the production of waste par excellence, these palaces of consumption are examined in the light of recent socio-economic trends that, in the context of the United States at least, have seen them threatened with the possibility of long-term extinction. ...

In the light of their horrific carbon footprint, both in construction and daily use, and in the context of the current economic conditions in the United States, Máté questions whether these 'spaces of consumption' may not be turned around and converted into 'places of production'. ...

The adaptation envisaged here of these existing buildings takes spaces that both produce waste and are in danger of becoming waste and questions how they may be radically reconsidered in the light of current socio-economic circumstances. She asks how they may be made sustainable.

Introduction

The typology of the shopping mall is an architectural phenomenon that has come to epitomise Western consumerist cultures across the globe. They are to be found on every continent in the world and, despite their short life, have become central to certain regional economies, generated numerous academic treatises and taken on a physical form that is instantly, and internationally, recognisable. However, the economic conditions which gave rise to their birth seem to be on the verge of collapse, at least in the country in which they were first established, the United States. The recent economic difficulties of many Western countries have led to numerous closures of malls and a certain crisis of confidence. In many areas, they are closing at a faster rate than they are being built.

These architectural monsters are often huge in size. They often occupy a no-man's land of suburban commercial space and, without a strong economy behind them, are in danger of becoming desolate places of neglect. This paper will both examine the history of malls as a product of a consumer boom and speculate on what their future may be in times of consumer austerity. We propose that the partial, and possibly only temporary, inversion of the economic conditions that gave them birth may facilitate their conversion from places of unbridled consumption to places of sustainable production. These symbols of consumerism, we suggest, may have the potential to remake themselves; to fold back their image as symbols of waste and decadence and become something quite different: places of real and symbolic sustainability.

First There Were Stones, Then There Were Malls

The translation of the activity of shopping into a physical form can be traced back to the first ancient Greek markets, where rings of stones were placed outside the city walls to mark out neutral territory for trade with other settlements.[1] The fundamental development of internal shopping spaces grew from marketplaces and bazaars to arcades, department stores, supermarkets and shopping centres and malls – each development separating itself continuously from the connections and limitations of urbanity and the unpredictable nature of climate. The development of the arcade in Paris in the late eighteenth century significantly changed retailing and shopping in Europe[2] and, for the first time, the urban experience was internalised and linked by spaces of consumption.[3] Customers were now able to traverse the city in an enclosed environment, separated from the noise and grime of the streets, and to concentrate their attention undividedly on one activity: shopping.[4] This retail form, enabled through new technologies and materials, spread across the globe over the next 100 years and created architecturally grand spaces for a 'growing middle class that marked itself through conspicuous consumption.'[5]

The opening of Bon Marché, the first department store in Paris in 1869, was a reinforcement of this new form of consumerism.[6] These new internalised spaces were dedicated to a new leisure activity of consumption, rather than to the more diverse and productive activities of the markets, bazaars and street shops which preceded them. They were the start of the modern culture of mass consumption.[7] The next significant development for retail forms was the supermarket, with the first opening in New York in 1930.[8] As these large interior spaces required land, they were mainly located on the urban fringes of cities and, as a result of their worldwide proliferation, their impact on the urban landscape was to be profound.[9] By 2008, there were approximately 85,400 grocery chain stores throughout America[10] and, in 2007, Australia – a much less populous nation – boasted over 6,000 similar supermarket and grocery retailers.[11]

The department store and supermarket are critical to the development of the shopping centre, as the relationship between these different entities is symbiotic. While the formative period for the development of the regional shopping mall in America was from the mid-1940s to the mid-1950s[12], the first enclosed mall[13] came into existence in 1956. It was Victor Gruen's Southdale mall in Minneapolis, USA. From this moment onwards, shopping could be completely internalised, the commercial streets of trade now captured within an artificially lit and air-conditioned island that, furthermore, could be surrounded by a sea of parked cars and an asphalt desert. To be fair to Gruen, his stated intention was to replicate the community life of markets and town squares and locate shopping centres alongside schools, offices, housing and open, landscaped spaces.[14] However, the reality became somewhat different. This growing internalised retail form, enabled through new technologies and materials, spread across the globe, creating architecturally grand spaces for a 'growing middle class that marked itself through conspicuous consumption'.[15]

Over the last fifty years, this typology has differed little from the initial concept, apart from becoming bigger and grander in scale, as exemplified by mega malls such as the Mall of America, USA, and the South China Mall, China. They now offer more 'variety', 'excitement' and 'entertainment' and continue to innovate and grow as they enter into ever more intense competition with each other. The focus on 'entertainment' seen in these more recent malls was first heralded in the 1990s with centres and malls offering anything from carousel rides to interactive demonstrations.[16] The Dubai Mall, for example, offers an ice rink and an aquarium and has been described as the Persian Gulf Complex, a complex that 'will have an indoor amusement park, a prayer room and a helicopter landing pad'.[17]

This shift in emphasis is seen in Australia in the projects of various shopping-centre developers, notably the Westfield Group. Westfield has been a leader in retail development and management internationally, creating a retail mix within the shopping-centre typology that has seen it grow into one of the world's largest retail property groups.[18] In recent years, the act of shopping, then, has correspondingly diversified, spreading from its traditional designated spaces into almost every arena of urban life such as airports, museums, train stations, hospitals, schools and even the military.[19] In this context, 'cities are no longer seen as landscapes of production, but as landscapes of consumption.'[20]

The modern-day shopping centre, whose evolution we have briefly sketched here, is so entrenched and so familiar a building form in most countries of the world (particularly the developed nations) that it is hard to believe that, within the living memory of those who today are sixty years or older, it did not exist. While this new way of shopping brought convenience, variety, comfort and a new shopping experience, the repercussions of its almost overnight infiltration and takeover of the retail experiences of the past were realised too late. In the last 20 to 30 years, however, there has been a growing concern in regard to mass consumption and its impact on our planet. As a temple of mass consumption, now that the world is entering an era where consumption is increasingly seen as a major prohibitory factor to a more sustainable future, the modern-day shopping centre could be vulnerable. In this context, we ask the question: like the industrial sites of past technologies, could shopping centres be adapted to become productive centres that contribute to sustainable physical, social and affective futures – without the need for a major reorientation in capitalism?

The Vulnerability of Shopping Centres and Malls

Shopping centres and malls are accustomed to change but are not always resilient to its effects. Being highly vulnerable to the variances of economies, demographics, local competition and trends, the shopping centre/mall is continually changing. These changes are evident in its internal environments, along with its organisational and technological systems, all of which have adapted in order to maintain economic viability and, ultimately, to survive.[21] However, many do fail to adapt. Between 2007 and 2009, more than 400 of the 2,000 largest malls in the USA closed their doors.[22] The last 'ground-up' mall to be built in the USA opened its doors in 2006.[23] At the start of the twenty-first century, industry speculated that the future of the omnipresent shopping mall in the USA was bleak;[24] a situation exacerbated between 2008 and 2009 by the global financial crisis.[25] In fact, malls in the USA continue to close at a faster rate than they are opening. The economy is the biggest killer for malls and the global financial crisis in the USA has seen many suffer.[26]

Anchor stores (usually a department store and/or supermarket) provide the traffic flow for the smaller shops within a shopping mall. If an anchor store leaves a mall, the smaller stores suffer and the mall itself falls into decline.[27] This has been happening with increasing frequency in the US in recent years. Other reasons malls have become less popular or failed are various: new malls opening in the area; new shopping experiences in other retail outlets; their mammoth size; their artificial interior environments; decreasing popularity of department stores; parking difficulties and customer preference for online shopping.[28] Furthermore, Ellen Dunham-Jones notes that many malls have also not been in keeping with the changing demographic and lifestyles of those living in the suburbs.[29]

In contrast to the difficulties of the mall in America, shopping centres in Australia rarely close: the problem of 'dead malls' is seen as an American phenomenon, with only pockets of retail closures and inactivity seen in Australia.[30] As Bird[31] explains, this is likely due to the retail mix found in Australian shopping centres, where general and luxury purchase items, as well as a variety of food outlets, cater for a greater proportion of consumer needs. This may offer some clues to what can be done in the US context to save the mall. However, it is unlikely to completely solve the problem and more radical solutions may be necessary.

Shopping Centres and Malls as Icons of Consumption

If, as Beth Blostein says, energy as an invisible product of consumption becomes visible through the production of 'stuff' and consumables,[32] then shopping centres are one of its greatest manifestations; and the speed at which they have become visible is astounding. The manifestations and growth of the shopping mall/centre have been almost parasitic. The number of shopping malls in the USA in 2005 (just shy of 50 years since the opening of the first mall) was 48,685.[33] This equates to over 900 malls for every year since 1956. Australia's shopping centres totalled 1,102 in 2007[34] and in the United Kingdom in 2009 there were 819 shopping centres and 1,340 retail parks. This equated to 17 per cent of all retail space being dedicated to shopping centres.[35]

Despite these impressive (or worrying) numbers, shopping centres and malls were created as part of an approach to consumption that, according to the marketing consultant and retail critic of the time, Victor Lebow,[36] demanded 'that we make consumption our way of life, that we convert the buying and use of goods into rituals, that we seek our spiritual satisfactions, our ego satisfactions, in consumption.' However, the world is moving towards a paradigm of sustainability according to which mass consumption is seen as one of the greatest barriers. As Migone points out: 'The high levels of consumption fostered by hedonistic consumerism lead to both an ecological and an economic crisis.'[37] The question is thus: can supermarkets and shopping malls continue to dominate retail in the face of such a radical paradigm shift, in a socio-economic environment in which:

> 'As the urgent state of ecological degradation and social inequity worldwide raise ever-more pressing questions about the methods, patterns, and consequences of global consumption, the subject of sustainable consumption has a become a focus of serious international attention.'[38]

Sustainability, Retail and Sustainable Consumption

The environmental impact of mass consumables is enormous and would far outweigh the impacts of the buildings they inhabit. Many retailers (Woolworths, Australia (Figure 1); Sainsbury's, Marks & Spencer (M&S) and Tesco, UK; Wal-Mart and Whole Foods, USA) are now addressing the environmental and social consciousness of their customers by ensuring that they provide alternative choices, such as products which are organically grown, fair trade, low carbon, water and energy efficient, or locally produced. Sustainable products are no longer the domain of the specialist eco and healthy-living stores of the late twentieth century. Even the world's largest retailer, Wal-Mart, is aware of the buying power of the LOHAS (lifestyles of health and sustainability) consumer; a figure who represents 16–20 per cent of all American consumers.[39] The extent of the environmental and social impacts of consumption is far reaching and the retail industry has only recently started addressing these issues beyond shelf products.

Energy, mainly from non-renewable and greenhouse-gas intensive sources, is used to maintain a constant internal temperature of big-box stores and shopping centres,

Figure 1: Woolworths Safeway Store, Melbourne, Australia

thus keeping perishables fresh. It is also used to illuminate stock to the maximum. Water use is another concern, particularly in food and beverage retail outlets where it is used for washing, cooking and ablutions. A similar concern is focused on the road transportation (the most carbon-intensive system possible) needed to deliver and purchase goods from stores. Furthermore, retail leases within centres and malls change rapidly – every five years on average in Australia.[40] This too leads to the use of excessive quantities of resources and materials and creates large volumes of waste on a continual basis. Beyond these material concerns, social sustainability is an issue of debate around the retail environment with 'non-buying customers' being made unwelcome and, in some cases, 'ostracised' in retail precincts. Furthermore, their tendency to become 'globalised' environments means that cultural diversity is also diminished inside their artificial confines.

According to Jones and Comfort,[41] many UK retailers have been addressing the three 'pillars' of sustainability (environment, society and economy) to tackle these issues. Companies such as Wal-Mart in the USA, M&S in the UK, Woolworths in Australia and global retail chains such as McDonalds and IKEA are global leaders in this area, significantly reducing their environmental and 'social' footprints. Sustainable consumption is taking varied and disparate forms as it steers away from years of conflicting messages and less-sustainable practices. The term is multilayered and subject to many interpretations, practices and imaginings which, as we have indicated, take on moral as well as material issues.[42] Two issues, however, are reasonably clear: the consumption of material products needs to be reduced (although to what level is arguable); and the environmental and social impacts of the things we consume should be decreased.

Growing evidence of new paradigms of sustainable consumption are emerging, then. These are often led by shifting consumer behaviours[43] which will assist in a reduction of overall consumption and likely further fuel the design of future retail environments.[44] Economics, politics, technology and changing consumer values are influencing the development of these paradigms and, in the process, instigate a parallel growth in the understanding of sustainable principles. Bansal and Kilbourne's[45] initial research into this area identified three critical differences between the current dominant social paradigm (DSP) and a new environmental paradigm (NEP): economics, technology and politics. The current DSP relies on economics formed by market-determined prices; technology focused on expanding productivity; and politics which is anthropocentric in nature. The NEP by contrast, shapes its economics on resource value and uses of technology aimed at improving quality of life and having a political focus that is ecocentric.

A retail system based on the NEP would be co-operative and community-orientated, would situate stores within communities and easily facilitate the transfer of goods and services. A greater responsibility to local communities would facilitate employment and support a stable eco-environment; and ecologically efficient technological and management systems would facilitate and encourage the reduction of ecological impacts. Finally, the merchandising of products would require life-cycle analysis to ensure a minimal ecological impact across their entire life cycle.[46] While Bansal and Kilbourne predict a new consumer paradigm through different approaches to economics, technology and politics, Blinkoff and colleagues use an ethnographic study in the USA to focus on a newly developing consumer identity.[47] This identity, they suggest, is based on changing values developed in the context of recent political and economic crises and is referred to as the 'grounded consumer'.[48] This new post has abandoned the economic past of *homo economicus* to form a new set of consumer values and qualities. Grounded consumers adhere to the following values:

1) *Know Thy Means: the Grounded Consumer fully understands their 'means' and lives within them;*

2) *Embraces a WE Economy: the Grounded Consumer embraces a 'We Economy' – balancing personal financial success with values of sociality, community, and well-being;*

3) *Lives an unSTUFFed Life: the Grounded Consumer fills their lives with more than just 'Stuff' (a 'technical' term from many in our study);*

4) *Walks the Talk: the Grounded Consumer does not sit on their new learning and skills but puts it all into action.*49

The work of Bansal and Kilbourne,[50] Blinkoff and colleagues[51] and others[52] shows compelling evidence that changes to consumerism and consumerist behaviour are being influenced by many factors. These include the growth of online shopping; the presence of new and developing technologies to enhance the shopping experience – both virtually and physically;[53] an increase in 'experiential' retail encounters; and global economic and political influences. These changes are producing a decline in conspicuous consumption and indicate that the current consumer paradigm in developed countries will soon be an model of the past.[54] These emerging consumer paradigms largely embody sustainable principles and values, and can broadly be grouped as follows:

1. Community-orientated consumption
2. Ethical and political consumption
3. The Experience economy
4. Prosumption.

Community-orientated consumption paradigms relate to behavioural changes that link people more closely in social and/or cultural terms. These can be virtual or face to face. Collaborative Consumption,[55] the 'Me' vs 'We' economies,[56] service economies,[57] the slow movement[58] and gift economies[59] are all examples of these emerging paradigms. In this context, Manzini argues that, in order to reduce consumption, we need to look at the systems and services we already have in place and use these more effectively.[60] Shared services such as car sharing, public bike hire, toy libraries and the like all result from these community consumer paradigms. Importantly, Botsman and Rogers also predict the use of the Internet for communication and obtaining information as important for a retail future based on collaborative consumption.

These ethical[61] and political[62] consumption paradigms reflect the deep values and beliefs held by consumers most clearly reflected today in the consumption of fair-trade, organically grown and locally produced food. Anti-consumption[63] addresses the ethical and political issues of over consumption head-on, avoiding the consumption of goods and also taking into account 'services' that can replace the 'purchase' of goods – for example libraries.[64] This paradigm will also expect transparency and authenticity of information[65] and will value honesty as a critical component and consider accessible information as key – either online or in-store.

These factors may be accompanied by what is known as the 'experience economy',[66] a phenomenon that takes on various guises. It includes providing entertainment to consumers while they shop,[67] providing information on various products through, for example, cooking shows and providing extras such as health services or health-insurance plans. The next generation of consumers will be looking for a memorable experience, service or event and will not necessarily be focused on the final product.

Figure 2: Whole Foods Store, Austin Texas, USA, in-store restaurants
Photographed by the author

In her article '2028: A Retail Odyssey', Dennis-Jones[68] predicts a future for retail in which shops are replaced by experiences, essential goods are delivered automatically to households as they are needed and shopping becomes an emotional experience that includes regular activities such as retail theatre, cooking demonstrations and fashion shows.

Prosumption (the final grouping) can be seen as the *'emergent orientation towards consumers as active value-creators.'*[69] Consumers in this category are actively involved in the production of their consumption, hence *pro*-sumption. Currently, the flat-pack, make-it-yourself furniture from companies such as IKEA is one of the few and limited examples of the potential of 'prosuming'. By adding value to the act of consuming, it encompasses many of the paradigms of the previous groupings and could be seen as one of the major consumer groups of the near future.

> *'"We are witnessing a 'prosumer' revolution; groups of active and engaged consumers are setting the agenda many mainstream consumers will eventually follow. They are demanding traceable or organic foods, they want to avoid malls and shop locally, they insist on a more personal level of service and they buy brands that demonstrate a clear ethical, social, civic and environmental agenda." The Future Laboratory'*[70]

Remediating Existing Shopping Centres and Malls for Sustainable Consumption

As we have argued, an increasing awareness and understanding of sustainability, its connection to the consumption of goods and changing values towards consumerism are all changing the values and behaviours of consumers. They are thus key factors in creating the current dominant retail paradigm. This is currently being reflected in changes to the manufacture and production of goods and services and, as we shall discuss now, by a growing number of retailers and shopping centres that address the consumptive output of their buildings themselves. These buildings attempt to reduce energy, water and material requirements and ensure that waste materials and pollution are dealt with appropriately.[71]

Cabot Circus (UK), Forum Duisburg (Germany) and Atrio (Austria) are notable examples of buildings that have been purpose built to integrate energy efficiency, alternative energy sources and natural daylighting. However, these efforts are limited and can be seen as little more than a 'band-aiding' solution. Furthermore, the problem remains of what to do about our existing malls, all of which need to be remediated.

The remediation of shopping centres/malls is not a new concept. In response to the 'dead mall' syndrome in Northern America, remediation of disused shopping malls and big-box retail has been occurring for a number of years. Julia Christensen[72] provides examples of new and productive uses such as the adaptive re-use of retail buildings as churches, schools, libraries and medical centres. Ellen Dunham-Jones, in her book *Retrofitting Suburbia*,[73] has documented case studies where entire shopping malls were transformed into living, 'walkable' communities and food courts. In these examples, the vacant interiors are replaced with quality restaurants that reflect the new suburban demographic of young professionals and 'empty nesters'.[74]

While several of these solutions address some of the needs of a sustainable consumption model for these buildings, they are largely changing the focus of use from the trade of goods and services to entirely new, singular-function or multi-functional precincts. In contrast to this, we suggest here that shopping centres and malls can be seen as places of consumption rather than production.[75] In existing centres, land, materials, goods, food, time, energy, personas and brands are consumed and very little is produced, save the unwanted remainders of consumption. However, by using Capra's principles of ecology as a basis, a secondary framework of 'productive urban ecologies' could be envisaged that would create positive, sustainably productive spaces that respond to evolving consumer needs and reduce the consumptive needs of the building industry through new builds.[76]

Retrofitting shopping centres and malls to make them places of production rather than places of consumption could be an option for a sustainable future. It is a change in the concept of a shopping centre as a 'production hub' that aligns with the theories of Bansal and Kilbourne on the NEP.[77] As production hubs, shopping centres and malls would be the 'producers' of much of the local community's food, goods and services,

Figure 3: Rouse Hill Town Centre, Sydney Australia, renewable energy sources and community kitchen garden

as well as the providers of their own (and possibly the local community's) energy and water requirements. Issues of waste would largely be dealt with on-site and could be used in the production of food, energy and/or goods. The interior environments for these shopping spaces might have to have a stronger connection with the exterior climate: air-conditioning, heating and lighting could be replaced with passive or mixed-mode designs that introduce fresh air and natural light into these formerly artificial enclosures.

These remediated shopping centres would provide greater and more diverse opportunities for employment within a local community, in areas such as farming, engineering and mechanical maintenance. In addition, there is more scope for voluntary and/or educational involvement from a larger proportion of the community – from small children to the elderly. The opportunity for the creation of small to medium-sized businesses would also be increased through the expanded diversity of goods and services and could include education, health and communication facilities. Politically, these urban/suburban production hubs could replace local governments and ensure the needs and well-being of individuals within a local community, rather than focusing only on services.

Figure 4: Student work, Alfonse Tran, UTAS: Adaptive re-use of Coates & Paton Building, Launceston, Australia, for sustainable consumption
Section showing vertical farm and diverse activities on each level

As production hubs, the large plots of land currently used as car parks could be more productively used as places of food production, reducing food miles by producing and selling the produce on-site and creating alternative occupations for local residents. Interior atriums could serve as internal vertical farms (Figure 4) and the large roofs could be transformed into productive green roofs, solar collectors and/or used to capture storm water for either the surrounding edible gardens or for distribution to surrounding communities. Energy production through renewable energy sources such as solar and wind farms could inhabit many of the extensive spaces of a suburban shopping centre/mall and potentially provide enough energy for not only their own needs but also those of the greater community. Furthermore, waste could be dealt with on-site as much as possible through composting (which would be the easiest to administer) but also by recycling and reusing items such as packaging.

Public transport systems and supported alternative private transport, such as pushbikes and walking, and shared private or semi-public systems such as car sharing would be required to supplement the loss of car parking. However, this would further reduce carbon emissions and reinforce a sustainable transport system. The use of 'plug and go' energy systems to recharge electric and solar-powered cars and trucks would further support the premise of the production hub and could be tied into a public semi-electric transport system. Further to this, community-orientated and ethical consumption paradigms could also be serviced through the re-use and adaptation of goods through repair, swapping and redesigning, thus further reducing pressure on resources and waste. Markets and light industry associated with product adaption and repair would also fit within this model as would designer maker studios, peer-to-peer services and exchange, loan and hire facilities, for example; all of which would facilitate local employment and provide a higher diversity of skills.

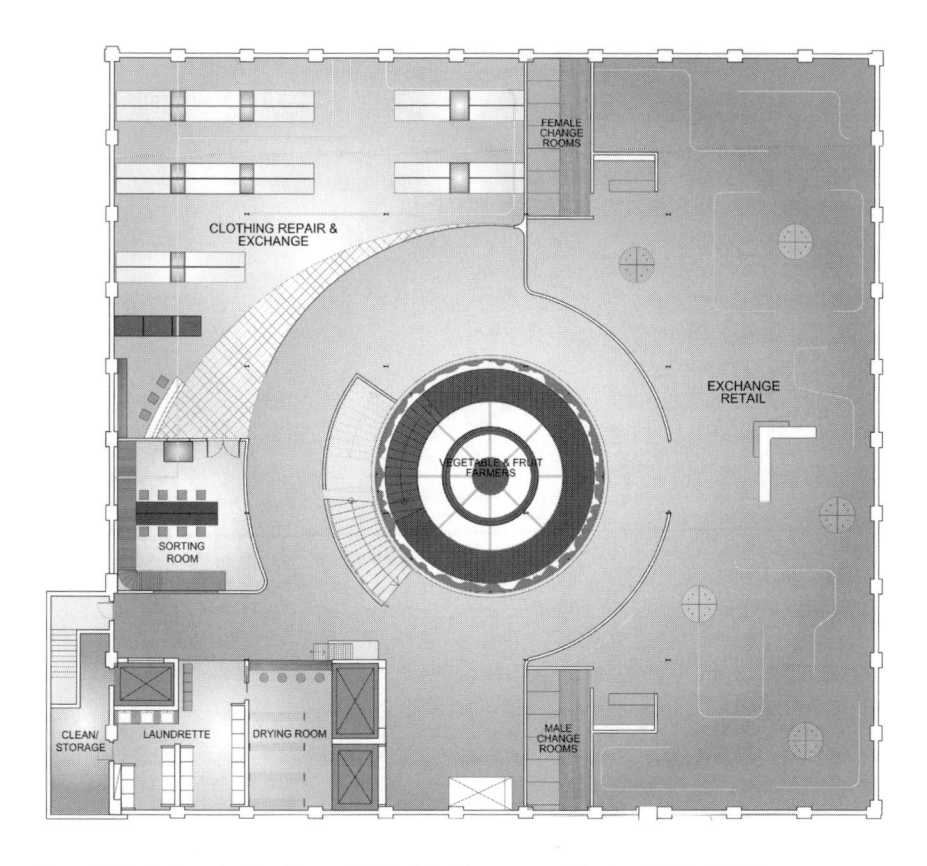

Figure 5: Student work, Alice Dwyer, UTAS: Adaptive re-use of Coates & Paton Building, Launceston, Australia, for sustainable consumption
Plan of clothing and exchange level

This diversification requires a corresponding variety of spaces for differing programs other than the display and storage of goods, as per the model of most current retail outlets. An example of this can be seen in the student project for a clothing exchange and repair outlet shown in Figure 5. The program includes sorting, laundering, repair facilities, pick up and delivery, storage, display and fitting rooms. For the designer makers involved, a diverse range of equipment and spaces would be provided including: kilns, timber- and metal-working machinery, textile equipment, water and wastewater facilities, computers, storage and safe working areas with natural light and quality ventilation (Figure 6). The use of technology such as mobile phone 'apps', social media and the Internet would play an important role in the project and help develop trade activities and community involvement.

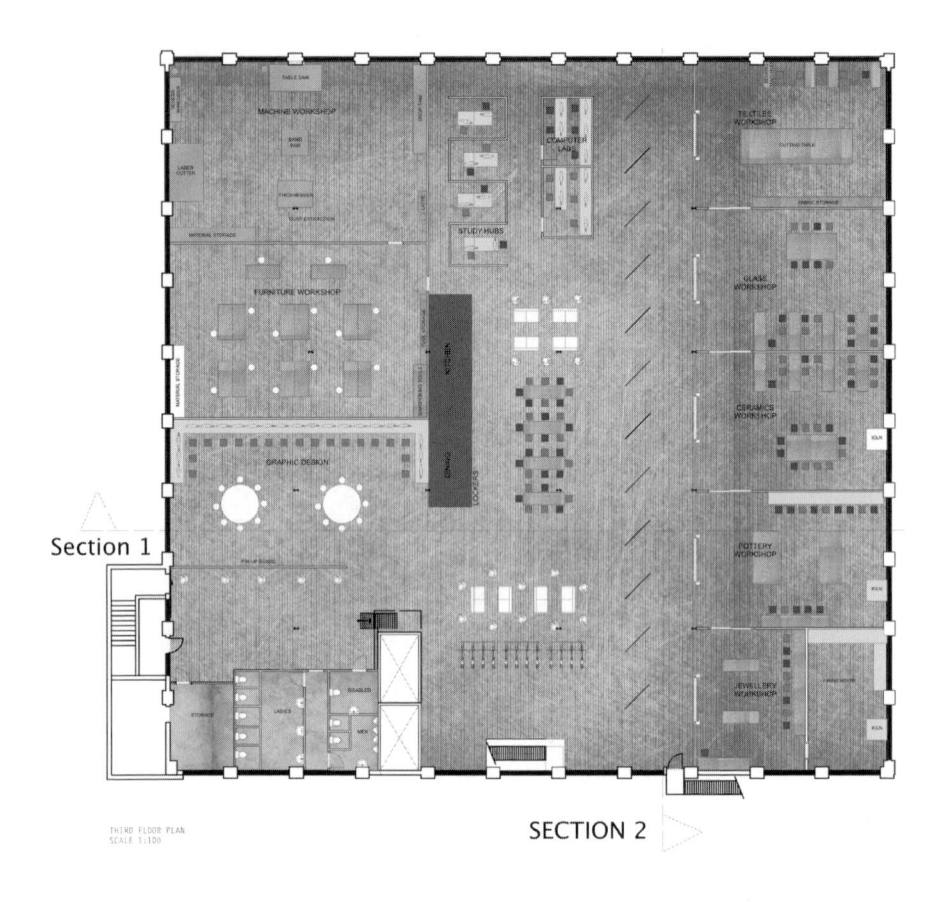

Figure 6: Student work, Ashleigh Elliott, UTAS: Adaptive re-use of Coates & Paton Building, Launceston, Australia, for sustainable consumption
Plan of designer makers' level

One already-evident consequence of the continued growth of online shopping is the increased focus on retail entertainment and other more socially inclusive activities that are replacing some of the more mundane shopping experiences. This is evidenced by the example of Stockland, the Australian property operator that recently announced a reduction in the retail floor areas of their venues so as to increase entertainment activities such as cinemas and restaurants.[78] Sustainably remediated shopping centres are likely to increase their social and cultural roles along related lines which, as we have indicated, may be more community based. 'Entertainment' activities likely to inhabit the production hub of these sustainable centres would include healthy and sustainable living entertainment shows for cooking, fashion design and cleaning. It may also include 'do-it-yourself' activities for local community groups as well as other entertainment facilities such as sports events, cinemas, restaurants, theatres and galleries.

Additionally, technology could ensure that the production hub remains a modern facility that utilises the benefits of the digital age for enhanced information provision and communication. The use of technology could play an important role in a sustainable retail future by ensuring the most efficient supply and delivery of produce; facilitating the development of smart packaging solutions; providing detailed information to customers through RFID coding; and enabling an increased use of the Internet and nanotechnologies to create intelligent products.[79] The production hub is proposed here as a part of the current economic paradigm in which money is largely exchanged for goods and services. However, it does not preclude the addition of other trade paradigms which may assist in maintaining lower consumption patterns such as bartering, the use of credit tokens and voluntary work schemes.

Furthermore, it does not presume that all the requirements of a community can be produced solely on-site and acknowledges that some goods and services will have to be brought to the site or completed offsite, in which case they would have to be vetted within a life-cycle assessment accreditation model such as Bansal and Kilbourne's NEP.[80] The production hub is also proposed as part of a modern community in which there is a diversity of needs, wants and desires. It does not presume that all members of the community will have an active role in the hub's activities but does suggest itself as a response to diverse consumption patterns and an uptake of sustainable consumption behaviour.

Concluding Remarks

As we have outlined here, the activity of shopping has seen a rapid global transformation in the space of half a century; a transformation epitomised by the emergence of the department store, the supermarket and the shopping mall. More recently, this transformation has seen an attitudinal change to consumption itself that has shifted from necessity to leisure.[81] Most recently, however, there has been a change in societal values regarding the use of technologies and, most importantly, around issues of a sustainability. In the last quarter of the twentieth century and into the twenty-first century, there has been a growing recognition of, and movement towards, a more sustainable way of life – particularly in developed countries, where rates of consumption outweigh the planet's ability to sustain itself into the future.[82]

Despite this, modern shopping centres and malls continue to try to sustain themselves through a growth in consumption. The remediation of these buildings into 'production hubs' can be seen as a means of enlivening and enriching these ageing monsters of consumption. We have suggested that their exterior spaces could be transformed into productive food, energy and water farms and their interior spaces could be adapted to an increased diversity of trade forms and light industries. To do this, their spaces would need to be more flexible and less wasteful. Perhaps they will need to integrate 'guerrilla'-type short-life stores and 'plug-and-play' concepts into the way they operate. Using ideas such as these, pre-formed interiors could be slotted into allocated modules so as to minimise resources and ensure re-use, recycling and biodegradability at the end of a store's lifecycle. Whatever the specifics of the approach applied, what we are proposing is the application of ideas and modes of operating that come from a field of study and activity normally completely disassociated from this building typology. The complexity and variety of the sustainable consumption solutions we have enumerated can, we suggest, create opportunities for change and a more inclusive and beneficial solution to the future of the shopping centres of the twentieth century. While this is not tabled as a solution to the problems of mass consumption per se, it is a change that could function as one of the many catalysts necessary for more profound changes within the current capitalist society.

Notes

[1] McMorrough, J. (2001) City of Shopping, in Chung, C.J., et al. (eds), *Project on the City 2 – Harvard Design School Guide to Shopping*, Köln, Germany: Taschen, pp.193–203.
[2] Chung, C.J., et al. (eds), *Project on the City 2 – Harvard Design School Guide to Shopping*, Köln, Germany: Taschen.
[3] McMorrough, 2001; Leong, S. (2001b) Mobility, in Chung et al., 2001, op. cit. (pp. 477–500).
[4] Leong, 2001b
[5] Jayne, M. (2006) *Cities and Consumption*, UK: Routledge, p.43.
[6] Humphery, K. (1998) *Shelf Life – Supermarkets and the Changing Cultures of Consumption*, Cambridge, UK: Cambridge University Press.
[7] Ibid.; Jayne, 2006
[8] Chung et al., 2001
[9] Humphery, 1998
[10] Anon. (no date) *Melbourne retail strategy 2006:2012*, Melbourne, Australia: City of Melbourne, State Government of Victoria and Melbourne Retail Advisory Board.
[11] Lennon, S. (2007) *National Association of Retail Grocers of Australia – The economic contribution of small to medium-sized grocery retailers to the Australian economy, with a particular focus on Western Australia*, retrieved from: file:///Users/kmate/Documents/Eco Info/Retail/Supermarkets:Large Chains/Economic_contribution_ SMEs_NARGA.pdf.
[12] Vernon, P. (2012) Shopping Towns Australia, *Fabrications: The Journal of the Society of Architectural Historians, Australia and New Zealand* 22(1), pp.103–21.
[13] In the USA and parts of Asia, the term 'shopping mall' is used for a building with an internal street of shops, usually with an anchor store such as a department store. This same form is called a shopping centre in Australia, the UK and Europe.
[14] Leong, S. (2001a) Gruen Urbanism, in Chung, C.J., et al. (eds), *Project on the City 2 – Harvard Design School Guide to Shopping*, Köln: Taschen, pp.381–7.
[15] Jayne, 2006
[16] Kavanagh, M. (2000) A Brief History of Shopping Centers, *ICSC News – The Impact of Shopping Centers*, retrieved from: http://www.icsc.org/srch/about/impactofshoppingcenters/briefhistory.html [accessed 24 November 2011].
[17] Anon. (2012) The 10 biggest shopping centres in the world, *Detail.de*, retrieved from: http://www.detail-online.com/architecture/topics/the-10-biggest-shopping-centres-in-

the-world-018606.html [accessed 1 October 2012].
[18] Shulman, C. (2010) *IBISWorld Industry Report L7714 Retail Property Operators in Australia*, Australia: IBISWorld.
[19] Koolhaas, R. (2000) Shopping, in Lavalou, A. (ed.), *Mutations*, Barcelona, Spain: ACTAR, pp.124–83.
[20] Zukin, S. (1998) Urban lifestyles: Diversity and standardisation in spaces of consumption, *Urban Studies (Routledge)* 35(5/6), p.825.
[21] Kavanagh, 2000
[22] Anon. (2009c) The vanishing shopping mall, *The Week*, retrieved from: http://theweek.com/article/index/94691/the-vanishing-shopping-mall [accessed 11 October 2011].
[23] Anon. (2011a) Last Stop: Turtle Creek, *Retail Traffic*, retrieved from: http://retailtrafficmag.com/development/analysis/last_stop_turtle_creek/ [accessed 15 October 2011]. A website, 'deadmalls.com', dedicated to the fall of shopping malls around the country documents this phenomenon: Anon. (no date) deadmalls DOT com, retrieved from: http://www.deadmalls.com/ [accessed 11 December 2011].
[24] Bodamer, D. (2005) The Mall is Dead, *Retail Traffic*, retrieved from: http://retailtrafficmag.com/mag/retail_mall_dead/ [accessed 7 December 2011]; Sokol, D. (2003) Longer Live the Mall, *MetropolisMag.com*, retrieved from: http://www.metropolismag.com/story/20030601/longer-live-the-mall [accessed 8 December 2011].
[25] Anon., 2009c; Benfield, K. (2009) R.I.P. the American Suburban Shopping Mall, *Kaid Benfield's Blog | Switchboard, from NRDC*, retrieved from: http://switchboard.nrdc.org/blogs/kbenfield/rip_the_american_suburban_shop.html [accessed 7 December 2011]; Gregory, S. (2009) The Last Shopping Mall? New Jersey Awaits Xanadu – TIME, *Time Magazine Business*, retrieved from: http://www.time.com/time/magazine/article/0,9171,1886537,00.html [accessed 7 December 2011]; Misonzhnik, E. (2010) Developers Rethink the Mall for the 21st Century, *Retail Traffic*, retrieved from: http://retailtrafficmag.com/news/developers_rethink_mall_06272010/index2.html [accessed 7 December 2011].
[26] Hudson, K. (2009) Recession turns US malls into ghost towns, *Wall Street Journal – Business*, retrieved from: http://www.theaustralian.com.au/business/recession-turns-us-malls-into-ghost-towns/story-e6frg8zx-1225714885352 [accessed 11 December 2011].
[27] Anon., 2009c
[28] Misonzhnik, E. (2011) Return of the Mall, *Retail Traffic*, retrieved from: http://retailtrafficmag.com/development/analysis/return_of_the_mall_05052011/index.html [accessed 7 December 2011].
[29] O'Connell, A. (2009) Architect Ellen Dunham-Jones on the future of retail in the post sprawl era – Harvard Business Review, *Havard Business Review – The Magazine*, retrieved from: http://hbr.org/2009/07/architect-ellen-dunham-jones-on-the-future-of-retail-in-the-postsprawl-era/ar/1 [accessed 8 December 2011].
[30] Productivity Commission (2011) *Economic Structure and Performance of the Australian Retail Industry Report 56*, Canberra: Australian Government Productivity Commission.
[31] Bird, J. (2009) The Dead Mall Syndrome, *New Retail Blog*, retrieved from: http://www.newretailblog.com/the-dead-mall-syndrome/ [accessed 11 December 2011].
[32] Blostein, B. (2010) Toward a Productive Excess, in Tilder, L., and Blostein, B. (eds),

Design Ecologies – Essays on the Nature of Design, New York: Princeton Architectural Press, pp.239–52.

[33] Anon. (2007) *Section 22 Wholesale and Retail Trade*, USA: US Census Bureau, p.661, retrieved from: http://search.census.gov/search?q=shopping+malls&btnG.x=9&btnG.y=14&btnG=Go&entqr=0&ud=1&output=xml_no_dtd&oe=UTF-8&ie=UTF-8&client=default_frontend&proxystylesheet=default_frontend&site=census [accessed 12 November 2011].

[34] Urbis JHD Pty Ltd (2007) *Australian Shopping Centre Industry – Information Update, March 2007*, Australia: Shopping Centre Council of Australia, p.1, retrieved from: http://www.scca.org.au/HTML%20Pages/Research.htm.

[35] Anon. (2009a) BCSC Retail Property Statistics Summary October 2009, retrieved from: www.bcsc.org.uk/.../download.asp?.../09RetailPropertyStatisticsSum... [accessed 12 November 2011].
A retail park is the equivalent of the Australian Supercentre and the American Power Center – a grouping of many retail warehouses. (Anon. (2011b) Retail park, *Wikipedia: the free encyclopedia*, retrieved from: http://en.wikipedia.org/wiki/Retail_park [accessed 11 December 2011]) Interestingly, in the UK, there is a different dynamic between shopping centres, the high street and retail parks from that in America and Australia.

[36] Lebow, V. (1955) Price Competition in 1955, *Journal of Retailing* (Spring).

[37] Migone, A. (2007) Hedonistic Consumerism: Patterns of Consumption in Contemporary Capitalism, *Review of Radical Political Economics* 39(2), p.185.

[38] Turner, R. (2010) Discourses of Consumption in US-American Culture, *Sustainability* 2(7), p.2,281.Turner, R. (2010) Discourses of Consumption in US-American Culture. *Sustainability*, 2(7), p.2281

[39] Interview with Gwynne Rogers, Lifestyles of Health and Sustainability Business Director, Natural Marketing Institute, 2010

[40] Anon. (2008) *The Market for Retail Tenancy Leases in Australia: Productivity Commission Draft Report*, Australian Government Productivity Commission, retrieved from: internal-pdf://Market for Retail Tenancy Leases in Aust-0402853888/Market for Retail Tenancy Leases in Aust.pdf.

[41] Jones, P., et al. (2005) Retailers and sustainable development in the UK, *International Journal of Retail & Distribution Management* 33(3), pp.207–14.

[42] Mansvelt, J. (2008) Geographies of consumption: citizenship, space and practice, *Progress in Human Geography* 32(1), pp.105–17.

[43] Bennie, F., et al. (2011) *Consumer Futures 2020 – Scenarios for tomorrow's consumers*, Forum for the Future, retrieved from: http://www.forumforthefuture.org/sites/default/files/project/downloads/consumer-futures-2020-full-document.pdf; Blinkoff, R., Johnson, T.P., Kabran, L., Gray, S., et al. (2008) *Grounding the American Dream: A Cultural Study on the Future of Consumerism in a Changing Economy*, USA: Context-Based Research Group & Carton Donofrio Partners, Inc, retrieved from: http://www.thegroundedconsumer.com/ [accessed 21 January 2012]; Goodman, J., et al. (2007) *Retail Futures – scenarios for the future of UK retail and sustainable development*, Forum for the Future, retrieved from: internal-pdf://Retail Futures Forum for Future-2483071744/Retail Futures Forum for Future.pdf.

[44] White, R. (2010) The future of shopping centers, retrieved from: http://www.whitehutchinson.com/leisure/articles/FutureOfShoppingCenters.shtml.
[45] Bansal, P., and Kilbourne, W.E. (2001) The ecologically sustainable retailer, *Journal of Retailing and Consumer Services* 8(3), pp.139–46.
[46] Ibid.
[47] Blinkoff et al., 2008
[48] Ibid., p.3
[49] Ibid., p.4
[50] Bansal and Kilbourne, 2001
[51] Blinkoff et al., 2008
[52] Black, I.R., and Cherrier, H. (2010) Anti-consumption as part of living a sustainable lifestyle: Daily practices, contextual motivations and subjective values, *Journal of Consumer Behaviour* 9(6), pp.437–53; Fraj, E., and Martinez, E. (2007) Ecological consumer behaviour: an empirical analysis, *International Journal of Consumer Studies*, 31(1) retrieved from: http://doi.wiley.com/10.1111/j.1470-6431.2006.00565.x [accessed 18 January 2012]; Jacobsen, E., and Dulsrud, A. (2007) Will Consumers Save the World? The Framing of Political Consumerism, *Journal of Agricultural and Environmental Ethics* 20(5), pp.469–82.
[53] Bennie et al., 2011
[54] Bansal and Kilbourne, 2001; Blinkoff et al., 2008; Botsman, R., and Rogers, R. (2010) *What's Mine is Yours – The rise of collaborative Consumption*, 1st ed., New York: Harper Collins; Goodman et al., 2007; White, 2010
[55] Botsman and Rogers, 2010
[56] Blinkoff et al., 2008
[57] Manzini, E., and Jégou, F. (2003) *Sustainable everyday: scenarios of urban life*, Milan, Italy: Edizioni Ambiente.
[58] Pietrykowski, B. (2004) You Are What You Eat: The Social Economy of the Slow Food Movement, *Review of Social Economy* 62(3), pp.307–21.
[59] Pinchot, G. (1995) The Gift Economy, *In Context: A Quarterly of Humane Sustainable Culture*, retrieved from: http://www.context.org/ICLIB/IC41/PinchotG.htm [accessed 4 January 2012].
[60] Manzini and Jégou, 2003
[61] Cherrier, H. (2007) Ethical consumption practices: co-production of self-expression and social recognition, *Journal of Consumer Behaviour* 6(5), pp.321–35; Newholm, T., and Shaw, D. (2007) Studying the ethical consumer: a review of research, *Journal of Consumer Behaviour* 6(5), pp.253–70; Woodruffe Burton, H., Eccles, S., and Elliott, R. (2005) Editorial, *Journal of Consumer Behaviour* 4(4), pp.221–2.
[62] Jacobsen and Dulsrud, 2007; Spaargaren, G., and Oosterveer, P. (2010) Citizen-Consumers as Agents of Change in Globalizing Modernity: The Case of Sustainable Consumption, *Sustainability* 2(7), pp.1,887–908.
[63] Black and Cherrier, 2010; Izberk-Bilgin, E. (2010) An interdisciplinary review of resistance to consumption, some marketing interpretations, and future research suggestions, *Consumption Markets & Culture* 13(3), pp.299–323.
[64] Ozanne, L.K., and Ballantine, P.W. (2010) Sharing as a form of anti-consumption? An

examination of toy library users, *Journal of Consumer Behaviour* 9(6), pp.485–98.
[65] Gilmore, J.H., and Pine, B.J. (2007) *Authenticity: What Consumers Really Want*, USA: Harvard Business School Press.
[66] Boswijk, A., Thijssen, T., and Peelen, E. (2007) *The Experience Economy: A New Perspective*, Amsterdam, Netherlands: Pearson Education; Pine, I., and Gilmore, J.H. (1998) Welcome to the Experience Economy, *Harvard Business Review* 76(4), pp.97–105; Lorentzen, A. (2009) Cities in the Experience Economy, *European Planning Studies* 17(6), pp.829–45.
[67] White, 2010
[68] Dennis-Jones, C. (2008) 2028: A Retail Odyssey, *Retail Week*, retrieved from: http://www.retail-week.com/2008/04/2028_a_retail_odyssey.html [accessed 5 October 2008].
[69] Anon. (no date) *Melbourne retail strategy 2006:2012*, Melbourne, Australia: City of Melbourne, State Government of Victoria and Melbourne Retail Advisory Board.
[70] Ibid.
[71] Yudelson, J. (2010) *Sustainable Retail Development: New Success Strategies*, New York, USA: Springer.
[72] Christensen, J. (2008) *Big Box Reuse*, USA: The MIT Press.
[73] Dunham-Jones, E., and Williamson, J. (2011) *Retrofitting Suburbia: Urban Design Solutions for Redesigning Suburbs*, 2nd ed., New Jersey, USA: John Wiley & Sons, retrieved from: http://books.google.com.au/books?id=1xH4b4pQzOkC&printsec=frontcover&source=gbs_ge_summary_r&cad=0#v=onepage&q&f=false [accessed 8 December 2011].
[74] O'Connell, 2009
[75] Glennie, P. (1998) Consumption, consumerism and urban form: Historical perspectives, *Urban Studies (Routledge)* 35(5/6), pp.927–51; Zukin, 1998
[76] Capra, F. (2003) *The Hidden Connections – A Science for Sustainable Living*, London, UK: Flamingo.
[77] Bansal and Kilbourne, 2001
[78] Schlesinger, L. (2011) Stockland plans smaller, regional shopping centres to combat online threat, *Property Observer*, retrieved from: http://www.propertyobserver.com.au/news/stockland-plans-smaller-regional-shopping-centres-to-combat-online-threat/2011081051105 [accessed 11 June 2012].
[79] Goodman et al., 2007; White, 2010
[80] Bansal and Kilbourne, 2001
[81] Chung et al., 2001; Jayne, 2006; Paquet, L.B. (2003) *The urge to splurge: a social history of shopping*, Ontario Canada: ECW Press.
[82] Anon. (no date) World Footprint, retrieved from: http://www.footprintnetwork.org/en/index.php/GFN/page/world_footprint/ [accessed 14 December 2011].

Bibliography

Anon. (no date, a) deadmalls DOT com, retrieved from: http://www.deadmalls.com/ [accessed 11 December 2011].
Anon. (no date, b) *Melbourne retail strategy 2006:2012*, Melbourne, Australia: City of

Melbourne, State Government of Victoria and Melbourne Retail Advisory Board.

Anon. (no date, c) World Footprint, retrieved from: http://www.footprintnetwork.org/en/index.php/GFN/page/world_footprint/ [accessed 14 December 2011].

Anon. (2007) *Section 22 Wholesale and Retail Trade*, USA: US Census Bureau, p.661, retrieved from: http://search.census.gov/search?q=shopping+malls&btnG.x=9&btnG.y=14&btnG=Go&entqr=0&ud=1&output=xml_no_dtd&oe=UTF-8&ie=UTF-8&client=default_frontend&proxystylesheet=default_frontend&site=census [accessed 12 November 2011].

Anon. (2008) *The Market for Retail Tenancy Leases in Australia: Productivity Commission Draft Report*, Australian Government Productivity Commission, retrieved from: internal-pdf://Market for Retail Tenancy Leases in Aust-0402853888/Market for Retail Tenancy Leases in Aust.pdf.

Anon. (2009a) BCSC Retail Property Statistics Summary October 2009, retrieved from: www.bcsc.org.uk/.../download.asp?.../09RetailPropertyStatisticsSum... [accessed 12 November 2011].

Anon. (2009b) Career Guide to Industries, 2010–11 Edition, Grocery Stores, Bureau of Labor Statistics, US Department of Labor, retrieved from: http://www.bls.gov/oco/cg/cgs024.htm [accessed 6 December 2011].

Anon. (2009c) The vanishing shopping mall, *The Week*, retrieved from: http://theweek.com/article/index/94691/the-vanishing-shopping-mall [accessed 11 October 2011].

Anon. (2011a) Last Stop: Turtle Creek, *Retail Traffic*, retrieved from: http://retailtrafficmag.com/development/analysis/last_stop_turtle_creek/ [accessed 15 October 2011].

Anon. (2011b) Retail park, *Wikipedia: the free encyclopedia*, retrieved from: http://en.wikipedia.org/wiki/Retail_park [accessed 11 December 2011].

Anon. (2012) The 10 biggest shopping centres in the world, *Detail.de*, retrieved from: http://www.detail-online.com/architecture/topics/the-10-biggest-shopping-centres-in-the-world-018606.html [accessed 1 October 2012].

Bansal, P., and Kilbourne, W.E. (2001) The ecologically sustainable retailer, *Journal of Retailing and Consumer Services* 8(3), pp.139–46.

Benfield, K. (2009) R.I.P. the American Suburban Shopping Mall, *Kaid Benfield's Blog | Switchboard, from NRDC*, retrieved from: http://switchboard.nrdc.org/blogs/kbenfield/rip_the_american_suburban_shop.html [accessed 7 December 2011]

Bennie, F., et al. (2011) *Consumer Futures 2020 – Scenarios for tomorrow's consumers*, Forum for the Future, retrieved from: http://www.forumforthefuture.org/sites/default/files/project/downloads/consumer-futures-2020-full-document.pdf

Bird, J. (2009) The Dead Mall Syndrome, *New Retail Blog*, retrieved from: http://www.newretailblog.com/the-dead-mall-syndrome/ [accessed 11 December 2011].

Black, I.R., and Cherrier, H. (2010) Anti-consumption as part of living a sustainable lifestyle: Daily practices, contextual motivations and subjective values, *Journal of Consumer Behaviour* 9(6), pp.437–53.

Blinkoff, R., Johnson, T.P., Kabran, L., Gray, S., et al. (2008) *Grounding the American Dream: A Cultural Study on the Future of Consumerism in a Changing Economy*, USA: Context-Based Research Group & Carton Donofrio Partners, Inc, retrieved from: http://www.thegroundedconsumer.com/ [accessed 21 January 2012].

Blostein, B. (2010) Toward a Productive Excess, in Tilder, L., and Blostein, B. (eds), *Design Ecologies – Essays on the Nature of Design*, New York: Princeton Architectural Press, pp.239–52.

Bodamer, D. (2005) The Mall is Dead, *Retail Traffic*, retrieved from: http://retailtrafficmag.com/mag/retail_mall_dead/ [accessed 7 December 2011].

Boswijk, A., Thijssen, T., and Peelen, E. (2007) *The Experience Economy: A New Perspective*, Amsterdam, Netherlands: Pearson Education.

Botsman, R., and Rogers, R. (2010) *What's Mine is Yours – The rise of collaborative Consumption*, 1st ed., New York: Harper Collins.

Capra, F. (2003) *The Hidden Connections – A Science for Sustainable Living*, London, UK: Flamingo.

Cherrier, H. (2007) Ethical consumption practices: co-production of self-expression and social recognition, *Journal of Consumer Behaviour* 6(5), pp.321–35.

Christensen, J. (2008) *Big Box Reuse*, USA: The MIT Press.

Chung, C.J., et al. (eds) (2001) *Project on the City 2 – Harvard Design School Guide to Shopping*, Köln: Taschen.

Dennis-Jones, C. (2008) 2028: A Retail Odyssey, *Retail Week*, retrieved from: http://www.retail-week.com/2008/04/2028_a_retail_odyssey.html [accessed 5 October 2008].

Dunham-Jones, E., and Williamson, J. (2011) *Retrofitting Suburbia: Urban Design Solutions for Redesigning Suburbs*, 2nd ed., New Jersey, USA: John Wiley & Sons, retrieved from: http://books.google.com.au/books?id=1xH4b4pQzOkC&printsec=frontcover&source=gbs_ge_summary_r&cad=0#v=onepage&q&f=false [accessed 8 December 2011].

Fraj, E., and Martinez, E. (2007) Ecological consumer behaviour: an empirical analysis, *International Journal of Consumer Studies*, 31(1) retrieved from: http://doi.wiley.com/10.1111/j.1470-6431.2006.00565.x [accessed 18 January 2012].

Gilmore, J.H., and Pine, B.J. (2007) *Authenticity: What Consumers Really Want*, USA: Harvard Business School Press.

Glennie, P. (1998) Consumption, consumerism and urban form: Historical perspectives, *Urban Studies (Routledge)* 35(5/6), pp.927–51.

Goodman, J., et al. (2007) *Retail Futures – scenarios for the future of UK retail and sustainable development*, Forum for the Future, retrieved from: internal-pdf://Retail Futures Forum for Future-2483071744/Retail Futures Forum for Future.pdf.

Gregory, S. (2009) The Last Shopping Mall? New Jersey Awaits Xanadu – TIME, *Time Magazine Business*, retrieved from: http://www.time.com/time/magazine/article/0,9171,1886537,00.html [accessed 7 December 2011].

Hudson, K. (2009) Recession turns US malls into ghost towns, *Wall Street Journal – Business*, retrieved from: http://www.theaustralian.com.au/business/recession-turns-us-malls-into-ghost-towns/story-e6frg8zx-1225714885352 [accessed 11 December 2011].

Humphery, K. (1998) *Shelf Life – Supermarkets and the Changing Cultures of Consumption*, Cambridge, UK: Cambridge University Press.

Izberk-Bilgin, E. (2010) An interdisciplinary review of resistance to consumption, some marketing interpretations, and future research suggestions, *Consumption Markets & Culture* 13(3), pp.299–323.

Jacobsen, E., and Dulsrud, A. (2007) Will Consumers Save the World? The Framing of

Political Consumerism, *Journal of Agricultural and Environmental Ethics* 20(5), pp.469–82.
Jayne, M. (2006) *Cities and Consumption*, UK: Routledge, p.43.
Jones, P., et al. (2005) Retailers and sustainable development in the UK, *International Journal of Retail & Distribution Management* 33(3), pp.207–14.
Kavanagh, M. (2000) A Brief History of Shopping Centers, *ICSC News – The Impact of Shopping Centers*, retrieved from: http://www.icsc.org/srch/about/impactofshoppingcenters/briefhistory.html [accessed 24 November 2011].
Koolhaas, R. (2000) Shopping, in Lavalou, A. (ed.), *Mutations*, Barcelona, Spain: ACTAR, pp.124–83.
Lebow, V. (1955) Price Competition in 1955, *Journal of Retailing* (Spring).
Lennon, S. (2007) *National Association of Retail Grocers of Australia – The economic contribution of small to medium-sized grocery retailers to the Australian economy, with a particular focus on Western Australia*, retrieved from: file:///Users/kmate/Documents/Eco Info/Retail/Supermarkets:Large Chains/Economic_contribution_ SMEs_NARGA.pdf.
Leong, S. (2001a) Gruen Urbanism, in Chung, C.J., et al. (eds), *Project on the City 2 – Harvard Design School Guide to Shopping*, Köln: Taschen, pp.381–7.
Leong, S. (2001b) Mobility, in Chung, C.J., et al. (eds), *Project on the City 2 – Harvard Design School Guide to Shopping*, Köln, Germany: Taschen, pp.477–500.
Lorentzen, A. (2009) Cities in the Experience Economy, *European Planning Studies* 17(6), pp.829–45.
Mansvelt, J. (2008) Geographies of consumption: citizenship, space and practice, *Progress in Human Geography* 32(1), pp.105–17.
Manzini, E., and Jégou, F. (2003) *Sustainable everyday: scenarios of urban life*, Milan, Italy: Edizioni Ambiente.
McMorrough, J. (2001) City of Shopping, in Chung, C.J., et al. (eds), *Project on the City 2 – Harvard Design School Guide to Shopping*, Köln, Germany: Taschen, pp.193–203.
Migone, A. (2007) Hedonistic Consumerism: Patterns of Consumption in Contemporary Capitalism, *Review of Radical Political Economics* 39(2), p.185.
Misonzhnik, E. (2010) Developers Rethink the Mall for the 21st Century, *Retail Traffic*, retrieved from: http://retailtrafficmag.com/news/developers_rethink_mall_06272010/index2.html [accessed 7 December 2011].
Misonzhnik, E. (2011) Return of the Mall, *Retail Traffic*, retrieved from: http://retailtrafficmag.com/development/analysis/return_of_the_mall_05052011/index.html [accessed 7 December 2011].
Newholm, T., and Shaw, D. (2007) Studying the ethical consumer: a review of research, *Journal of Consumer Behaviour* 6(5), pp.253–70.
O'Connell, A. (2009) Architect Ellen Dunham-Jones on the future of retail in the post sprawl era – Harvard Business Review, *Havard Business Review – The Magazine*, retrieved from: http://hbr.org/2009/07/architect-ellen-dunham-jones-on-the-future-of-retail-in-the-postsprawl-era/ar/1 [accessed 8 December 2011].
Ozanne, L. K., and Ballantine, P.W. (2010) Sharing as a form of anti-consumption? An examination of toy library users, *Journal of Consumer Behaviour* 9(6), pp.485–98.
Paquet, L.B. (2003) *The urge to splurge: a social history of shopping*, Ontario Canada: ECW Press.

Pietrykowski, B. (2004) You Are What You Eat: The Social Economy of the Slow Food Movement, *Review of Social Economy* 62(3), pp.307–21.

Pinchot, G. (1995) The Gift Economy, *In Context: A Quarterly of Humane Sustainable Culture*, retrieved from: http://www.context.org/ICLIB/IC41/PinchotG.htm [accessed 4 January 2012].

Pine, I., and Gilmore, J.H. (1998) Welcome to the Experience Economy, *Harvard Business Review* 76(4), pp.97–105.

Productivity Commission (2011) *Economic Structure and Performance of the Australian Retail Industry Report 56*, Canberra: Australian Government Productivity Commission.

Schlesinger, L. (2011) Stockland plans smaller, regional shopping centres to combat online threat, *Property Observer*, retrieved from: http://www.propertyobserver.com.au/news/stockland-plans-smaller-regional-shopping-centres-to-combat-online-threat/2011081051105 [accessed 11 June 2012].

Shulman, C. (2010) *IBISWorld Industry Report L7714 Retail Property Operators in Australia*, Australia: IBISWorld.

Sokol, D. (2003) Longer Live the Mall, *MetropolisMag.com*, retrieved from: http://www.metropolismag.com/story/20030601/longer-live-the-mall [accessed 8 December 2011].

Spaargaren, G., and Oosterveer, P. (2010) Citizen-Consumers as Agents of Change in Globalizing Modernity: The Case of Sustainable Consumption, *Sustainability* 2(7), pp.1,887–908.

Turner, R. (2010) Discourses of Consumption in US-American Culture, *Sustainability* 2(7), p.2,281.

Urbis JHD Pty Ltd (2007) *Australian Shopping Centre Industry – Information Update, March 2007*, Australia: Shopping Centre Council of Australia, p.1, retrieved from: http://www.scca.org.au/HTML%20Pages/Research.htm.

Vernon, P. (2012) Shopping Towns Australia, *Fabrications: The Journal of the Society of Architectural Historians, Australia and New Zealand* 22(1), pp.103–21.

White, R. (2010) The future of shopping centers, retrieved from: http://www.whitehutchinson.com/leisure/articles/FutureOfShoppingCenters.shtml.

Woodruffe Burton, H., Eccles, S., and Elliott, R. (2005) Editorial, *Journal of Consumer Behaviour* 4(4), pp.221–2.

Yudelson, J. (2010) *Sustainable Retail Development: New Success Strategies*, New York, USA: Springer.

Zukin, S. (1998) Urban lifestyles: Diversity and standardisation in spaces of consumption, *Urban Studies (Routledge)* 35(5/6), p.825.

Marc FURNIVAL

Urban Design Practitioner

ON HUMAN ACTIVITY AND DESIGN – TOWARDS MORE SUSTAINABLE DEVELOPMENT

Sustainability also plays a central role in the arguments put forward by the urban designer Marc Furnival. He outlines a project that envisages the renovation of a small existing barn in a semi-rural town as a key element in a much broader sustainable tapestry. Indeed, Furnival's principal argument is that the renovation of buildings should never be considered as separate from that broader tapestry – one that, as an urban designer, he engages with on a daily basis. …

In these final comments, however, Furnival not only calls for interior designers and interior architects to consider more than the building as an 'object' when they engage in renovation: he proposes the necessity of reconsidering the nature of community itself. Just as buildings have to adapt to the changing socio-cultural and economic factors around them, so too do some of our more conceptual notions of living and working that are bound up with them. Thus, he suggests, a project that envisages the re-use of an existing derelict barn can become a key component in something much bigger and, in a sense, much more important: a project that helps rebuild a community.

Introduction

Sustainability is a complex and much misunderstood concept. It has been, and is, subject to multiple and often contradictory definitions. At its most basic and generic level, sustainable development has been described as 'development that meets the needs of the present without compromising the ability of future generations to meet their own needs'.[1] Some have defined it in political terms as a 'journey' or 'process' leading towards a form of ecological utopia[2] whilst in the 'Earth Charter' it was described as 'a global society founded on respect for nature, universal human rights, economic justice, and a culture of peace.'[3]

In these definitions, the commonly accepted umbrella terms of sustainability are used: social, economic and environmental.[4] Beyond these vagaries, however, it is often seen as a purely ecological question and, as such, is seen to be antithetical to any sort of economic activity in the context of capitalism.[5] The material published around this perspective is extensive and has its roots in the ecological community and its struggle to raise awareness about the misuse of the earth's resources over a number decades and even centuries. However, more recently, sustainability has also become generally accepted as a social issue and thus one intrinsically linked with economic development questions.[6] In this regard, communities, towns, infrastructure and building projects of all types are seen as fully integrated into questions of economics at local, regional, national and international levels.

How all of these elements contribute to the creation of beneficial places and ongoing healthy lives in a way that is not detrimental to others, either now or in the future, can also be called sustainability; an integration not just of social, economic and environmental factors but also of physical, cultural and political issues, albeit in an imperfect balance that will necessarily vary between places and through time. In this context, the big question is often seen to be the emerging mega-cities of the present and the near future. The work done in this context includes analyses of the conditions of cities in the developed world, as well as those burgeoning cities of countries such as China, Brazil, India and South Africa, to name just a few.[7]

In the UK, perhaps the most high-profile engagement of politics and urban design in the sustainable agenda came in the form of the Richard Rogers led 'task force', set up by the Tony Blair Labour government in the late 1990s. Leading to government white papers and the setting of national policy, *Towards a Strong Urban Renaissance*, published in 2000 and again in 2005[8], argued for an approach to urban design that coincided with many of the ideas found in Richard Rogers' earlier book, *Cities for a Small Planet*.[9]

As in architectural circles in the past, the principal area of interest, and the scene of Rogers' major debates, was the city.[10] It is now the consensus that we have passed the point where over half of the world's population live in an urban environment.[11] Whilst this is undoubtedly significant, it still leaves over three billion people in a predominantly rural or semi-rural situation. Whilst our understanding of rural may be more or less clear, what we define as semi-rural is a little more ambiguous. Here, we will define it as a collection of small market towns and villages acting in concert.

If 'semi-rural' areas could become more viable as places to live for a wider sector of society, some of the issues facing expanding cities[12] might also be addressed, at least in part. One of the main benefits from regenerating semi-rural areas as places to live and work would, naturally, be to stem the migration of people to our cities, thus relieving pressure on already stressed physical and social infrastructures.

In terms of sustainability, the challenges faced in semi-rural areas are very different to those faced in our cities and the ways of responding to them must similarly different and diverse. In a sense, they begin not with the collective area of living, whether that be defined as the region, a town or a village, but rather with the question of what to do about their innumerable individual buildings that are falling continually into disrepair and ever-deeper states of abandonment. The questions that need to be dealt with, then, begin on the interior: inside the numerous desolate, derelict and abandoned buildings that now litter the rural and semi-rural landscapes of Europe.

Starting here, with the renovation of a crumbling infrastructure, we may begin to build an approach to dealing with the much broader issues of sustainability; issues that affect our towns, our cities, our regions and even, in extreme cases, our countries and our planet. However, it is important to bear in mind that this is not the solution in itself and, too often, produces more problems than it solves – particularly when individual buildings are not considered as part of a bigger tapestry of socio-cultural and economic issues. As an urban designer, the author of this paper deals with this conundrum on a daily basis. The attitude of interior designers and architects, then, is often seen as problematic; as too focused on isolated physical objects; on buildings.

What this paper intends to do is call on interior designers and architects to consider their work as part of this bigger picture – as a potentially integral part of constructing sustainable infrastructures and economies and, just as importantly, sustainable and viable communities. It will do so in the context of a project, or rather a series of integrated projects, in a semi-rural mountainous area of Span: Cabrales, Asturias. It will document an attempt led by the author to renovate an individual building in an ecologically responsible way which, more importantly, forms part of a bigger plan to help economically regenerate a region and, furthermore, contribute to the creation of a new set of sustainable communities. It is a speculative and ambitious project that remains in its early stages; but it is hoped that, if successful, it could offer a template for integrated sustainable development for more than just this individual region.

With this emphasis on integration in mind, the structure of the arguments and the description of the project presented here are sequential; one idea and argument flows into another with the point of intersection being seen more like a change of 'plateau' than an abrupt shift in subject or tone. It is intended to reveal the project, and the approach behind it, as based on the belief that the particular cannot be divorced from the universal: that for genuine sustainable development to be possible, individual projects at the scale of renovation need to relate to the economic viability of regions. Furthermore, it hopes to underline that such material social consequences also form a part of the development of something more intangible: sustainable communities.

Our three steps, then, begin with an overview of the project's beginning: the renovation of a barn building in Cabrales. As an attempt at renovation, this was an ultimately foiled first step and, as we shall see, the project had to redirect itself very early on and become a re-build rather than a renovation project. Nevertheless, this first engagement with the physical infrastructure of the region will enable the project to progress to its second stage: an attempt to implement a series of building renovations as part of a region-wide regeneration project based on using the cultural industries as a driver toward supporting and reinforcing semi-rural economies.

This stage of the project is dealt with in the second part of the paper, in which we discuss proposals for the re-use of a number of diverse buildings spread out over the geographical area of the region; a proposal in which the individual building discussed in detail is an integral part. Finally, this will lead us to our third part, in which some deeper considerations are raised. These issues go beyond either the re-use of a particular building or the re-use of numerous buildings as part of a region-wide regeneration scheme. We will examine how renovation projects such as these sit within our understanding of 'community' and how they may contribute to the creation of this perhaps intangible notion.

What we present here, then, is a paper that begins with the specific – a renovation project – but which argues that such projects are in themselves nothing more than a drop in the ocean when it comes to the economic or social issues of regeneration, sustainable infrastructure or community building. On the basis of this, we underline how such individual projects must be considered as part of a larger plan and a deeper understanding of place. It is an approach that reveals the thinking of the author who, despite being involved in the renovation of the building we look at initially, comes from the world of urban design and thus sees such projects as inseparable from an altogether different and richer tapestry.

Plateau 1 – Case Study of a Mountain House

The project documented here began in 2005 and has progressed slowly through a number of variations. It involves the re-use of small buildings, barns and outhouses in Cabrales, a valley of 19 villages with a population of around 2,250 people. The buildings themselves lie in a small village of fewer than twenty people, just off the main valley road. It is the last village before the national park boundary, which is a half hour's walk away. And whilst the main road through the valley has some public transport, as with many rural areas, a car is necessary for general transport. Although, the villages have a system of mobile shops – trucks that come to each village once every two weeks – people tend to rely on their cars to get to the nearby market towns.

The project has begun with the use of one of the buildings in the village as a house and the conversion of one other building into an artist's studio and an exhibition space (only the first of these has been constructed thus far). It is premised on the eventual creation of an art and design foundation that will provide a residence, studio space and an exhibition venue for guest artists who will occupy the site and its buildings for three-

Figure 1: View from the mountain house showing the original barn roof

to-four-month tenures. This timescale is intended to provide enough time to produce work but also to allow for concurrent exhibitions throughout the year, each exhibition overlapping with a different residency.

With the reinstatement of a barn and its conversion into a residence, we begin the project at the smallest scale. At this scale, one of the key issues in terms of our broad and varied definition of sustainability is the quality of construction in the adaptation; an issue that focused attention initially on practical questions and the ecological/environmental side of sustainable construction. In this case, this focus on quality construction resulted in a longer development period so as to allow for the development of a high-quality design, the achieving of good quality construction and, importantly, the construction of the project within budget.

This insistence on high standards of design and construction was not only a personal decision or an architectural preference: it was essential to cultivating additional benefits such as helping to raise the quality of the local housing stock, attracting more investment for the project and improving/expanding local construction knowledge – as local builders and trades people adapted to sometimes-new techniques.[13] In this regard, the house has been a success. It has a number of things that were relatively new to the area including aero-thermal heating[14] and exposed concrete floors that use a local mineral by-product as their mass, in an attempt at minimising the negative impacts of the use of concrete in terms of the project's carbon footprint.

However, the project was not only concerned with introducing new ideas of construction to the area. It was also concerned with learning from the past and has re-introduced some things that are now only seldom used by local trades and crafts people but that were once more common in the area. The building's stone cladding and lime plaster is a prime example; as is its use of old local construction details which have recently fallen out of favour, such as the local stone steps. As a result of this, the house is already acting as a showcase for local people looking to develop their own homes and local trade's people looking both to expand and to recuperate their own knowledge base.[15]

This dual approach of considering the introduction of new techniques whilst simultaneously examining the knowledge and techniques of the past was key to the development of the building project at this stage. One of the things it revealed, for example, was the tendency of the buildings in the area to suffer from damp. The buildings in this area can be cramped and dark and the construction techniques used, whilst being robust, are not ideally suited to the heavy rainfall and humidity of the area. [16] There are numerous recently renovated buildings in the area that suffer from poor insulation and low levels of natural light, as well as a lack of views to the landscape. This last was not originally a priority for these houses as most people saw them as retreats from the outside, where they worked for large parts of the day. This insight was to prove crucial.

Although it is preferable to retain an existing structure for reasons of carbon footprint, local pride and, possibly, aesthetics, we took the view that 'sentimentality' regarding the notion of 'retention' or the 'traditional' would not influence our approach.[17] As a result, once the various pros and cons had been weighed up, the decision was taken to reject the option of adapting the building and it was demolished with a view to reusing as many of the existing materials as possible. The decision was a difficult one but was ultimately taken on the basis of a number of points: full access to the rear was required for the construction of a retaining wall; new window openings in the main facade were required and would constitute most of the overall surface area; and, as revealed by the local people themselves, there was a tendency for adapted building shells in the area to continue to suffer from humidity. Given that the building would only be used intermittently in its first years, it would have to be extremely well insulated and damp-proofed to avoid future issues with damp.

In this case then, the options for adaptive re-use were considered limited. It was, of course, structurally feasible but would have meant an unbearable additional cost for a project on such a limited budget. Furthermore, it would not have been possible to

Figure 2: New house – principal façade from the south-east corner

reach the standards of thermal insulation required to be considered even remotely environmentally sustainable in terms of use. This did not mean, however, that the project completely rejected the notion of re-use. On the contrary, it was simply reframed in different terms: referring to the 're' employment of local skills and labour, the re-use of the demolished stone and the renovation of local infrastructures which were redeveloped to facilitate the connection of utilities and the access of vehicles to what is, more or less, an isolated site.

The development of the project at this stage, then, was informed by the external eye and knowledge of the designer but, crucially, also be the insider knowledge and depth of local understanding offered by the people of the region; the designer pushing for the use of new construction techniques whilst always listening and responding to the knowledge inherent to the region. It is a dualistic or integrated approach evident in multiple ways and is clearly reflected in the building's aesthetic, albeit in a literal sense: the interior and exterior were envisaged as complementary but distinct. It was to be mostly traditional in appearance on the outside but with some contemporary aspects; and mostly contemporary on the inside with some traditional aspects.

With regard to the interior, the aim of the project was not a stereotypical 'homely aesthetic', typical of houses and renovation projects in the area, but rather an interior ideally suited to 'human use'. Indeed, aesthetically, the design can be considered somewhat sparse and lacking in 'warmth', a reading further accentuated by the natural lime plaster walls and exposed concrete floor. The aesthetic was so unlike that typical of the area that, upon entering the building, many of the local residents commented that it was still 'unfinished'. The builders too did not understand the distinction made between an interior 'fit for home use' and one that looks homely; they sketched details

Figure 3: New house – main living space from the kitchen area

on walls and hammered nails around the windows into finished surfaces that they assumed were incomplete.

By contrast, the much more 'traditional' exterior has, despite a use of modern motifs, been easily absorbed, passers-by commenting upon it as a 'good version of the local house'. This is, in part, the result of the use of adapted vernacular details. The scheme used an idea we call 'markers', a term that refers to an aspect of the house that is recognisable as having being used in other designs of a similar ilk. One example is the window detailing, a modern reinterpretation of a feature that appears familiar to both locals in the village and design professionals, both groups of people recognising different features. Other markers include the vertical slot window in the front door and graphite-grey metal window frames.[18] However, the acceptance of the building by local people is most obviously the result of the re-use of the stone from the original building, a decision that also allowed us to employ the local stonemason who lived in the village.

Despite our general intentions of making the project ecologically sustainable, there were many compromises made in this regard. One example is found in the windows just mentioned, which were ultimately sourced in Germany.[19] Another compromise was in the use of a concrete floor and yet another – perhaps the most important – was the decision to move towards a re-build project. The building also failed to reach the exacting standards set initially on energy efficiency, with an uneven distribution of insulation across the floor, walls and roof being one example of this.[20]

Certain aspects of the design had to be changed, or accepted, due to lack of day-to-day project management. Such things included the positioning of various elements, such as utility-meter cupboards, in places that were very obvious and thus weakened the 'sense of repose' sought in the original brief. More significantly, it also included changes to the insulation of the building that diminished the thermal efficiency achieved in the walls and roof. Successes in this regard, however, were achieved with the new wall-construction technique based on that used at *The Prince's House* at the Building Research Establishment Innovation Park. Another success in this sense was the use of a highly efficient aero-thermal heating system.[21]

Clearly then, from a purely environmental perspective, the project described here cannot be considered carbon neutral or completely in line with a strict sustainable agenda. The compromises made to cost, local building practices and the professional skill of the designer as an architect all affected the project in this regard. However, as mentioned at the beginning, our principal argument here is that sustainability should not be considered in one-dimensional terms and that these issues are only parts of a bigger picture which, in this case, involves seeing the individual building, and its individual design decisions, in the context of a broader social-cultural approach whose second plateau we deal with now.

Plateau 2 – Cultural Intervention in the Country

The broader proposal within which the house project sits is one intended to operate at the level of regional regeneration. It involves implementing a sustainable economic development plan that uses the role of 'creatives' as part of its regeneration initiative. [22] It should be noted before proceeding, however, that whilst considering the wider context for an individual building project in this sense can offer greater possibilities of integration, it can sometimes lead to more deeply entrenched problems too. One example of this potential pitfall occurred as a result of European LEADER grants to invigorate rural communities across Spain a generation ago, the consequences of which are still being felt.

The grants available were for 100 per cent of the cost of renovating and converting abandoned rural buildings into tourist accommodation. This produced an oversupply of mediocre bed spaces not commensurate with the high quality of the landscape the area enjoys. Today, many of these tourist accommodation projects struggle to be filled for more than a few months a year. Furthermore, they have only managed to instigate the emergence of subsistence type of services, amenities and facilities around them; there are eating, drinking and sports facilities but not much that is culturally related, for example. That said, there are now signs of a second generation of hotels and restaurants emerging in this particular region that raise the quality of accommodation and service provision to a level more consistent with the landscape. They are beginning to attract a different type of more affluent and 'culturally aware' tourist; and it is within this context that the project envisaged here may be able to succeed.

In the second half of the twentieth century, the industry that the area of Cabrales was well known for went into substantial decline.[23] This led to an exodus to countries such as France, Belgium and Germany of a large part of the workforce, many of whom have now returned in retirement. In many cases, these people have had children who were born abroad and are thus highly unlikely to return to Spain, as it is not the country of their birth. This represents a situation distinct from the more common exodus of the younger generation from areas such as this where unemployment, or at least the perception of a lack of employment opportunities, keeps people away.

Consequently, it is highly unlikely that there will be any significant increase in population through people native to the area returning because they are now, in effect, foreigners. Despite this, the area is reasonably vibrant and operates as a coherent place through the winter, avoiding the 'tourist town' winter shut-down typical of many parts of Spain. Because historically this area was primarily a farming region, many families tend to have multiple properties; a characteristic that reflects the farmstead structure of house, winter barn and summer refuge. Because farming has also gone into substantial decline, however, many of these buildings have been left empty, as in the case of the project we have been describing here.

Despite the outwardly negative situation this represents, these properties do have potential and could be re-used in a way that economically invigorates the area as a whole. Our proposal involves using a series of these buildings as public galleries organised by a contemporary art and design foundation – managed from the building(s) described earlier. With the intention of developing programmatic links to larger institutions in the district and regional capitals, the schemes proposed here are to be embedded at the lower end of the hierarchy of towns and villages – in the smaller and more isolated areas.

The idea is that, through the establishment of a number of similar individual small-scale projects throughout the region, local people could find out about other events at the larger facilities and at other similarly sized small venues. A small part of an exhibition could be displayed in each of these renovated spaces, allowing art to be on display in each of the villages as a sort of 'taster' to bigger exhibitions. Inserting cultural hubs into smaller towns and villages would naturally increase the prevalence of cultural and art works in the region but these would have to be timed to coincide with of people's use of these facilities: that could be daily, weekly, monthly, seasonally or annually, depending on the area.

Our re-use proposal at this regional scale, then, involves the adaptation of several buildings as part of a coherent culturally led regeneration scheme. However, key to that scheme is our notion of 'a lorry load of art': the use of shipping containers to

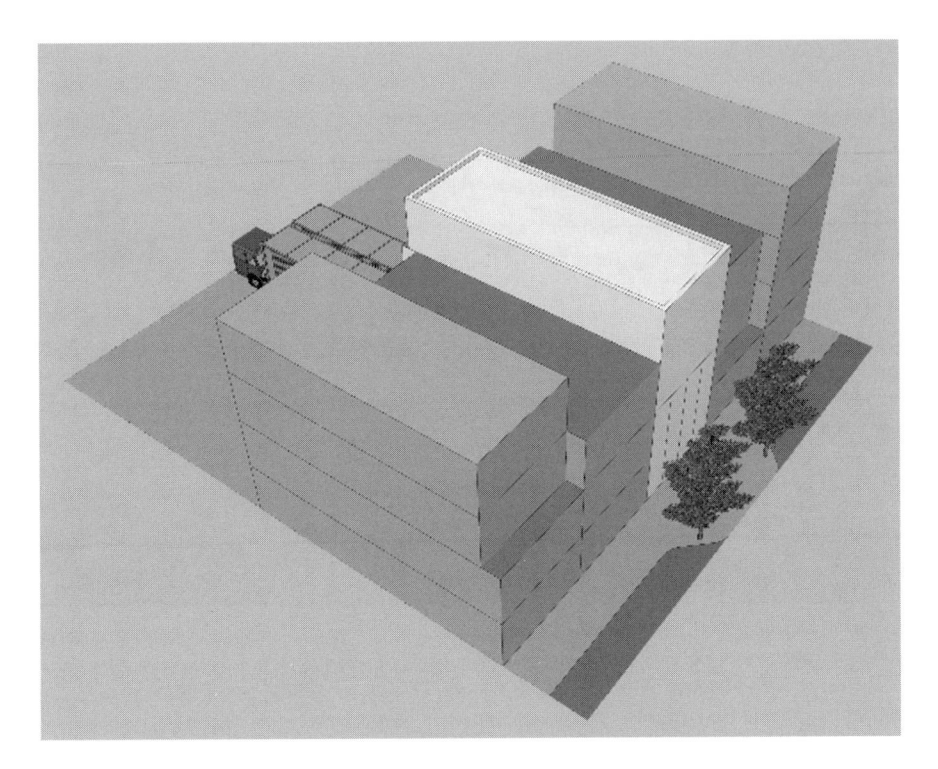

Figure 4: Concept for use of empty local shops as a cultural centre with plug-in gallery

transport the art around the different venues. It is a scheme that involves adapting these buildings so that they work in conjunction with 'mobile galleries'. The shipping container offers a standardised way to transport goods and has been put to various alternative architectural uses in recent years.[24] If used as a 'ready-made' gallery as we envisage here, containers offer transportation, an appropriately sized display space and enough programmatic flexibility to accommodate art of different types.

Containers would work in conjunction with the existing adapted architecture by simply 'plugging in'. They could work in conjunction with both the larger and smaller venues and could offer Internet access to these relatively remote areas. They could host readings, performances and give information about a whole variety of issues, such as education, health, employment or entertainment. They could also function as shops and administrative centres for the project in general.

As mentioned earlier, as part of our initial stage of this project, we propose to convert at least one other building into an artist's studio and residence, the intention being that artists could take up residencies of three-to-four months' tenure. By providing both a studio and a residence, as well as a location that is relatively isolated and devoid of distractions, the artists-in-residence would be able to focus on developing their work.

Figure 5: Montage of retained stone barn renovated as an artist's studio

We do, however, intend to convert one other building into an exhibition space as well, which would be the one physically integrated into the mobile 'lorry load of art' concept. There would, of course, be almost no passing footfall in the normal high-street sense for these exhibition spaces and it is for this reason that the mobile nature of the project must be implemented successfully.

The establishment of regional art networks would also be key to the success of the vision we describe here. Artists-in-residence would often come with their own networks established, of course; but it would be fundamental that the art foundation we hope to set up to manage this project should be linked into the regional and national art scene. These networks act as support and knowledge-sharing avenues, offering streams of information about grants and, crucially, publicity.

The business plan, or rather intuitive vision, we are setting out here will, of course, emerge and evolve slowly. We have not even finished the first stage yet. However, the potential exists in this region to build slowly; to attract one artist and a little bit of funding; to finish the small exhibition space and develop a regional reputation; to attract tourists and bigger art curators to the area. The effort needed and the time required to achieve 'critical mass' may be more than we expect but it can be done.

All this said, the project we describe here is not a panacea for the region's problems. The art and design foundation is not intended as a full solution to the difficulties faced by the local economy. It is seen more as a marker; an indication of a change in the dynamic of the locality and the outlook of its people and politicians. It hopes not only to attract 'creatives' but also to cultivate them. It is not just about the local consumption of art but its local creation and, in this sense again, we return to the principles of sustainability, only this time, considered from a social and economic perspective.[25]

Seen in this context, the initial building project we described clearly becomes irrelevant if seen in isolation. It can play no real or genuine role in the regeneration of the area or its economy if it is not seen within a broader framework – even if that framework can seem speculative and possibly even utopian. The individual building and the art project we describe here are inseparable: two sides of the same coin that propose an engagement with the area of Cabrales through the adaptation and re-use of its architectural heritage and infrastructure, on the one hand, and its creative, innovative and dedicated inhabitants, current and future, on the other. It is our belief that it is only through thinking of individual building renovation or reinstatement in this broader context that attempts at building in a sustainable, or at least semi-sustainable, way will really make an impact at fundamental levels.

Plateau 3 – Human Activity and Community

Our insistence here is that individual building renovation is important to questions of sustainability but that it is also essential that architects and interior designers do not work in isolation. It is fundamental if we wish to build more sustainable futures that thinking in one discipline is not isolated from those around and related to it. In terms of building projects such as renovations, this generally means understanding or placing the built project in a broader context of regeneration which, as in this case, may only exist as possibilities at the point of physical construction.

This integrated approach is certainly at the heart of sustainability and is nowhere more clearly expressed, albeit with a different sense to that employed here, than in Geddes' internationally famous catchphrase: 'think globally – act locally'.[26] By using Geddes' concept to look at both specific examples of design and the context of development at large, we are encouraged not only to explore the links between the diverse factors that contribute to any social or economic situation but to look at the small and the large as integrated.

In our context, this is most pertinent when applied geographically: we are acting initially on one building in a small village but the implications of what we propose and intend operate in a wider geographical sphere. However, Geddes' notion does not just open up the question of scale into our thinking but also allows us to consider the more-intricate and less-obvious connections such as the link between specific building projects and ideas that are perhaps less fixed and less tangible: the notion of community and community building, for example.

It is not, and never has been, our intention with this project to consider only the use of the region's physical infrastructure or its economic viability. It is our intention to consider our initial isolated project and its bigger programmatic framework as something integral to the idea of community; as individual components in the tapestry of this more intangible and perhaps undefinable concept. Given the nature of the migration away from Cabrales and the unlikelihood of a return of former local residents, the sense of community that is possible to restore or develop in Cabrales is, in all probability, going to be one reliant on new definitions of the term. It is certainly going to be reliant on new people: foreigners, tourists, artists and so forth.

This is an important issue in the context of Cabrales that it is fundamental to understand if we are to consider how we can use the design of individual buildings, with particular functions, to build a sense of place and community. A statement such as 'the nature of a place flows from the activities it contains', on face value, may seem obvious and almost trite. However, accepting *more explicitly* that the nature of a place is a consequence of the functions and specific activities for which its buildings and spaces were designed leads to a wider deliberation.

By adopting a line of thought that suggests we consider specific or local activity as the kernel of building functions, a link between building forms, external spaces, the communal gathering they facilitate and, subsequently, a sense of place and community is identified. The specific is linked with the general, the small with the large and the concrete with the abstract. What emerges is an interrelated conception of how and where we live and, ultimately, who we feel we are. This then links our thinking about the key aspects of buildings to our understanding of neighbourhoods, our sense of place and our notions of, and connection with, community.

By taking human activity and its implications as the primary source from which good design stems, we reject the primary importance often given to buildings *as objects* in the design of the built environment and find a way to prioritise people, act locally and have an effect globally.[27] It is this, then, that underlies our insistence that the design of buildings and their interior spaces is less important than the human activities they house and the context they exist in. It is these issues that should be the drivers for our spatio-physical-design-based work. It is, ultimately, these issues, that create community. It is human activities that produce the healthy socio-economic situation necessary to fuel and lubricate both the measureable notion of local and regional economies and the more intangible sense of communities we should seek to create with every one of our physical interventions; even at the level of individual house renovations like ours.

Returning to our point about Cabrales and its migrated population, we are faced with a situation in which the restoration of community cannot be based on previous models of human activity. These have evolved, died, migrated. Perhaps then, our sense of community must evolve and migrate. Perhaps 'place-bound' notions of human activity, and thus community, also need to evolve. We are far from being constrained by the mediaeval boundaries of parishes or communes that once tended to keep most of us in one place and involved in the same activities throughout our lifetime. Whilst it is easy for some to view such changes as the 'break down of society' and lament the loss of 'traditional community and values', such an outlook may be too rigid to accommodate the needs of today.

If we are to develop an evolved notion of community, it may be necessary to develop an equally evolved notion of place. In both cities and rural areas, for example, we are increasingly living across wider and wider distances, both in a general and a daily sense; travelling significant distances between home and work; living a long way from other members of our families; going further to visit friends – whether that be across town for a meal or across a continent for a long weekend. These wider movement 'nets' are ones in which home, socialising and work are located in many different areas and are overlaid on top of each other to form a rich nexus. Within this nexus, places are constituted by the nodes of these nets. Merely because people 'in' a place do not live, socialise and work in that locale permanently or throughout their lifetime does not invalidate it as a cohesive and valid arena of activity: a community.

Emerging Social Organisation

These wider living networks mean that groupings are less isolated, in that certain aspects of us are plugged into various places and groups. So whilst we may be less integrated from a 'traditional' perspective, we are actually immersed in a greater variety of arenas and activities. Lives comprising increasingly numerous places resist traditional definitions and thus the challenge is to reconsider the notion of community. Accepting this increased complexity as part of community may be necessary to understand better how to create, augment or just improve the places that we use through our daily lives.

Thus, when we propose the renovation of a barn in a semi-rural location so as to make it capable of functioning as a locale in which an international artist can work for a limited amount of time, we are not necessarily proposing an idea that accepts the death of the village's community. On the contrary, this proposal is based on an interpretation of modern life, and thus a modern sense of community, that is less place bound, less fixed in time; something more malleable, fluid and, perhaps, ever changing. It is based on an amorphous and integrated view of community and its relationship with regional regeneration, individual buildings and their specific activities. It is based on the idea of sustainability not understood as an issue of ecology or environmental efficiency, or as a question of economic regeneration and continued growth. It is based on an understanding of sustainability as integrated thinking on multiple levels and in multiple directions.

When we consider the renovation of a building, as at the beginning of this paper, we are forced to consider it as an individual project that responds to this globalised social dynamic. Rather than be considered as isolated buildings that house 'foreigners' in what, for these inhabitants, becomes an isolated tourist environment, these buildings are considered as a small but integral parts of an overall regenerative and continually rearranging sense of place and community. It is conceptualised as a project operative on multiple geographical levels; a project that engages with economic issues on at least three levels: the local, the regional and the national.

Furthermore, this project responds on an even deeper level to our need to form part of a community – albeit a sense of community that challenges traditional geographically fixed definitions. It is an isolated building project that attempted to renovate a building, that forms part of a broader regional regenerative initiative (in the physical and economic spheres) and that responds to a reworked notion of community. All of these things respond to a reimagined definition of sustainability, one that may begin with an approach to the re-use of existing buildings but which is inevitably linked to broader and deeper economic and social issues.

What we have, then, is a project that attempts to investigate thinking across scales – something we argue is essential to sustainable regeneration. It is important to stress that designers from all spheres should work together and cooperate with each other. The interior designer cannot work in vacuum, the architect must partake in development planning and the urban designer concerned with creating 'community' must develop an appreciation of more aesthetic and specific criteria. It is equally important to stress the need for them to learn to engage with the local communities with which they work, to learn from local practices and identify that development and sustainability – considering the social, economic and environmental – are two sides of the same coin. At the end of the day, 'sustainable design' is just 'design' – but design is both local *and* global; concrete *and* intangible.

Notes

[1] Brundtland Commission of the United Nations (1987, 20 March) Report of the World Commission on Environment and Development: Our Common Future, *Annex to document A/42/427*, New York: United Nations.

[2] Markus, J., Milne M.K., Kearins, K., and Walton, S. (2006, November) Creating Adventures in Wonderland: The Journey Metaphor and Environmental Sustainability, *Organization* 13(6): 801–39.

[3] The Earth Charter was published in 2000 as the result of a four-year consultation process by the Earth Charter Initiative. For more information, see: www.earthcharterinaction.org. Corcoran, P.B. (ed.) (2007) *The Earth Charter in Action: Toward a Sustainable World*, Amsterdam: KIT Publishers.

[4] Knox, P.L., and Heike, M. (2009) *Small Town Sustainability – Economic, Social and Environmental Innovation*, Basel: Birkhäuser.

[5] This argument can be found in works such as: Porritt, J. (2006) *Capitalism as if the World Mattered*, London: Earthscan; Redclift, M. (2005) Sustainable Development (1987–2005): an Oxymoron Comes of Age, *Sustainable Development* 13(4): 212–27.

[6] This type of analysis and definition can be found in works such as: Bookchin, M. (2008) *Social Ecology and Communalism*, Oakland: AK Press; Dillard, J., Dujon, V., and King, M. (eds) (2008) *Understanding the Social Dimension of Sustainability*, Routledge: London.

[7] In this regard, some typical examples of the material available are: Li, R.Y.M. (2011) *Building Our Sustainable Cities*, Illinois: Common Ground Publishing; Stern, R., and

Polese, M. (eds) (2008) *The Social Sustainability of Cities: Diversity and Management of Change*, Toronto: University of Toronto Press, Scholarly Publishing Division.

[8] In 1998 the Deputy Prime Minister, John Prescott, set up the Urban Task Force with Richard Rogers at its head. Its aims were 'to identify causes of urban decline and establish a vision for cities, founded on the principles of design excellence, social wellbeing and environmental responsibility within appropriate delivery, fiscal and legal frameworks'. See: Rogers, R. (2005) *Towards a Strong Urban Renaissance* – an independent report by members of the Urban Task Force chaired by Lord Rogers of Riverside.

[9] Rogers, R. (1998) *Cities for a Small Planet*, London: Icon Books.

[10] The most famous example of the predominance of the city as an area of concern for the designers of the built environment in recent decades is of course CIAM (Congrès Internationaux d'Architecture Moderne). In many ways the concerns of today, as evident in the arguments put forward by the Urban Task Force, invert the initial proposals of the modern movement as evident in the Athens Charter, 1933. For more information, see: Mumford, E. (2000) *The CIAM Discourse on Urbanism, 1928–1960*, Cambridge: MIT Press.

[11] Grahame Shane, D. (2011) *Urban Design Since 1945 – A Global Perspective*, New York: Wiley.

[12] Lim, C.J., and Liu, E. (2010) *Smart Cities + Eco-warriors*, New York: Routledge.

[13] On this project we employed locally all of the main trades, including those of stone mason, plumber, electrician and carpenter. Their knowledge from having worked in the area proved useful to the project by understanding issues ranging from prevalent weather conditions to suitability and availability of materials and equipment.

[14] Aero-thermal heating is based on an air-to-water heat pump exchange system, similar to that used by fridges, and can extract heat from the outside air down to temperatures below freezing.

[15] It has been visited by local people who have commented that they find it 'in-keeping' with the area. The carpenter features his work on the house on his website and the plumber has brought prospective clients to the house to see the heating system.

[16] Many of the existing houses are over 100 years old and consequently built at a time of traditional stone-wall construction without insulation in the modern sense. Windows were also a large source of heat loss and were consequently minimised, serving as ventilation rather than maximising views. Additionally, the area is very mountainous and so many properties are at least partially built into the mountain side, which can lead to damp penetration.

[17] This is, of course, a contentious position. The heritage debate has raged since the time of Ruskin and Viollet le Duc, see: Scott, F. (2008) *On Altering Architecture*, London: Routledge. More recently, contextualism and heritage in the UK has been kept on the media agenda by Prince Charles and the group of architects that form his intimate 'design circle'. For these designers, issues such as 'tradition' and 'retention' are paramount – as they are, of course, for groups such as English Heritage.

[18] The windows are not too dissimilar to ones found in the region but also pay homage to Japanese 'En' space, or 'window threshold' space. For an overview on 'En' and other

Japanese concepts of space (that less directly influenced the design of this project) see: Yoshida, T. (1955) *The Japanese House and Garden*, London: The Architectural Press; Engels, H. (1964) *The Japanese House: A Tradition for Contemporary Architecture*, Tokyo: Charles E Tuttle Publishers; Fawcett, C. (1980) *The New Japanese House – Ritual and Anti-ritual Patterns of Dwelling*, London: Granada.

[19] This decision obviously represents a compromise. Although not directly related, the local window factory has since gone into receivership, affecting five households, highlighting the fragility of the local economy as Spain goes deeper into recession but also the preference of sourcing locally whenever possible.

[20] This phase of the project was a personal build project with the client and designer based in the UK and the builders in Spain. Inevitably, issues arose which caused delays and, as in this case, mistakes undermining the design and attempts at a more sustainable approach.

[21] This was used in place of a geo-thermal system that uses the more constant temperature underground as a heat source or heat dump.

[22] Bishop, P., and Williams, L. (2012) *The Temporary City*, London: Routledge.

[23] European Commission. (2006) General Format, URBAN II Evaluation, Case Study: Gijón, retrieved from: http://ec.europa.eu/regional_policy/sources/docgener/evaluation/expost2006/urban_ii_en.htm
See also: http://europa.eu/legislation_summaries/employment_and_social_policy/social_inclusion_fight_against_poverty/g24209_en.htm.

[24] Container City in London is perhaps one of the most high-profile examples of the creative re-use of shipping containers in recent years. See http://www.containercity.com.

[25] For a discussion on this type of issue, see: Bishop, P., and Williams, L. (2012) *The Temporary City*, London: Routledge.

[26] The original phrase 'think global, act local' has been attributed to Scots town planner and social activist Patrick Geddes. Although the exact phrase does not appear in Geddes' 1915 book *Cities in Evolution*, the idea (as applied to city planning) is clearly evident: '"Local character" is thus no mere accidental old-world quaintness, as its mimics think and say. It is attained only in course of adequate grasp and treatment of the whole environment, and in active sympathy with the essential and characteristic life of the place concerned'. Geddes, P. (1915) *Cities in Evolution*, London: William, p.397.

[27] 'To approach a city… as if it were [an] … architectural problem… is to make the mistake of attempting to substitute art for life…. The results… are neither life nor art. They are taxidermy.' Jacobs, J. (1961) *The Death and Life of Great American Cities*, New York: Random House, Chapter 19.

Dr Nuala ROONEY
University of Ulster

RE-PRESENTING THE *TITANIC*

[T]he role a single building can play in the economic regeneration of an area, and a sense of community, is taken up by Nuala Rooney, who examines a very different building typology and a very different geographical place. With Rooney, we move from small-scale interventions in semi-rural areas to large-scale and high-profile museum projects in a definitely urban industrial context: the city of Belfast. Rooney examines the recently opened Titanic Belfast, an £100-million museum and tourist attraction opened near the site of the Titanic's construction.

In particular, she questions the role of its major design feature, an interior inside an interior: the reconstructed 'grand staircase' of the Titanic. This has been reproduced in full scale and in all its original detail as the museum's principal attraction. Considering this simulacrum first in the context of the arguments of Debord, Baudrillard and Eco, she identifies our tendency to see it as a consumerist folly, a kitsch and tawdry attempt to create (or re-use) the 'real thing' in a world of consumer spectacle. However, she also points out that this feature could be central to the financial success of the project. Thus the possibility that the simulacrum may have a social utility is brought into debate.

Introduction

It is now some fifty years since the ideas of Guy Debord, and later of Jean Baudrillard and Umberto Eco, began to inform debates on architecture and interior design as reflections of culture. In their terms, we had come to live in a society of the spectacle, a consumer culture characterised by the simulacrum and a form of hyper-reality in which notions of the fake, the copy and the replica had supplanted genuine experience and human engagement. This new artificial state of affairs was seen as most clearly manifest in architecture through the literal decorated shed as highlighted and praised by Robert Venturi in the late '60s and early '70s. However, it is perhaps most conspicuously evident and repeatedly used in interior design, the ephemeral nature of the interior fit out being perfect for the constant recreation of artificial, replica environments such as the themed bar or restaurant.

For Debord, Baudrillard and Eco, this new post-modern repeated replica condition was seen as negative; a reflection of a loss of authenticity and a passive role for the public in a consumer-led and capitalist-controlled economy. For Venturi and the designers and theorists who would associate themselves with the trends he set, it was the reflection of societies that were beginning to question modernity and its insistence on rejecting of the past. In terms of architecture and interior design, this meant there was an opportunity, and perhaps a need, to reference history as well as, at times, recreate it directly. Given that this tendency was primarily occurring in countries like the United States and the UK, it was directly associated with capitalism and the free market. Architecture and interior design were tools for the creation of wealth through consumption.

This paper will examine a recent project opened in Belfast, Northern Ireland that, to an extent, offers a more contemporary manifestation of some of these ideas and theories: Titanic Belfast, a £100-million visitor attraction opened in March 2012. However, rather than examine the project in the terms of Debord, Eco, Baudrillard or Venturi, here we examine it under a slightly different gaze: as a project with the potential to aid in the economic regeneration of a city with a troubled past, on the one hand; and on the other, as a building with a major design feature (the replica of the *Titanic*'s 'grand' staircase) that reflects a real human need, and tendency, to engage emotionally with the past and, indeed, the human condition. It thus offers up this project as an example of how this approach to architecture and interior design may, despite the severe questions raised about it, function in positive and beneficial ways in the early twenty-first century.

Northern Ireland: The Context

As many major cities look to recreate their very own 'Bilbao effect'[1], architectural design has been re-evaluated and given prominence in the re-branding of the old to the new, in order to boost visual recognition and esteem and to reflect a progressive cultural image of innovation. With its recent troubled past, Belfast arguably needs this more than most cities. It needs to be seen to present a more positive image worldwide if it wants to attract visitors. It also needs to develop and regenerate existing sites for a tourism-based economy. As Northern Ireland emerges from decades of social and civil conflict, tourism has been strategically highlighted as a means upon which to develop the economy. The Northern Ireland Tourist Board's designated slogan for this year – 'NI 2012: our time, our place' – urges the public to help to change the negative connotations of Northern Ireland.[2] Given the highly contested histories, dates, traditions and places that exist within the province, this initiative represents a focused

Figure 1: *Titanic Belfast*. N. Rooney

effort to re-brand Northern Ireland and to shift attention towards more inclusive events and regenerated spaces. This positive investment in tourism has already resulted in the construction of several major new public buildings opening in 2012: the Giant's Causeway Visitor Centre, the MAC Arts Centre and the new Titanic Belfast visitor centre.

Rather than being known throughout the world for conflict and sectarianism, Northern Ireland is actively re-negotiating its heritage. Central to this is Titanic Belfast, a multi-million-pound attraction which opened in time to mark the one hundredth anniversary of the sinking of the RMS *Titanic*. Lost on its maiden voyage, the ship was built in Belfast by Harland and Wolff, which at that time was one of the biggest shipbuilders in the world. With the decline of shipbuilding in Belfast, the industrial land was left derelict and the area run down. However, with the *Titanic* anniversary looming, this huge 185-acre site was designated for re-development and, re-named the *Titanic* Quarter, swiftly became a vision for brand-new uncontested spaces for commercial property, retail and housing.

As a world-class exhibition, Titanic Belfast sets out to celebrate the culture and history of shipbuilding in Belfast but will focus specifically on the RMS *Titanic*,[3] because that is what visitors to Northern Ireland will *come* to see. In the media frenzy surrounding the *Titanic*'s centenary, Belfast aims to build on the brand-worthiness of the ship to ensure that the city becomes known as the place where it was designed and built. The building itself, designed by the American architect Eric Kuhne, is a four-pointed steel-clad structure inspired by 'ice crystals, icebergs, timber scaffolding and the gantries on which the *Titanic* was built'.[4] The shiny metal chunks cut into a diamond glass box were developed in plan from the points of the compass and the star of the White Star line logo; the imagery is said to suggest the hulls of the great ships built on this site.

The impressive use of sleek, sharp steel forms is a huge gesture on a highly visible site yet this monumental exterior gives little away as to the interior experience. Inside, the design of the public spaces contrasts with the clean steel lines of the exterior, more obviously referencing the imagery of shipbuilding with walkways and escalators dissecting the space at different levels within the five-storey atrium. These features reference the past but do not explicitly copy it. The totally opposite approach, however, is taken with regard the project's principal interior feature: the 'grand' staircase replica. Consequently, we can see a double referential approach in both the exterior and the interior design strategy.

For interior designers, 'heritage design' already suggests a conflict of resolution in bringing together the past and the present. It raises the issues of the levels of intervention a designer should take in relation to renovation and preservation, innovation and tradition. This is especially true if it is an existing heritage space and where a particular design interpretation might be judged to be 'wrong' or not in sympathy if it deviates wildly from the order. Borrowing, referencing, copying or re-using a period style sets levels that have either obvious or subliminal recognition value.

This is also true, albeit in a different sense, when we consider the other extreme: the themed space and the all-out replication of a recognisable style. The themed space is perhaps more an assembly of standard parts drawing on a preconceived image and format, so that it virtually designs itself. A typical example of this might be the 'Irish theme pub', a vague culturally referenced style of an indeterminate past with incredible mass appeal and global recognition. These venues can appear in even the most unlikely cities around the world, yet still project a welcoming 'traditional' image of Ireland abroad. Themed interior spaces such as these provide a faked experience that sets an illusion of the past. They appeal to the imagination and help people to relax because it is all so removed from real life. The popularity of such spaces (because they are familiar settings) reminds us that the public has diverse tastes in interior design, high and low. They also hold strong preconceptions about how certain spaces should look in order to feel right.

Umberto Eco[5] described America as a country 'obsessed with realism', the demand for the 'real thing' resulting in the fabrication and acceptance of the 'absolute fake'. The widespread use and acceptance of themed museum spaces with replicated interiors presents the visitor with a hyperreal experience. This gives them an immediate visual and physical connection to something that no longer exists in order to foster a sense of the past – much like the Irish pub. Coming from a European country steeped in authentic ancient artefacts and buildings, Eco was astounded at the brazen attitude to reproduction in a cultural context but at the same time amazed at the liberating boundaries of kitsch: a new-world attitude to the old world. It forced him to question whether the designed neutral museum space was a better solution – or indeed just one solution. America's approach to the hyperreal has given the rest of the world an expectation for culture with an entertainment/experiential/interactive dimension. Inevitably, as this has proved to be a successful and profitable medium, it has set a precedent that has been widely used and copied elsewhere.

Titanic Belfast

Titanic Belfast is not a museum[6] as there are no original artefacts; rather, it aims to engage visitors experientially through an interactive spectacle created using cutting-edge digital forms and design. In the high-pressure world of leisure tourism, the competition and success of such exhibits depends on their ability to provide the viewer with a different experience, that is, something that cannot be accessed elsewhere or, indeed, at home. The media- and techno-savvy public are both demanding and fickle in how they expect to be entertained and informed – if they are to be engaged. The free dissemination of images reduces the need for the original (there being only ever one) and the emphasis on its unique presence. This means that the narrative can be developed and expanded in places not limited by any authentic geographical or personal connection to present multiple interpretations, to attract and appeal to wider audiences. The use of technology in exhibition design has created a need for spaces to be flexible. Often the requirement for the interior is simply for it to be an empty black box; a dark, windowless space. Inside, the visitor may be largely unaware of the material specification or whether it is day or night outside. This contrasts with a more traditionally conceived museum and gallery space where the joy of the experience is as much about the strength and quality of the interior architecture, of moving from room to room, and the placement of an artefact in that space.

Leading artists, such as Olafur Eliasson, have challenged the notion that museums must be about collecting real objects but that they should be 'part of the times in which we live'[7] and viewed from 'where we are today'. The design freedom that comes from exploring new media and interpretations, audio, visual, interactive seems limitless insofar as the speed of technology continually adds new means that can be used to inspire and bring to life ideas, places and things. Images can be made to seem real. They can be designed into the space and be spatial but they are not three dimensionally *of* the space. The beauty of new media is that it can be easily changed to refresh the viewer experience. The problem is: when it malfunctions, the space serves no purpose, because there is nothing (else) to see.

In Titanic Belfast,[8] the sequential galleries have been arranged so that visitors begin their journey in Belfast of the early 1900s, establishing the period and something of what life was like for people at that time. The immensity, scale, sounds and excitement of the shipbuilding industry are highlighted in the 'shipyard ride', a moving pod/car through which the visitors' view is controlled and where they experience the shipyard processes and activities. In addition, there is a gallery dedicated to the fit-out that celebrates the 'sumptuous luxury and superb craftsmanship associated with the cabins and public rooms'. This is largely recreated using 'an eclectic range of exhibits, models, reconstructions, holograms, interactive databases and elaborate CGI imagery'. It also includes examples of interior styles from first, second and third class where, it is claimed, 'exceptional detail is key to the authentic representation'. The exhibition then takes the visitor through the maiden voyage, the sinking, the aftermath, the myths[9] and legends and through to the haunting images of the *Titanic* as it is now. The aim is to enable the spectator to connect to the event on many different levels (social, historical, physical, experiential) so they will make a strong contemporary association between the *Titanic* and Belfast.

As a state-of-the-art attraction, and to ensure it will attract the crowds, the centre must appeal to as wide a range of the people as possible. From enthusiasts and experts, to thrill seekers of all ages, if it is to satisfy a public used to, and demanding, high levels of visual stimulus and digital contact, the method of communication has to be varied and cutting edge. In this hyperreal environment, the presentation and absorption of facts, images and stories of the *Titanic* are based on the immersion of the spectator as participant. Through this method, as Van de Vell comments:

> 'Digital imaging techniques are employed to create spectacular and overwhelming experiences; these annihilate the distance between the spectators and representation that might give them the latitude for contemplative thought about what they see.'[10]

As the viewer is fully absorbed by the journey from one spatial experience to the next, they lose their sense of time and place. The viewer drifts through a world expressed through the digitally imagined past. Moving from one big visual/spatial wow factor to another, the visitor experiences the interior space *as* the exhibition design, so that the visual quality of the space is secondary to the impact of the images, which are carefully designed to achieve maximum theatrical effect. This blending of spatial installation and art form undoubtedly presents fantastic opportunities to introduce a playfulness in the design, exploring new methods and means to utilise technology to push the visitor/user experience and communication of information in new and exciting ways. The danger is that the visitor may suffer from technology fatigue and need some physical and visual relief from the excitement overload. Relief comes as a break between certain galleries where the viewer is encouraged to pause and look out across the city as it is now. What perhaps the visitor is missing from the whole experience is the sense that comes from something real, that can be touched, in the form of material that draws from the period, the past and memory.

The Replica

Contrasting with the exhibition space, on the top floor in the banqueting hall, the *Titanic*'s main first-class staircase[11] has been re-built as a central focus of the space. The staircase featured prominently within the publicity hype associated with the new

Figure 2: Rendered image "Grand Staircase" *Titanic Belfast*, Titanic Belfast®

building and so there was much anger and frustration, played out through the local media, when visitors discovered that the staircase was only to be used for private events and was not part of the tour covered by their entrance fee. Denied access to the image of what they 'thought' they were going to see, the public clamoured to see the staircase to the extent that the centre had to offer special Sunday visits to view it on a limited-ticket basis.[12] The developers and designers clearly underestimated how strongly people would feel about its separation from public view. The images of the staircase were so widely publicised as being 'of' the building that the public felt they were missing out, indeed, being cheated of their *Titanic* experience. Such was the public awareness of the staircase made real that in the opening weeks this issue seemed to diminish the impact of the entire exhibition. The staircase was tantalisingly beyond reach, creating a 'them and us' social and spatial division, fuelled by the public's desire to see it, but blocked by the restricted access. The demand was for something that was literally, physically, unequivocally based on their image of the ship; rather than symbolically, as it is represented by the building's exterior form, or by a 2D image.

Based on the demand, the marketing team have since capitalised on the themed aspect of the space by introducing over the summer period of 2012 'Afternoon Teas by the Grand Staircase'. This event responds to the projected fantasy played out by the theme and widens access to the space for those who are prepared to pay the five-star-hotel prices. The presence and function of the staircase also ensures that this interior space stands apart from the rest of the building's interior in image, design, context and style.[13] Constructing the staircase was an impressive task yet, *in situ*, there is no doubt that it stands somewhat anachronistically within the contemporary design of the banqueting suite. As a major design gesture in this space, the staircase's main function is to provide something tangible and 'real' to remind diners of the theme of the building. Yet, built only as the staircase, without the surrounding first-floor gallery and the full integration of the domed glass ceiling, the 'grand' staircase as we know it is truncated, the original proportions are compromised and its position, wedged into a corner of the space, disappoints. Overall, it is oddly caught between the image of an Edwardian music-hall stage and a public-school assembly hall, rather than as a functioning architectural element.

The staircase was designed to create a physical impact in a way that CGI cannot. Although it is built to a scale of 1:1, in this form it sadly loses its drama; it appears inauthentic and an interpretation, rather than an imitation of the original. Its status as simulacrum imposes itself.[14] Despite this failing, however, it may be that we are not tuned to understanding the potential deeper values carried by 'replicas'. In *On Altering Architecture*,[15] Fred Scott explores this by drawing attention to the Japanese Shinto Temple of Ise and the art of re-building it every twenty years in the 'spirit of renewal'. As Scott points out, the fact that it is a copy not an original, weathered and worn over time, may be at odds with Western views of 'style' being separate from form and structure but, in the Japanese context, what is appreciated is the 'intangible essence within its style' rather than the structure itself. The 'design' of the original lives on through the knowledge and ability to re-make and re-new it.

In this respect, recreating the style of this staircase to represent the spirit, or 'essence', of the *Titanic* means that it lives on as something that can be experienced today: touched and walked on and seen in three dimensions. For visitors, it provides a sense of realism that may prompt a level of romantic escapism and nostalgia, drawing from the image of the period style. In its intricate design, it may also challenge our idea of quality in material finish, contrasting as it does with more contemporary interior spaces in its use of ornamentation and detail. In terms of smell, colour, shininess and smoothness, this replica staircase must reflect something of the quality of the original staircase in its fresh and pristine 1912 state. For now at least, it is as new as the *Titanic* staircase was when it sank. Clearly, far from viewing the replica as a tawdry commercialised attempt at cashing in on the heritage industry, this more oriental perspective allows us to contemplate a potentially deeper significance embedded within the project.

The Grand Staircase

At this point, it is useful to consider the function and purpose of the original staircase in the context of the ship. On the *Titanic*, first-class passengers (who were the last to embark) entered the ship (from the Boat Deck or A Deck) into an interior that had to set the right level of prestige, opulence and luxury through an extravagant gesture of space. Reminiscent of the halls of the great country houses, the most high-ranking

Figure 3: Olympic: First Class Main Staircase
HOYFM.HW .H1578 © National Museums Northern Ireland Collection Harland & Wolff,
Ulster Folk & Transport Museum

first-class passengers would be guided on board first and personally presented to the captain and main officers. The importance of creating this sense of arrival encouraged a sense of personal attention to help connect passengers with the space and the ship, enabling them to make a poised and grand entrance as they took their place on board.

The class and social conventions of the day were strictly maintained in the physical divisions between the passengers, though this was less rigid between the first and second than between the second and third classes. Second- and third-class provision on the Olympic-class ships were much more generous in terms of space and superior in terms of facilities and comfort than on other ships of that time. Although US immigration laws required segregation of emigrants to prevent the spread of disease, passengers were advised to remain within their class section throughout the journey, unless invited to do otherwise. Beveridge[16] suggests that the high level of fatalities amongst third-class passengers may have been compounded by their reluctance to enter into areas they saw as being restricted, in part because they were conditioned not to do so without permission and also because they were unfamiliar with the escape routes.

Those areas to which they were forbidden access were of course of an opulence they could perhaps only imagine. Nowhere was that opulence more evident than in the lavish interior design of the First Class Lounge to which the grand staircase led. There were in fact two staircases.[17] Both of the first-class main staircases[18] extended from the Boat Deck and comprised six steps to the half landing followed by 11 steps (separated by a handrail) which fanned out for a dramatic flourish to A Deck.[19] Designed in the style of William and Mary but supported by lighter wrought-iron balustrades in Louis XIV, with flourishes of bronze, the graceful lines of the stairs in carved oak were accentuated by columns of composite material mounted on oak pedestals. On the landing, the carved centrepiece 12-foot-high arched panel featured a clock surrounded by carved winged figures representing Hope and Glory.[20] Overhead, the staircase was topped by an Adam-style white-glass, brass and iron dome with a chandelier fixed to its centre. At the foot of the stairs, there was a pedestal-mounted bronze cherub holding aloft a torch.[21]

Despite this very detailed description, there are no known photographs of the *Titanic*'s forward grand staircase. Most of the recognisable images that feature so strongly within the minds and imagination of the public are actually of the *Titanic*'s sister ship, the RMS *Olympic*, which was the first of the Olympic class ships and was at the centre of the original White Star publicity campaign before its maiden voyage in 1911. Experts consider the ships to be almost identical in design and quality: the *Titanic* had some modifications in finishes and layout but was essentially a design replica. Both were built primarily as immigration ships whilst also being designed to define the luxury market as palatial hotels. The production of ships renowned for their size and the beauty of their interiors was a deliberate marketing strategy adopted by the White Star Line, which knew that it could not compete with the speed of its main competitor's ships, the Cunard Line's *Lusitania*, *Mauretania* and *Aquitania*.

The *Shipbuilder* was lavish in its praise for the décor and the stance the White Star Line had taken to upgrade all areas on board the *Olympic*, proclaiming that:

> 'Everything has been done to make the accommodation superior to anything previously seen afloat.'[22]

On board, there were new and exciting design innovations in the ship's structure, engineering and facilities, with the introduction of a swimming pool, lifts, Turkish bath, barber shop, photographers' dark room, telephone installation, electric light and wireless equipment. However, the interiors were neither cutting edge nor modern. The design was conservative and traditional, referencing styles from the past such as Jacobean, Renaissance, Queen Anne and such like. As a luxury fit-out, they played safe with styles that were already tried and tested but built with the highest-quality materials and craftsmanship.[23] In this respect, the first-class state rooms were required to be beautiful, to be in a range of different styles, but not *too* different or outré. It was imperative, however, that they impress.[24]

Real and Not Real

When the *Titanic* sank, its claim to be the most luxurious ship of all time was also firmly fixed. Unlike other ships, including the *Olympic*, this image could not be affected by the subsequent and competing design trends, innovations and needs that shape the lifetime of most interior spaces. Each photograph taken on board the *Titanic*'s short maiden voyage is a valuable commodity in itself, with reproduction rights fiercely protected.[25] When the ship was rediscovered in 1985,[26] having been hidden from view for seventy-three years, it reappeared as a hollow wreck, stripped to its barest bones, with little evidence of the fit-out left.[27] Thus, inevitably, the original *Titanic* grand staircase no longer exists.[28]

As the ship dropped two and a half miles to hit the bottom of the sea with considerable force, the images that have emerged of its broken hull, at a depth where the darkness is complete, appear ghostly and unreal. Far removed from any human contact, in this hostile and remote environment, the *Titanic* is revealed through the light of the submersibles, significantly adding to its theatrical and other-worldly presence. To make sense of these images, we look for recognisable elements of the interior space for traces of human life or habitation. We see the void that once housed the staircase and accept this as significant – because it is the place where it *used* to be. In the presence of absence, we make a connection between the shell of what it *is* and the images we have seen of what it *was*, connecting the *Titanic* of the present to the *Titanic* of the past. The discovery of the ship finally answers the questions: what does it look like now and how much of it is there left?

As it is, removed from everyday access and seen up close only by very few, we can only view the wreck in the form of disseminated images rather than as something we can go to see for ourselves. It is this spatio-temporal contrast between the *Titanic* in its extreme states of pristine luxury and as a wreck which adds resonance to the myth – and creates a fascination for the original, true spatial experience. As Baudrillard states:

> 'When the real is no longer what it was, nostalgia assumes its full meaning. There is a plethora of myths of original and signs of reality – a plethora of truth, of secondary subjectivity and inauthenticity. Escalation of the true, of lived experience, resurrection of the figurative where the object and substance have disappeared.'[29]

Nostalgia and empathy are emotions central to the connection that people feel towards the ship. The *Titanic*, in its final resting place, continues to deteriorate and decay. Experts estimate that there will be a gradual collapse of the ship and it will eventually be lost – again. However, we may also speculate that if it ever were raised (as a huge rusting heap), it could lose much of its allure. Remaining removed from view adds to the *Titanic's* air of mystery, fuelling desire for the discovery of new artefacts, knowledge and images to spin new narratives and romantic nostalgia as to what actually happened.

Ballard was adamant that his expedition should not be a salvage operation and argued that the ship should remain undisturbed as an archaeological site. However, the discovery in itself was not enough to satisfy public curiosity and events such as the 1987 live TV opening of a safe from the *Titanic* attempted to manufacture a sensational historical moment as a big reveal. Subsequent expeditions, recognising the commercial opportunities of the wreck, have raised hundreds of artefacts which have now become collector and museum items. On offer today are items such as pieces of coal inset into silver bracelets but also a carved rosette from the grand staircase, which recently sold for £20,000.[30] These are not 'treasure' in the traditional sense of objects possessing intrinsic worth; they are valued not for what they actually are (fragments and debris) but sentimentally for what they represent as items and artefacts that were once part of the event, and brief life, of the *Titanic's* maiden voyage.[31]

The sense of discovery (or re-discovery) of salvaged items seems to bring new insights and evidence of life on board, from the kitchens below decks, where different sets of crockery were used for each class, to the items that can be connected to a specific and identified place on board denoting who (or at least, what type of person in terms of class or rank) might have used it or come into contact with it. Touring exhibitions of artefacts raised from the ship attract crowds to view authentic personal items, often related back to the original owners, whose own personal histories have become part of the narrative, before and after the event. Similarly, photographs of people taken on board the vessel – mostly the first-class passengers and crew – resonate as persons who could be named and seen to be part of the maiden voyage and, specifically, as the only *ever* people to sleep in this stateroom, to use the dining room, to walk up and down the staircase in the first-class section. The interior seems to come alive once it is known who exactly inhabited the space. Then, it is not just a space but a place where real people lived and where their lifestyle and position in society was bound up in how that space was designed and looked.

The Myth

The public seem to crave this personal and human connection to the *Titanic* story. There are an astounding number of knowledgeable experts and enthusiasts throughout the world who possess an in-depth understanding of every detail, archive and aspect, from the ship's engineering to survivors' stories and the social, political, cultural and historical contexts.[32] This widespread sharing of information through the media ensures that the ship remains in the consciousness of different generations, each output feeding the next wave of interpretation – stimulating interest and creating the potential to for its development across wider audiences within leisure and tourism.

According to Neill,[33] the popularity of the *Titanic* can be considered under three main themes. First, it reflects the twenty-first century anxieties on progress and a loss of confidence in modernity.[34] Second, he proposes that the tragedy of the *Titanic* reflects the 'ultimate fate of mankind'. This is reinforced by the haunting images of the *Titanic* wreck which suggests how our eventual demise is unknown – a powerful fate, drawing on an empathetic emotion that applies across all cultures. His third point claims that we still respect the *Titanic* for its stories that reflect courage, duty, honour, stoicism and resilience in the face of adversity – though the concept of chivalry may not be as prevalent today in a more egalitarian, less-class-structured, peace-time life where old standards and principles have radically changed.[35]

Lubin[36] suggests that James Cameron's 1997 blockbuster film *Titanic*, with its mass appeal, offers audiences 'a way to *think about* relevant modern issues of culture and class.' He claims that people identified with the simple message of love across the great class divide, the meaning of sacrifice and the modern obsession of technology over nature. In effect, it was the nostalgic assertion of these old-fashioned qualities and meanings from a bygone age that created its resonance, sentiment and success.

Cameron went to great lengths (based on many dives to the wreck) to reproduce the scale and quality of the interiors in order to add authenticity to the film.[37] His enthusiasm upon seeing the original fittings within the wreck reflects how deeply his research interpreted what he saw – and also how he was going to sell this to audiences worldwide:

> 'On D-deck, one of the swinging vestibule doors still hangs from its hinges, complete with its ornate bronze screen. Through this door Molly Brown and John Jacob Astor would have passed as they boarded from the tender ship Nomadic at Cherbourg.'[38]

At three-and-quarter-hours long, viewers who have seen the film (often repeatedly) identify not just with the characters, fictional and real, rich and poor, the action and the event and narrative, but also with the spaces in which it was enacted. The first-class staircase, in particular, is used to great effect to demonstrate the way status affects behaviour, showing how the first-class passengers pose in full evening dress as they descend the staircase dressed for dinner. By contrast, we also witness the staircase later in the film through powerful images of destruction, as many people (and the main characters) are submerged by the incoming water and experience the panic and fear of the sinking ship.

It is in the very last scene that the staircase becomes the final stage for the most powerful and lasting 'memory' of the film. As the elderly Rose sleeps (or dies), we are taken through the ruined shipwreck which then visually merges back into ship in all its glory. A door opens and we enter onto the grand staircase surrounded by smiling people: crew and passengers from all classes who we know, or assume, died at sea. Once we reach the landing, the young Rose is reunited with Jack (her long lost love) to great applause from everyone standing all around them in the gallery. As the emotive climax to the film, the ending effectively eradicates the tragedy and presents a fantasy of what might have been. In this emotionally charged scene the staircase almost becomes a 'sacred place' where the characters can go on to fulfil their lives together, having changed history and time.[39]

Re-presentation

The fact that the *Titanic* was bound for New York has undoubtedly contributed to the strength of the *Titanic* myth,[40] especially in the US. Behind all this lies the powerful message of the 'American Dream' and the opportunities for emigrants to make a better life for themselves – like so many people before them. While Titanic Belfast sets out to be a contemporary iconic building and 'The World's Largest *Titanic* Experience', the precedence has already been set by the 'World's Largest *Titanic* Museum' attractions in Branson, Missouri and Pigeon Forge, Tennessee, which are housed in half-sized, front-half *Titanic* replicas complete with iceberg.[41] Situated on Highway 76, the Branson Strip, there is no mistaking that this building is all about the *Titanic*. It is an unsubtle and literal interpretation of the ship that is both blunt and to the point. In a country where the car dominates over the pedestrian, the building has to shout out its presence and, in doing so, as Venturi and colleagues comment, the building *is* the sign. It was not designed to be high architecture; it was designed to be easily recognised, to make commercial sense.

Though there is no known authentic connection between either of these places and the *Titanic*, it suggests that the ship goes far beyond a specific or localised heritage. Wholly embracing the opportunity to bring to the people a version that equates to the original, the culture of reproduction and theme parks in the US has been well documented. As Umberto Eco comments, the issue is not that the reproduction substitutes the original but that it serves to satisfy the needs of people to have access to the original. He points out that 'for the reproduction to be desired, the original has to be idolized'.[42] The unprecedented attention the ship has received from the Cameron film and the lead up to the centenary commemorations has, in the past 15 years, given the ship a massive profile to boost its recognition, both as a physical entity and historical event.

As recreational simulacra, these places explore and interpret the ship's history in their own way and their appeal suggests they respond well to a gap in the market for those who enjoy all things *Titanic*.43 The interior spaces are conceived of as a staged exhibition where the visitors are actors, made to feel they are re-enacting actual experiences from life on board. The effect has to be realistic, but must also feel larger than (real) life, so that it is hyperreal. Although there are also beautifully reconstructed rooms and artefacts housed within this space, it is the replica grand staircase that is the major highlight of the tour. Its authenticity is established by its being 'constructed from the original Harland & Wolff plans' and it is described as 'The *Titanic*'s defining element of luxury and grace'.[44]

Here, the concept of wealth, and the class system, reflected in the contrasting décor and design of the *Titanic*, is a key to connecting visitors through a glamorous re-imagining of the myth. The staircase 'led First Class passengers into the heart of shipboard society where the rich and richer mingled before dinner'. It is played up as 'a spectacular staging area for guests to make their evening appearances.' Highlighting passenger names such as Guggenheim, Astor, Widener and Straus, who were some of the richest people in the world at that time,[45] helps personalise the attraction to give visitors a sense of a contained world within the *Titanic* designed specifically for people used to such luxury. Perhaps this is the crux that sustains the myth. People want the escapism and romance of a selective history. The replicated *Titanic* answers that need. The original was promoted as the epitome of interior-design luxury and quality but today everyone can access this social/spatial world as it 'was', unrestricted by time, class or location.

Figure 4: Grand Staircase, Titanic Branson, Branson, Missouri
Photo Credit: Titanic Museum Attraction - www.TitanicAttraction.com

As in Titanic Belfast, the 1:1 scale allows the spectator to move inside and be part of the space. It also enables the viewer to absorb something of the original passengers' true experience. They engage experientially with the space: standing, descending, gazing over, up and down. Like Titanic Belfast, the new brass hand rails comply with contemporary health and safety regulations reminding us that an old design model must be made to fit in with our (new) views of design. Overall, the US version appears to be a more faithful replica of the original, and a more complete space, as it also incorporates the first floor gallery and overhead dome. It is a contained space rather than one designed to be a feature placed within a bigger space that must also function as a banqueting suite. This means that it has no other purpose than to be viewed, admired and walked on (when permitted) as a discrete artefact.

As Eco comments, the prevalence of full-scale authentic copies suggests 'a philosophy of immortality as duplication.' He adds that:

> 'for historical information to be absorbed, it has to assume the aspect of reincarnation. To speak of things that one wants to connote as real, these things must seem real. The "completely real" becomes identified with the "completely fake". Absolute unreality is offered as real presence.'[46]

To heighten the link to *Titanic*, drawing directly from the film, the 'romance' of the grand staircase is fully exploited and marketed for the use of weddings and vow renewals.[47] An ordained 'Captain' in period costume will conduct the ceremony on the staircase in a setting of 'First-Class luxury' so that people 'feel that they too can be part of an image, myth, legend.' They too can be part of 'history' and their wedding marked as a defining event. Despite the fact that this is a replica staircase in a themed attraction on dry land, the association of the staircase transcends the reality. It looks the part, it sets the scene and, as it fulfils visitors' expectations, it enhances and validates their experience. This is not just the site of a superficial engagement with the *Titanic* myth, at least not always. It is the site through which, as Neill identified, our 'anxieties about progress and a loss of confidence in modernity', our consideration of the 'ultimate fate of mankind' and our empathy with 'courage and stoicism in the face of adversity' are all channeled.

Conclusion

The apparent need to recreate the *Titanic's* grand staircase over and over again reflects how much this 'grand' gesture in the interior design has become blurred by the cultural memory of the ship, of history and of the film. It is presented as a 'real life' tangible form of an image to enhance the hyperreal experience of 'being there', of being 'inside'. Made real, it brings people closer to the ship as it was. This indicates that a strong connection can still be established by degrees of associated authenticity reinforced by clever marketing: based on the original… from the original plans… the very place where it was built… from the hands of the same artisans… and so on.

With tourism as the focus of plans to breathe new life into Belfast, the once-successful shipbuilding industry has now been re-told by the story of what is, arguably, its least successful ship. With the break out of the 'Troubles' from 1969, local priorities were largely focused elsewhere so that, ironically, when tourists came looking for authentic connections to the ship there was nothing much left for them to see. The Thompson Dry Dock and Pump House have only recently been brought into use as a café and visitor centre and now feature as part of a walking tour of the area. Sadly, the old Harland and Wolff Drawing Office, the most significant building from the time of the *Titanic*, still lies empty, despite various re-development options that have been considered over the years. Located right beside the new Titanic Belfast building, it begs the question: why was *it* not re-developed as the new visitor centre?

Having already proved to be a big success with visitors in the US, in Belfast, the investment in tourism centred on the *Titanic* story also appears to have paid off. Visitor numbers to Titanic Belfast have been higher than expected and the spin-off effects of this can be seen all over the city in the number of new hotels and restaurants that have sprung up offering greater diversity in dining experiences and design. The *Titanic* theme has also caught on, with a new commemorative memorial, a re-branded railway station, street sculptures and theme pubs re-presenting the city in 2012. The original ship has long since gone but now the city has embraced its shipbuilding past, on the back of the *Titanic*, and is cashing in. It is arguable that the focal point of this broader phenomenon is the grand staircase; this interior in an interior; this simulacrum.

'Fake', 'theme' and 'copy' are all associated with low design and kitsch and, given the often ephemeral nature of interior design, it is often seen as the most potent channel for manifestation. However, in this context, 're-using' or 'making use of' can also be construed in the widest sense as appropriating or exploiting (the *Titanic*) literally and symbolically, physically and subliminally in various forms. Extending the presence of something that no longer exists by drawing on its mythic qualities is helping to reinvigorate space and place on both social and economic levels. The designing and re-designing of heritage that this interior reconstruction represents not only benefits the design industry by creating more work across a wide range of related sites, new and old; it may also be capable of achieving something more, at least in certain moments. It may be capable of reconnecting us with a sense of the sometimes laudable and powerful human condition – Neill's sense of pathos. In these terms, what is an authentic experience, and what is not, seem to matter less than the context in which the artefact or space is presented, how the wider public might view this within the narrative and, ultimately, how seriously people take it.

Understanding these broader potentials of the 'replica', the interior within an interior and its relationship with the original may have implications for the architectural and interior-design industries. As revealed by the case of the Titanic Belfast and its 'grand' staircase, these industries, their activities and production are associated with much bigger issues. Understanding this may well help us as designers to navigate the potentially difficult and contradictory terrain of design in a commercial context. It is just possible that this project gives us a glimpse of how to work within today's commercially cultural context in ways that still allow us to engage with more significant emotive and socio-economic questions.

Notes

[1] Rybczynski, W. (2002) The Bilbao Effect, *Atlantic Monthly* 290(2), pp.138–42.
[2] The 'our time, our place' campaign shown on TV and the Internet also includes four other motivational straplines: 'A year of exceptional opportunities'; 'Our time to turn the tide'; 'A chance to change perceptions'; and 'Your invitation to be part of it'. (Northern Ireland Tourist Board (2011) General format, retrieved 17 July 2012 from: http://www.discovernorthernireland.com see also http://www.nitb.com/ni2012/.)

[3] Howells, R. (1999) *The Myth of the Titanic*, Basingstoke: MacMillan Press.
[The three new White Star Line ships were the *Olympic, Titanic* and *Gigantic* (re-named the *Britannic*). Although the *Titanic* was the world's largest liner when it was launched (surpassing the *Olympic*), it too would have been surpassed, in 1913, with the launch of the Hamburg-America Line's *Imperator*.
[4] Harron, P. (2012) Titanic Belfast, *Perspective*, May–June (special supplement), pp.4–11.
[5] Eco, U. (1987) *Travels in Hyperreality*, trans. W. Weaver, London: Picador.
[6] There is one other long-standing *Titanic*-based exhibition in Northern Ireland, at the Ulster Folk and Transport Museum. It links in with a late-nineteenth, early-twentieth-century living museum comprised of re-constructed homes and buildings reflecting the local town and country experience at that time. (National Museums Northern Ireland (2011) General format, retrieved 18 November 2011 from: http://www.nmni.com/titanic.)
[7] Samis, P. (2008) The exploded museum, pp.3–17 in Tallon, L., and Walker, K. (eds) *Digital Technologies and The Museum Experience*, Plymouth: Altamira Press, p.3.
[8] Titanic Belfast (2011) retrieved 20 November 2011 from: from http://www.titanicbelfast.com.
[9] Many authors have explored the *Titanic* as a phenomenon of twentieth-century popular culture, for example: Howells, op. cit.; Foster, J.W. (1997) *The Titanic Complex: A Cultural Manifest*, Vancouver: Belcouver Press.
[10] Van de Vall, R. (2008) *At the Edges of Vision*, Aldershot: Ashgate, p.6.
[11] Beveridge, B., Andrews, S., Hall, S., and Klistorner, D. (2008) *Titanic: The Ship Magnificent, Volume 2: Interior Design and Fitting Out*, Stroud: The History Press, p.224.
[12] *Belfast Telegraph* (2012) retrieved 20 September 2012 from: http://www.belfasttelegraph.co.uk/news/nostalgia/titanic/rush-of-requests-as-titanic-staircase-sundays-launched-16150378.html.
[13] Designed at a time when the hand-crafted joinery skills to create such fine detail were readily available, the original *Titanic* staircase showcased local expertise and artistry to a wider and luxury market. Harland and Wolff were able to buy in specialist joinery fittings or fabricate them within the shipyard as required but were themselves highly experienced builders and renowned for quality finish and workmanship. For the joiners today, however, building this 'near replica' staircase for Titanic Belfast, proved to be quite a challenge. Used to contemporary joinery processes and tools, they had to work with more traditional techniques and levels of craftsmanship than they might normally employ. The task at hand was difficult, time-consuming and ultimately expensive. Comprising over 10,000 parts and built in the main within a workshop, the staircase was dropped by crane through the roof into the banqueting suite and finished on site. The making of the staircase was featured in the local media and greatly added to the excitement in the lead up to Titanic Belfast's grand opening. (BBC Newsline (2011) General format, retrieved 5 October 2011 from: www.bbc.co.uk/news/uk-northern-ireland-15185888.)
[14] While the grandeur, luxury and quality of detail in the staircase are evident, the Edwardian style jars as a themed and decorative feature so that it looks at odds within this space. It has been faithfully recreated to 'look' like the original but it has no real function, because it does not seem to lead anywhere. It fails to resonate as *the* staircase

of the *Titanic*, because it appears incomplete and, in this vast space, is something of an anti-climax. As a backdrop for photographs viewed up close with a narrow focus lens, it may look the part: after all, it is a physical recreation of the image that people hold of the original in terms of scale, materiality, finish and detail. Yet when viewed from further back, it is shown to be a simulacrum.

[15] Scott, F. (2008) *On Altering Architecture*, London: Routledge.

[16] Beveridge et al., op. cit.

[17] There were two so-called 'grand' staircases on the *Titanic*, forward and aft. Although neither Harland and Wolff nor the White Star Line ever referred to them as such, the staircases assumed this title, automatically adding a sense of importance and status through a definition of scale, quality and craftsmanship. For a virtual rendered tour of the forward grand staircase from all floors (Boat Deck to E Deck), see Titanic Grand Staircase for the Mafia Titanic Mod – a brief tour (2010) General format, retrieved 2 December 2012 from: www.youtube.com/watch?v=A20tMxvINJw.

[18] Beveridge et al., op. cit.

[19] This 'grand' sequence continued as far as D Deck for the forward staircase, and from E to F decks as a set of straight stairs. The aft staircase continued as far as C Deck in its 'grand' double staircase form.

[20] This panel featured only in A Deck. Lower floors in the forward staircase had paintings on the half-landing. The aft staircase had a less-elaborate feature clock on A Deck.

[21] In the forward grand staircase, the cherub holds the torch in his left hand; in the aft staircase he holds it in his right.

[22] Cited in Chirnside, M. (2004) *The Olympic Class Ships: Olympic, Titanic, Britannic*, Stroud: The History Press, p.54.

[23] Beveridge et al., op. cit., p.59. The interiors were built and designed by Harland and Wolff, though six of the special state rooms that signified the luxury of the vessel were fitted out by H.P. Mutters and Zoon of Holland. The style on board was opulent, late Edwardian drawing on a mixture of periods from Louis X1V, Louis XV, Louis XVI, Adam style, Italian renaissance, Georgian, Regency, Jacobean, Queen Anne, Modern Dutch and Old Dutch, eleven period styles plus Harland and Wolff's own design, reminiscent of Louis XV in Bedrooms 'A' and 'B'. This mix of design styles in the Edwardian era, Long suggests harks back to a nostalgia for the past and sense of security, in a time of flux. Jacobean, Louis XV, Georgian, Sheraton, Hepplewhite and Adam interior design styles all feature in the ideal Home Exhibition catalogue 1912. (Long, H. (1993) *The Edwardian House: The middle-class in Britain 1880–1914*, Manchester: Manchester University Press.) Service also observes that the design and style options used in wealthier late Edwardian homes were broad and conservative. (Service, A. (1982) *Edwardian Interiors: Inside the Homes of the Poor, the Average and the Wealthy*, London: Barrie & Jenkins.)

[24] The subsequent forensic notoriety that befell the White Star Line and the *Titanic* after it sank contrasts with the relatively anonymous existence of most of its other ships, and the *Olympic* in particular. Known as 'Old Reliable' for her steady and industrious service, that also served her well as a troopship during the WW1, the *Olympic* is normally only ever mentioned in relation to the *Titanic*. When the *Olympic* was finally retired in 1937, its interior fixtures and fittings went to auction. Some of these were bought and installed

in the dining room and staircase of the White Swan Hotel at Alnwick, which today advertises its *Titanic* connection. These original fittings, from the same era, craftsmen and materials as those of the *Titanic*, add authentic value not only through their own intrinsic antiquity and history but also in the way that they are able to re-make this land-based space (and the hotel itself) in the borrowed reflection of the *Olympic*'s more-famous sister ship. The *Titanic* staircase carries a strong image. By association these *Olympic* staircase fixtures are also noteworthy – despite the fact that in the White Swan Hotel the staircase has been re-built as a single flight, which physically makes it quite dissimilar from what we recognise as the original. (See Chirnside, op. cit.)

[25] O'Donnell, E. (1997) *Father Browne's Titanic Album*, Dublin: Wolfhound Press. Father Frank Browne boarded the *Titanic* in Southampton and disembarked in Queenstown (Cobh). While on board, he took many photographs of his trip, of the interior, decks, passengers, crew and quaysides. These images have proved to be an invaluable record of the life and times of *Titanic*'s maiden voyage.

[26] Ballard, R.D. (1989) *The Discovery of the Titanic*, London: Hodder & Stoughton. This expedition was led by Robert Ballard from Woods Hole Oceanographic Institution in the US together with IFREMER (the French National Institute of Oceanography).

[27] NOAA Titanic Expedition 2004 (2007) retrieved 20 November 2011 from: http://www.youtube.com/watch?v=6Z7REEnwKOQ. For a closer look at the aft grand staircase as a wreck, see: Titanic WHV (2008) General format, retrieved 20 November 2011 from: http://www.youtube.com/watch?v=GaojDBM_U04.

[28] Fragments of the staircase(s) that have been found include sections of wrought iron and gilt bronze balustrades from the aft grand staircase, patterned lino tiles, light fittings and the bronze cherub presumed to come from the B Deck of the aft first-class staircase. These have all been cleaned up and exhibited widely. Each piece and part (some more recognisable than others) are valued as a composite of the original, from what was once a major feature of the ship.

[29] Baudrillard, J. (1994) *Simulacra and Simulation*, trans. Sheila Faria Glaser, Ann Arbor: University of Michigan Press, pp.6–7.

[30] Titanic Stories (2010) General format, retrieved 28 November 2011 from: http://www.the-titanic.com/Gallery/Videos/Titanic-Memorabilia.aspx.

[31] Gronberg, T. (1999) The *Titanic*: An object manufactured for exhibition at the bottom of the sea, in Kwint, M., Breward, C., and Aynsley, J., (eds) *Material Memories: Design and Evocation*, Oxford: Berg, pp.237–51. Gronberg also highlights the effect of the cult value of the *Titanic* artefacts as souvenirs and the impression of the 1994–5 'Wreck of the Titanic exhibition' at London's National Maritime Museum. He comments: 'However "authentic" these objects, they were obviously mundane; in nearly every case such exhibits were neither intrinsically precious nor beautiful to look at. It was through their identification with this particular instance of death that they derived their fascination.' (p.243)

The New York based RMS *Titanic*, Inc. is the legal holder of the ship's salvage rights. The company claims it is dedicated to preserving the legacy of the ship, wreck, site and all her passengers and crew through educational, historical, scientific and conservation-based programs. (RMS *Titanic*, Inc (2011) General format, retrieved 20 November 2011 from: http://www.rmstitanic.net/about-us.html.)

[32] Foster, op. cit. In addition to the academic texts and journals, the *Titanic* disaster has inspired a whole host of musicals, plays, films, songs, cartoons, jokes, paintings, documentaries, poems and works of fiction. Foster explores the range of cultural outputs that have been closely, widely and loosely connected with or based on the *Titanic*.

[33] Neill, W. (2011) The debasing of myth: the privatization of *Titanic* memory in designing the 'post-conflict' city, *Journal of Urban Design* 16(1), pp.67–86.

[34] In this technological age, there is a romantic fascination for a perceived golden era preceding WW1, before lifestyles, gender roles and culture changed so dramatically. The current appeal for the ITV series *Downton Abbey* also suggests a similar high regard for a time when there was a strict class system in place and a sense of craftsmanship and quality (at least, for the wealthy) before widespread mass production and consumption. The notion of this ship as the epitome of luxury at that time adds to the allure and arguably remains unchallenged as it was in near-perfect condition when it sank. In this respect, its interior style has gained an appreciated mythic value beyond its actual significance and design worth.

[35] The *Costa Concordia* sank off the coast of Italy on 13 January 2012 but, unlike in the case of the *Titanic*, the captain did not go down with his ship or remain the last person to be evacuated. Thirty-two people lost their lives.

[36] Lubin, D. (1999) *Titanic*, London: British Film Institute, p.12.

[37] Marsh, E.D. (1997) *James Cameron's Titanic*, London: Boxtree.

[38] Ibid., p.xii

[39] Middleton, P., and Woods, T. (2004) Textual memory: the making of Titanic's archive, in Bergfelder, T., and Street, S. (eds) *The Titanic In Myth and Memory: Representations in Visual and Literary Culture*, London: I.B. Tauris.

[40] Howells, op. cit., pp.58–9. Howells interprets the story of the *Titanic* as a 'modern myth, communicated, encoded and preserved in popular culture'. In this particular context, his second point indicates: 'although myths still have a complex relationship with the past, that past is partly idealized, invented, selectively remembered or reanimated in the interests of the present.' This also links to his last point that myths 'are a result of social need, and are used to spin "webs of significance" out of the raw materials of lived experience. In this way, they reanimate the actual to construct order and meaning from an arbitrary world.'

[41] Venturi, R., Scott-Brown, D., and Izenour, S. (1972) *Learning from Las Vegas: The Forgotten Symbolism of Architecture*, Cambridge, Mass: MIT Press. The half-sized, front-half ship replica may be seen as a good example of their categorisation of a building as a 'duck', rather than a 'decorated shed'.

[42] Eco, op. cit., p.19

[43] The format of the visit has been developed as an experience that trades on the emotions as a journey through the space. As people arrive, they are given the name of a passenger or crew member from the *Titanic*'s maiden voyage and it is only when they complete their journey that they discover if that person survived or not. Throughout the visit, actors in period dress and assumed character guide visitors to add to the 'real life' living theatre aspect in simulating the past. Through a series of different

spaces the *Titanic* experience is reinforced contextually, physically and emotionally to fully engage the visitor through the process of simulation: firing coal, attempting to stand up on a sloping deck, touching a iceberg, sending an SOS signal and sitting in a life-sized lifeboat. (Titanic Branson (2011) General format, retrieved 20 November 2011 from: http://www.titanicbranson.com/titanic-branson-tour.php. See also: Titanic the Experience (2011) General format, retrieved 20 November 2011 from: http://titanictheexperience.com.) RMS Titanic Inc, a subsidiary of Premier Exhibitions, currently stages eight *Titanic* exhibitions throughout the US. These have been built around their sponsored research expeditions and artefacts raised from the depths specifically for the purpose of exhibition within the leisure/entertainment industry. (RMS Titanic (2012) op.cit.)

[44] *Titanic Branson*, retrieved 20 November 2011 from: http://www.titanicbranson.com/titanic-weddings/titanic-branson-weddings.php.

[45] Howells, op. cit., p.86. Howells comments that in the late Edwardian period the popular interest in the *Titanic* was largely focused on the stories associated with the rich, documenting their survival or final moments in relation to their passage, lifestyle and status.

[46] Eco, op. cit., p.7

[47] At Titanic Branson, the wedding package is sold as 'an experience of pure romance, beauty and elegance' in a 'gilded age of magnificent excess'. (Titanic Branson (2011) General format, retrieved 20 November 2011 from: http://www.titanicbranson.com/titanic-weddings/titanic-branson-wedding-packages.php.)

Bibliography

Ballard, R.D. (1989) *The Discovery of the Titanic*, London: Hodder & Stoughton.

Baudrillard, J. (1994) *Simulacra and Simulation*, trans. Sheila Faria Glaser, Ann Arbor: University of Michigan Press.

BBC Newsline (2011) General format, retrieved 5 October 2011 from: www.bbc.co.uk/news/uk-northern-ireland-15185888.

Beveridge, B., Andrews, S., Hall, S., and Klistorner, D. (2008) *Titanic: The Ship Magnificent, Volume 2: Interior Design and Fitting Out*, Stroud: The History Press.

Chirnside, M. (2004) *The Olympic Class Ships: Olympic, Titanic, Britannic*, Stroud: The History Press.

Eco, U. (1987) *Travels in Hyperreality*, trans. W. Weaver, London: Picador.

Foster, J.W. (1997) *The Titanic Complex: A Cultural Manifest,* Vancouver: Belcouver Press.

Gronberg, T. (1999) The *Titanic*: An object manufactured for exhibition at the bottom of the sea, in Kwint, M., Breward, C., and Aynsley, J., (eds) *Material Memories: Design and Evocation*, Oxford: Berg, pp.237–51.

Harron, P. (2012) Titanic Belfast, *Perspective*, May/June (special supplement), pp.4–11.

Howells, R. (1999) *The Myth of the Titanic*, Basingstoke: MacMillan Press.

Long, H. (1993) *The Edwardian House: The middle-class in Britain 1880–1914*, Manchester: Manchester University Press.

Lubin, D. (1999) *Titanic*, London: British Film Institute.

Marsh, E.D. (1997) *James Cameron's Titanic*, London: Boxtree.
Middleton, P., and Woods, T. (2004) Textual memory: the making of Titanic's archive, in Bergfelder, T., and Street, S. (eds) *The Titanic In Myth and Memory: Representations in Visual and Literary Culture*, London: I.B. Tauris, pp.507–26.
Neill, W. (2011) The debasing of myth: the privatization of *Titanic* memory in designing the 'post-conflict' city, *Journal of Urban Design* 16(1), pp.67–86.
NOAA Titanic Expedition 2004 (2007) General format, retrieved 20 November 2011 from: http://www.youtube.com/watch?v=6Z7REEnwKOQ
O'Donnell, E. (1997) *Father Browne's Titanic Album*, Dublin: Wolfhound Press.
RMS Titanic (2012) General format, retrieved from: http://www.rmstitanic.net/expedition/
Rybczynski, W. (2002) The Bilbao Effect, *Atlantic Monthly* 290(2), pp.138–42.
Samis, P. (2008) The exploded museum, in Tallon, L., and Walker, K. (eds) *Digital Technologies and The Museum Experience*, Plymouth: Altamira Press, pp.3–17.
Scott, F. (2008) *On Altering Architecture*, London: Routledge.
Service, A. (1982) *Edwardian Interiors: Inside the Homes of the Poor, the Average and the Wealthy*, London: Barrie & Jenkins.
Titanic Branson (2011) General format, retrieved 20 November 2011 from: http://www.titanicbranson.com/titanic-weddings/titanic-branson-weddings.php.
Titanic Stories (2010) General format, retrieved 28 November 2011 from: http://www.the-titanic.com/Gallery/Videos/Titanic-Memorabilia.aspx.
Titanic the Experience (2012) retrieved from: http://titanictheexperience.com
Titanic WHV (2008) General format, retrieved 20 November 2011 from: http://www.youtube.com/watch?v=GaojDBM_U04.
Van de Vall, R. (2008) *At the Edges of Vision*, Aldershot: Ashgate.

Monica DI RUVO and
Amanda BREYTENBACH
University of Johannesburg (SA)

SOUTH AFRICAN PUBLIC INTERIORS: REDRESSING THE PAST, CRAFTING THE PRESENT

In her explanation of a contemporary project that incorporates visual references to the past, with the aim of boosting the economy on the one hand and creating a new image for its region on the other, Rooney's essay again overlaps with our following one. In this case, this latter is a text whose geographical focus is on a completely different continent. ... [Di Ruvo and Breytenbach] offer socio-political interpretations centred on three government buildings: the Mpumalanga Provincial Legislature, the Northern Cape Provincial Legislature and the Constitutional Court. ... [T]hey identify how these buildings were intended to showcase South African arts and crafts as part of a drive to promote a new creative economy in the country that would move it away from low-mark-up agricultural production to high-mark-up designed and manufactured goods. ...

Beyond the purely economic, however... [they show how these buildings] were seen as symbols of the South African majority regaining power and were intended to present an image that celebrated liberation but which also celebrated the recuperation of the past.

Introduction

This chapter considers the approach South African architects and designers took when tasked by government in the 1990s to design buildings representative of a new democratic South Africa. We will identify that this approach looked to the surrounding context and included local craft and skills into designs that resulted in a synergy between local arts and contemporary design. This extensive use of craft will be examined in the interiors of the three public buildings commissioned by the democratically elected South African Government since 1994: the Mpumalanga Provincial Legislature building (1999), the Northern Cape Provincial Legislature building (2003), and the Constitutional Court (2004) in Johannesburg. These buildings have become recognised architectural symbols of a new South African but a key aspect of their designs has yet to receive significant attention: their interiors. This chapter therefore focuses on their interior spaces and aims to provide deeper insights, as well as a critical discussion, on their inclusion of local craft and craft skill. As a result, it will identify the role of interiors in the development and presentation of a new South African identity.

South African Government and the Craft Industry

In 1994, the post-apartheid government was faced with huge challenges. Amongst these were regaining ethnic individuality undermined during apartheid rule, the creation of a new shared democratic national identity and the creation of skills training and employment opportunities.[1] Given the large numbers of economically disadvantaged, unskilled and unemployed people found in South Africa at this time, the government identified the labour-intensive craft industry as offering potential for addressing these issues. In 1998, the Department of Art, Culture Science and Technology commissioned a report, *Creative South Africa*, which researched the cultural industries and proposed strategies for their growth and development.[2] According to this report, the craft sector was identified as a predominantly rural industry with women being the key producers. It thus offered a wide range of positive social and economic spin-off effects. The *Creative South Africa* report further indicated that 'the craft sector can serve as an indigenous research and development arm for South African innovation'.[3] This report informed the government's agenda towards job creation and the promotion of an arts-and-crafts economic sector which remains active today.

Ten years later, the Gauteng Department of Sports, Arts, Culture and Recreation commissioned a further study. *The Gauteng Creative Mapping Project: mapping the creative industries in Gauteng, 2008* was conducted by the Afro Micro Economic Research Umbrella (AMERU) at the Witwatersrand University in conjunction with Culture Arts and Jobs and the British Council. It found that creative industries, which include the design and craft sectors, contribute in excess of 33 billion South African Rand (ZAR) to the province's economy and create direct employment for over 60,000 people.[4]

Using these reports to inform strategy and obtain statistics for the craft industry, the South African government has focused on, and invested in, this sector. It sees it as a means of creating employment, increasing economic growth through export earnings, as a vehicle for 'nation building' and as an aid in the creation of an 'understanding of the nation's identity'.[5] This investment is evidenced by the increasing prevalence of craft exhibitions such as the Design Indaba Expo, held yearly in conjunction with the

Design Indaba Conference in Cape Town, and the South African Handmade Collection, an initiative by the Department of Trade and Industry at the Decorex trade fairs held yearly in Johannesburg, Durban and Cape Town. Pavilions representing each province showcase the work of craft artists.[6] Craft centres have been initiated across the country such as the Gauteng Craft and Design Centre in Sandton, a highly populated business destination in Johannesburg. These ventures have served not only to create employment but also to create awareness amongst designers, specifiers and architects of the wide range of skills available to them.[7]

Craft centres offering training in skills such as mosaic work, colour exploration, sewing-machine skills, beadwork and embroidery have also played a social role whereby community projects are used as platforms for adult education, providing support around daily issues affecting the lives of members of the project. One such project, the Boitumelo sewing project, carries the slogan 'Stitching our lives together'.[8] In an interview, Erica Luttich, creative director of the Boitumelo project, explains that project participants are actively engaged in discussing and working with the community on a range of social issues including family relations, group work, social awareness and environmental pressures. In the process, they create a wide variety of functional products and art pieces that are sold to the public. Now in its tenth year, Boitumelo offers a six-month training course that includes various arts-and-craft skills to any person who needs skills development. Through skills training and various workshops, it offers the participants the possibilities of exploring social problems within the community. Community members are involved in preparatory exploratory workshops concerning themes dealing with history, identity and key social issues relevant to the participants. As such, the participants themselves begin to explore these selected themes and develop essential skills to engage positively with the serious social problems they face on a daily basis.

The inclusion and exploration of reflective themes is also evident in other regions. In her study of the Mapula embroidery project in the Winterveld region, Brenda Schmahmann[9] describes embroideries which have documented various themes over the years: politicians and symbols of nationhood, advertisements, aids awareness, sport, self-representation, and local and international news.[10] She states that the selection of themes depicted is informed by experience and that the act of representation provides women with 'opportunities to articulate concerns they feel unable to discuss in everyday discourse'.

The craft theorist Sue Rowley explores the relationship between collective memory and artefacts, and the concept of narrative identity, which suggests that 'we know who we are by the stories we tell' and that our 'present sense of identity is grounded in our knowledge of the past.' Crafted objects, therefore, are integral to the sense of identity of the people who produce them.[11] Traditionally, whether produced for domestic use or in large quantities for sale, craft objects or artefacts show little or no variation in style or technique between one craft artist and the next.[12] Sue Rowley states that this repetition of form along with a resistance to innovation that is often attributed to craft indicates a cultural value invested in these forms rather than their lack of originality. These objects signify the continuity of traditional values and thus become effective symbolic signifiers of identity.

The Role of Local Craft in the Drive Towards Sustainable Design

Social and environmental responsibilities have received attention since the 1960s; however, only in the 1990s did extensive evidence determine that the world had gone into 'overshoot'. Mathis Wackernagel and William Rees presented these results and indicated that humanity's ecological footprint had exceeded the global carrying capacity of the Earth.[13] These revelations urged people across the globe to embrace a paradigm shift and transform from being environmentally irresponsible to environmentally responsible. The United Nations Agenda 21, a comprehensive plan of action for sustainable development, was adopted in Rio de Janeiro in 1992. This was signed by 178 governments and reaffirmed in Johannesburg, South Africa in 2002.[14] Now with 195 member governments, the United Nations Framework Convention on Climate Change held its December 2011 convention in Durban, South Africa.[15]

These global efforts to address climate change have contributed to growing social awareness amongst consumers. With a greater interest in sustainable products, designers have responded with a return to a more labour intensive, handmade approach to manufacturing decor items for use in interiors. The industrial designer Steven Burks calls this 'design with a conscience'.[16] According to Kamphuis, designers are rediscovering traditional and regional handiwork techniques in a response to the increasing uniformity of our environments caused by mass production, industrialisation, globalisation and commercialisation.

In South Africa, local designers such as Haldane Martin started making use of locally available materials, recycled products and local craft techniques in contemporary designs in the 1990s. Martin's Zulu Mama chair, designed in 2006, is an exploration of an indigenous Zulu basket-weaving technique adapted for weaving recycled plastic onto a recycled stainless steel frame.[17] Haldane Martin's design could be compared to solutions provided by international designers such as the Campana Brothers' Transplastic chairs[18] and Birsel + Seck's Madame Dakar range of chairs[19] for Moroso – contemporary designs using sustainable materials that help create employment in rural areas.

This global paradigm shift towards sustainable design occurred at the same time as the transformation and rebuilding agenda proposed for the new South Africa and thus resonated with the national agenda for the craft industries. Both these issues were to play a central role in determining the nature of the three public buildings we consider in detail here, each of which responded positively to a complex range of expectations and demands brought to the fore by these geo- and socio-political circumstances.

Searching for a New National Identity

After the democratic elections in 1994, the provincial borders of South Africa were revisited and the former four provinces were reconfigured into nine smaller ones. As a result, many of these provinces required new governmental offices, many of which were inserted into repurposed existing public buildings. Such buildings have historically functioned as vehicles for constructing national identity and, according to Federico Freschi, these buildings expound 'the cultural and historical virtues of the nation state'. [20] South African colonial architecture was largely adopted by the apartheid regime which, during the mid-twentieth century, morphed into a brutalist style which can be said to have serviced the ideals of apartheid. As Walter Peters has argued: 'like all aspects of South African life, architecture was created with conscious political effects'. [21] Similarly the interiors of these buildings were functional and characterised by large expanses of un-rendered concrete with little or no applied ornamentation.

Lawrence Vale argues that postcolonial states are rarely culturally homogenous[22] and, in response to this, the slogan 'rainbow nation', as used in 1994 by then Archbishop Desmond Tutu, was introduced in South Africa as an attempt to reconcile the many cultures present in the country and create a mood of peace and 'unity in diversity'.[23] This notion introduces an additional aspect of the postcolonial discourse which deals with hybrid space. According to Homi Bhabha,[24] this is a space in which the sovereign state and the colonial subject are not exclusive alternatives but the construction of their identities involves 'mutual contamination'. This third space was viewed by Bhabha as a potential site of resistance; one of struggle and negotiation. This notion is relevant in the South African post-apartheid context due to its multifaceted and multicultural population that for so long had been denied a voice by the apartheid regime: this was a space where reconciliation could take place.

Freschi states that 'new' South African nationalism is less about ideology than it is about identity.[25] Furthermore, he suggests that the process of nation building has had to take place in an increasingly post-national world, where the creation of national identity is positioned amongst other collective notions such as gender and ethnic, ecological and global identities. In this instance, the context is no longer one of resistance against the apartheid regime but rather of reconciliation and filling the cultural gaps left by the apartheid system. Three decades later, this too could be seen as a new type of hybrid space: a fourth space in the South African postcolonial discourse?

Jonathan Noble also reflects on hybrid representation, using the metaphors of skin and mask to describe these buildings. He concludes that they represent the simultaneous appropriation, inclusion and subversion of the dominant so as to render a 'layering of form, an inclusion of difference and a resistance to closure'.[26] He refers to the multiple symbolic references made in these buildings as 'African expressions' and 'identifications' rather than 'identity and style'.[27]

According to Valéria Salguiero, allegorical visual language has been utilised in the decoration of buildings since Renaissance times and this is particularly evident at those moments when a rupture with the past has required new formulations.[28] Sometimes, in order to imply rupture with the past, new symbols and devices may come into existence as part of the process of building nationality, such as a national anthem, a national flag or the personification of a nation in a symbol or image. South Africa was no different and its architects and designers all engaged in a use of symbols and devices to develop an appropriate design identity. That identity reflects on local culture and tradition, relates to community and takes into account specific economic, social, environmental, cultural and technological conditions prevailing in the 'new post-apartheid South Africa'.[29]

Mpumalanga Provincial Government Complex

The Mpumalanga Provincial Legislature building is located in Nelspruit on a site that overlooks the convergence of the Nels and Crocodile Rivers and which is surrounded by indigenous flora and fauna. The brief for the design competition referred to the natural beauty of the site and the need to preserve the indigenous flora and fauna protected by a thirty-meter buffer zone from the river. Noble indicates that, apart from technical and programmatic requirements, the brief for the Mpumalanga Legislature did not present any expectations or guidance with regards to the symbolic significance or the architectural aesthetic of the building.[30] Reflecting this – but also the cultural importance of symbolism – Patrick McInerney, the project architect, has expressed the importance of the geographical context in the interpretation of the brief: 'there was a desire to incorporate the place, the people and the identity of the province'.[31]

The resultant complex, completed in 1999 by Meyer Pienaar Tayob Schnepel Architects and Urban Designers, relied on an inclusive, participatory design process and included crafts from the local communities to create decorative elements within the building. Tapping into the artistic skill inherent in the local community and allowing people to contribute to the building served to give the complex a contemporary cultural expression and resulted in ownership of the building by the community.[32] The design development was seen to emerge as an attempt to hybridise established architectural patterns with elements from material, cultural and historical contexts and incorporate these in the design of the buildings.[33] A strategy was developed for the incorporation of local finishes which, materially and metaphorically, were divided into three themed categories – earth (rock mud or clay), grass (woven fabrics and patterns derived from weaving) and reed – and represented as vertical elements on the edge of the space.[34]

The interior decoration is visible in three forms: decoration associated with building materials; decoration applied by craft; and decoration derived from contemporary South African art. The diagonal pattern from early iron-age pottery which was excavated on the site informed many of the decorative elements used in the interiors.[35] According to Noble, the introduction of an element dating from a 'pre-colonial past' becomes relevant to a society trying to free itself from connections with colonial and apartheid rule and he argues that the implementation of such signifiers has become a prominent feature in South Africa's new political imagery.[36] This pattern, applied

Figure 1: Mosaic 'rugs' along passage

Figure 2: Mosaic detail resembling a hand-woven basket

to various surfaces, becomes an imagined rather than a purely tectonic signifier. It becomes an identifying mark operating like a 'signature, stamp or seal'. Noble views this as an important turning point in South African architectural discourse as it links a 'poetics of place' to identifications with pre-colonial history. It is an attempt to fuse nature with history, material context with pre-colonial identity, architecture with an authenticity derived from a parent culture which existed before colonialisation.[37]

On one level, Patrick McInerney states that the interiors evolved from the functional requirements of the program.[38] However, fully integrated into this thinking was an awareness of symbolism. The design of the dome, which echoes the granite outcrops in this region, offered acoustic challenges which led to the design of triangular woven acoustic panels. These in turn led to the development of the motif of the woven basket which was then carried through to the mosaic flooring patterns. The integration of craft in the interior finishes is evident in the carved and pigmented plastered panels used on the interior walls of the chamber which, although contemporary and not specifically traditional in pattern, are reminiscent of decorative techniques used to adorn the mud walls of traditional dwellings. It is also evident in the intricate marble mosaics on the floors that mimic the patterns of woven grass baskets traditionally created by women in the region and which are positioned as if they are decorative mats along passageways.

In the main lobby, the mosaic floor represents the sweeping movements traditionally made by women smoothing layers of clay and dung onto the floors of dwellings. Yet another mosaic floor depicts the natural grasses of the surrounding landscape swaying gently in the wind.[39] A notable example of a community development project is the thirty-five-meter-long embroidered panel which tells the history of the Mpumalanga region. The horizontal panel articulates the public gallery in the legislative assembly chamber. This panel was co-ordinated by the Department of Sports, Arts, Recreation and Culture in 1999 and executed by fifty-six rural women.[40] Numerous artworks and traditional craft pieces from the region are displayed in custom-designed showcases along the main walkways. In 2004, in a further attempt to showcase and promote the work of local craft artists, a retail outlet was added at the entrance facing the courtyard to be used as a showcase for local craft products.

The Northern Cape Provincial Legislature

The Legislature of the Northern Cape Provincial Government building is located in Kimberley and was inaugurated in 2003. Designed by Luis Ferreira da Silva Architects, this was the second large-scale public building commissioned by the post-apartheid government. According to Noble, this brief differed from that of the Mpumalanga Provincial Government Complex as it elaborated on political ambition, empowerment, public symbolism and architectural character, as well as the natural, cultural, political and historical heritage of the province.[41]

Freschi reflects on the role that the decorative programmes for public buildings play in the 'construction of a national imaginary of unity in diversity' in contemporary

South Africa and makes explicit reference to the Northern Cape Provincial Legislature buildings.[42] According to Freschi, public buildings bring into sharp relief debates about the role of public art and architecture in the construction of national identity. Public buildings raise questions regarding ownership, access, identity and power and these questions are mediated by decorative elements such as the elaboration of the façade or other user-oriented aspects of the building. He argues that architectural ornament has the potential to be politicised and thereby we can gain insight into a regime's political ideology by analysing how it decorates what it builds.

In this building, a new imagery is created which attempts to show a break from the past. This was achieved through the innovative architecture conceived by throwing shapes of modelling clay onto the floor, in the same way as a traditional Sangoma (diviner) would throw bones to communicate with the ancestors.[43] It was a technique that resulted in a cluster of buildings, each housing a particular function and linked by external walkways and gathering spaces. The artist Clive van den Berg was invited to collaborate with the architects from the early conceptual stages of the competition bid and the result is evident in the integration of surfaces that have been handcrafted as part of the architecture.[44]

Iain Low states that Ferreira da Silva's work seems to respond constructively to Paul Ricouer's challenge of 'becoming modern without losing contact with our origins'[45] which, in effect, was the challenge facing the emerging post-apartheid nation. Low is of the opinion that the architect has 'moved away from the functionalist agenda of modernism and embarked on a re-writing of the architectural type in a space that straddles the subjective expression and the objective imperative of collective necessity'.

Van den Berg proposed a training workshop to run simultaneously with the building programme. After a tour of the craft facilities in the province, twenty people from surrounding communities were invited for a one-week workshop from which a team of eleven were selected to work on the project. The intention, according to Van den Berg, was to give these artists the skills training and confidence necessary to apply these skills in future.[46] Mosaic is extensively used on the heroes' wall, for the portraits of the democratically elected presidents, as well as for relief panels used as details on walls. Materials were restricted and selected based on suitability for skills transfer and techniques such as casting, mosaic tiling and welding were utilised to execute the installations, many of which are located on the exterior of the building.[47] Round glass-blown orbs or 'beads', inspired by the beadwork and decorative use of safety pins on traditional Xhosa blankets, were also 'stitched' to the plastered surface of the exterior wall of the tower with metal pins.[48] As a result, art, craft, interior and architecture can all be seen to merge.

Van den Berg's interest in the reciprocal relationship between the built environment and the life of its inhabitants, his interest in spaces as the repository of memory and his concern for the sculptural and narrative potential of architecture all informed his approach to the project. The integration of art into the building fabric adds accents and layers of meaning to the built surface and the artworks become echoes of archaeological, geological and biological elements. Found as patinated traces in the landscape, these elements or sculptural applications are intended to be added to with the passing of time.[49] Noble comments on this as an interesting point, regarding it as the creation of an open narrative which can be added to through time.[50]

With the inclusion of art, Van den Berg explains the need to visualise art and design outside of colonial and apartheid templates so as to ensure that the post-apartheid landscape looks different from what existed before.[51] He describes his approach by quoting Edward Said on the danger of being surrounded by the carefully selected images of the ruling power: in time, one comes to believe in them simply because it is difficult to imagine an alternative. Van den Berg questions how one might constitute a vocabulary that is not just based on iconography. If meaning for the visual arts and architecture is as much formed by the materials of speech as by iconography, then we also need to think about how climate, light, materials and space are reconstituted as a post-apartheid language.[52] Not only were colonial and apartheid traditions to be avoided but also the over-used imagery of African-themed casinos or lodges characterised by masks and the addition of oversimplified geometric chevron designs as decoration.

Figure 3: Exterior view of glass 'beads' stitched to the plaster and mosaic portraits of past (and future) presidents

Figure 4: Woven wattle acoustic wall treatment in the chamber

On the floor of the public gallery, metal inlays are noticeable among the polished slate floor tiles. These have been cast in bronze and depict the San engravings and glaciated paving found at Driekopseiland in this region.[53] Intricately detailed mosaics are strategically placed at the entrance to the chamber while, inside, coloured fluorescent lights hang like mobiles and acoustic panelling is crafted out of panels of woven wattle branches. These weaving traditions, historically used for mats in the 'matjieshuise of the Griqua' of the region, are also represented here in the acoustic treatment along the walls.[54] Where possible, surfaces make reference to indigenous craft and decorative traditions whilst carefully avoiding obvious traditional solutions.[55]

The Constitutional Court

The Constitutional Court, by OMM Design Workshop and Urban Solutions Architects and completed in 2004, has since become the 'architectural symbol of democratic South Africa'.[56] This project differs slightly from the preceding examples as the site identified for this development was already a national monument: the Old Fort in Braamfontein, Johannesburg. At first a prison, then fortified and expanded into a complex of prison buildings historically used to detain political prisoners of the apartheid regime, it already had a symbolically laden reputation. The brief described

Figure 5: Hand-carved entrance doors

the context, the historical importance of the site, the technical and special requirements of the users as well as material and climatic concerns.[57] Inevitably, the use of such a historically significant site brought into play difficult and polemic questions of heritage and re-use.

The resultant court building makes use of the reclaimed bricks from the awaiting-trial block which was demolished in order to create a paved gathering space in front of the building. The 'reclaimed brick' wall forms a curved feature wall visible on the interior of the court. Reclaimed red brick also inscribes the footprint of the demolished building in the paving in front of the new court building.[58] In response to the brief, which required that many people should finally contribute to the design and building of the Constitutional Court, the architects identified areas in which artworks could be incorporated. These were put to open tender and, as a result, community workshop crafters were engaged to work alongside established professional artists to realise many of the decorative items in the building.[59]

According to Andrew Makin, the foyer is the primary mechanism for communicating the building's symbolic intent.[60] It is here that craft is evident in numerous custom-made elements of the interior décor: the over-scaled entrance doors, designed by Andrew Verster and Andries Botha and executed by a team of eight wood carvers being the best example.[61] The doors are made up of twenty-eight panels, one for each of the rights enshrined in the constitution and an additional one in braille at door-handle height.

Wire-work chandeliers mimicking the patterns made by the shadow under the leafy canopy of a tree by artist Walter Oltmann hang over the lobby; woven metal wire and wicker lampshades by Lindelani Ngwenya are placed along corridors; slanted supporting columns, representing the trunks of trees under which the court would have traditionally been held, are clad with mosaic. The artists behind this last piece were inspired by how the sun fell onto the columns and decided to treat these in divided sections. They also looked to indigenous trees for inspiration and applied the mosaic so as to represent tree bark and leaves.[62]

To the northern side of the foyer is an open gallery housing a notable South African art collection. This collection was never part of the original design programme: however, during the design process, numerous artworks were donated and therefore needed to be accommodated.[63] The western glass facade of the gallery is screened by

Figure 6: Slanted supporting columns in the foyer

hand-crafted metal sun louvres designed by the architect Lewis Levin. Some panels are perforated and others are engraved by the artist Patrick Rorke with narratives he obtained by talking to people in the community and illustrating their stories.[64]

The floors in the main foyer are of the same polished slate tile with cast-metal inlays as used in the Northern Cape Provincial Legislature. In this instance, the metal inlays are used as stair nosings designed by Jabu Nala, a potter who formed the nosings out of clay prior to making the brass castings.[65] The doors to the courtroom are clad with engraved copper panels inspired by traditional Ndebele beadwork designs, executed by a team of six South African artists. In the court room, there is a large beaded flag as well as hand-stitched tapestries which hang as acoustic banners. These were made by rural craftswomen in small panels which could be carried home and then delivered once completed. Moreover, as in the Mpumalanga Provincial Legislature, traditional craft items are also on display as artworks in selected areas and in appropriate display cabinets.

In the opinion of Freschi, the function of this building as a symbol of a new democratic South Africa is achieved almost exclusively through the building's decorative programme.[66] He notes that the physical act of walking into, around and out of the building creates the opportunity to experience and interpret its various symbols, no matter how subliminal the visual points of reference implied by the decorative programme can be in some instances. Offering a slightly different interpretation, Noble maintains that architectural identity constructed here is not self-defining but rather involves a relation to something external, material, cultural or historic.[67] It involves a chain of signifiers which are linked to local experience.

Conclusion

In these public buildings, we see how South African interior designers and architects tapped into local skills traditionally used to create functional household objects and incorporated them in buildings to create decorative surfaces for contemporary interiors. However, not every technique employed comes from these roots. Mosaic tiling, for example, is not a craft skill historically practised in South Africa but has been incorporated into all three of the building interiors. The mosaic process is labour intensive yet relatively easy to learn. It was thus seen as ideal for use alongside carving, weaving and embroidery in the interiors of these public buildings as a means of skills transfer and job creation. Furthermore, it facilitated the creation of new imagery not linked to a colonial or apartheid past. In contrast to this, the hand-crafted surfaces represent ties with a pre-colonial heritage belonging to the geography of the region and its traditional values and have been a successful signifier of local identity allowing South Africans to remember and commemorate the past. By making use of these diverse techniques and cultural references, these projects were able to answer the requirements of the government both at a socially practical level, through the creation of jobs and the development of skills, and at a socially symbolic level, through the use of deep cultural references.

The approach to the inclusion of craft differs in each these examples in that they have each been designed as a response to their local setting. In the Mpumalanga Provincial Legislature, craft is employed to practically all the finishes of the interiors and its employment was so extensive it had to be carefully managed by the design team. In every case, including those instances when commercially produced items such as the mosaic floors were employed, the references to the history of traditional crafts were brought to the fore and space was deliberately made available in display cases to highlight craft objects as art. This was to be further reinforced by opening a shop which was seen as helping highlight the commercial benefits available through seeing and using crafts as industry – something that has not yet been as successful as intended.

In the Northern Cape Provincial Legislature buildings, craft was again applied as a surface decoration as well as presented as art in its own right. In this building, some wall spaces are left clean and function as a blank canvas for future arts-and-crafts features to be added by other artists. As in the Mpumalanga Provincial Legislature, the application of these features is not traditional or literal but rather a poetic, contemporary application of craft that avoids stereotypes and one-dimensional interpretations of South African traditional cultures. In this case, however, the interior plays a lesser symbolic role than the exterior: no interior designer worked on the interior, the interior furnishings did not form part of the competition brief and the building does not house an art collection. Furthermore, the training programme designed to equip members of the community to be able to undertake future commissioned work by government has not been implemented and none of the open spaces left for the addition of further embellishment have been filled to date. Nevertheless, the potential exists and it is to be hoped that the continued decorative embellishment will be taken up again in due course.

In the case of the Constitutional Court, the approach towards the use of craft has similarities to that already described: spaces were earmarked by the architects and then artists were invited to make proposals. The interiors are contemporary in style and a limited palette of materials was employed. Here, there are no decorative architectural elements but the building does house sub-collections as a way of creating separate identities.[68] Examples of these sub-collections include a variety of hand-woven loose rugs, each inspired by a fragment from a different artist's painting, and the security gates to the judges' individual chambers which each have a different hand-crafted design. Traditional craft is only displayed as artwork in the judges' lounge, with smaller pieces in glass-topped displays serving as coffee tables.

In each case, there is a tangible surface quality to the finishes, a richness of colours and textures and a fascination to be found in the labour-intensive handmade decorative finishes that make up the interior and its symbolic message about the new South Africa. The hand-crafted surfaces serve to inform and remind the public of traditional culture and heritage, as well as cultivating a new sense of identity and pride in buildings that visually break from the austerity of the past. The hand-crafted surface decoration used in the interiors fills the spaces left by the apartheid regime and conveys a new attitude, one in which 'many pairs of hands' are involved in the building of the new nation.[69] This new nation, like the interiors themselves, is colourful and multifaceted.

All of these buildings have received national and international architectural acclaim since their opening approximately a decade ago and most of the craft skills applied to their interiors have filtered into contemporary South African corporate, retail and hospitality design. Numerous examples of their specific features have reappeared in a whole range of other projects, from ornately decorated bush lodges and hotels to sedate and sophisticated corporate environments. Despite the evident success of these projects in initiating a design trend and an awareness of crafts at an industrial level, the government has missed the opportunity these projects opened up with regard their potential to kick start skills development programmes aimed at the building industry and thus, ultimately, to help increase employment levels.

Upon visiting these buildings, it became evident that initiatives undertaken by the newly elected government at the time these buildings were constructed have not been maintained by successive staff. In Gaylard's review of the craft industry after ten years of democracy – conducted, coincidentally, in the same year that the Constitutional Court building was completed – he notes that the poor performance of this sector is largely due to a loss of skilled craftsmen to migrant labour and a tendency to focus on the supply of crafted products rather than the generation of greater demand, particularly internally.[70] This situation persists despite the example offered by these projects of how design innovation, the integration of craft skills with contemporary building projects and the creation of an internal market can come together in practical and symbolic ways. The South African interior-design industry is one avenue through which this can happen. It is, however, indicative of how it could happen.

Notes

[1] Cultural Strategy Group (1998) The South African craft industry report, retrieved from: http://www.info.gov.za/vie/Download FileAction?id70487.
[2] Cultural Strategy Group (1998) Creative South Africa, retrieved from: http://www.info.gov.za/view/DownloadFileAction?id=70493.
[3] Cultural Strategy Group (1998) The South African craft industry report, retrieved from: http://www.info.gov.za/vie/Download FileAction?id70487.
[4] AMERU (Witwatersrand University) and Culture Art and Jobs (2010, 10 October) The Gauteng creative mapping project, retrieved from: http://srac.gauteng.gov.za.
[5] Molewa, E. (2009) Archives for Future Generation, retrieved from: http://www.info.gov.za/speeches/2009/09021316451004.htm.
[6] South African Handmade Collection (2011) Retrieved from: http://www.sahc.org.za/ASPX/Public/Home.aspx.
[7] Mungoshi, R. (2009) Craft Centre opens in Sandton, retrieved from: http://www.joburg.org.za/index.php?option=com_content&task=view&id=37338&Itemid=193.

[8] Luttich, E. (2012, 2 July) Creative director of the Boitumelo project, Johannesburg: Interview with author.
[9] Schmahmann, B. (2006) *Mapula Embroidery and Empowerment in the Winterveld*, Parkwood: David Krut Publishing.
[10] Ibid.
[11] Rowley, S. (ed.) (1997) *Craft and Contemporary theory*, NSW: Allen & Unwin.
[12] Ibid.
[13] Wackernagel, M., and Rees, W. (1996) *Our ecological footprint: reducing human impact on earth*, Gabriola Island: New Society Publishers.
[14] UN Economic and Social Development Division for Sustainable Development (2010) Retrieved from: http//:www.in.org/esa/agenda21/.
[15] United Nations Framework Convention on Climate Change, retrieved from: http://unfccc.int/essential_background/items/6031.php.
[16] Kamphuis, H. (2010) Boundary-breaking crafts, *Frame 73* (March–April), pp.202–7.
[17] Martin, H. (2010) Contemporary South African Furniture Design, retrieved from: http://www.haldanemartin.co.za/zulumama.php.
[18] Designboom (2007) Transplastic recent work by the Campana brothers, retrieved from http://www.designboom.com/contemporary/transplastic.html.
[19] Moroso does Africa (2009) *Design Indaba Magazine* (Quarter 3), p.7.
[20] Freschi, F. (2006) Imagining unity: the construction of an imaginary of 'unity in diversity' in the decorative programme of the Northern Cape Legislature building, *Southern African Humanities* 18(2) December, pp.155–72.
[21] [21] Peters, W. (1991) South Africa Architecture of Symbiosis, in *Architects of South Africa*, Mulgrave: The Images Publishing Group, p.23.
[22] Vale, L.J. (1992) *Architecture, power and national identity*, New Haven: Yale University Press.
[23] Freschi, 2006, op. cit.
[24] Yacobi, H. (2008) Architecture, Orientalism and identity: The politics of the Israeli built environment, *Israel Studies*, Volume 13, (Number 1), pp.94–118.
[25] Freschi, 2006, op. cit.
[26] Noble, J. (2011) *African identity in Post-Apartheid Public Architecture: White Skin, Black Masks*, Surrey: Ashgate, p.265.
[27] Ibid., p.264
[28] Salguiero, V. (2006) Visual culture in Brazil's First Republic (1889–1930): Allegories and elite discourse, *Nations and Nationalism* 12(2), pp.241–60.
[29] Marschall, S., and Kearney, B. (2000) *Opportunities for relevance, architecture in the new South Africa*, Pretoria: University of South Africa.
[30] Noble, 2011, op. cit.
[31] McInerney, P. (2011, 7 June) Partner at Meyer Pienaar Architects & Urban designers, now Co-Arc International Architects Inc, Johannesburg: Interview with author.
[32] Malan, C., and McInerney, P. (eds) (2001) *The making of an African Building, the Mpumalanga Provincial Government Complex*, Johannesburg: Meyer Pienaar Tayob Schnepel Inc.

[33] Noble, 2011, op. cit.
[34] Ibid.
[35] Malan and McInerney, 2001, op. cit.
[36] Noble, 2011, op. cit.
[37] Ibid.
[38] McInerney, 2011, op. cit.
[39] Ibid.
[40] Sellschop, S., Goldblatt, W., and Hemp, D. (2002) *Craft South Africa, traditional/transitional/contemporary*, Hyde Park: Pan Macmillan SA.
[41] Noble, 2011, op. cit.
[42] Freschi, F. (2007) Post-apartheid Publics and the Politics of Ornament: Nationalism, Identity, and the Rhetoric of Community in the Decorative Program of the New Constitutional Court, Johannesburg, *Africa Today* 54 (Winter), pp.27–49.
[43] Ferreira da Silva, L. (2011, 25 August) Partner at Luis Ferreira da Silva & Johnston Architects, Johannesburg: Interview with author.
[44] Van den Berg, C. (2012, 31 July) Artist, Johannesburg: Interview with author.
[45] Low, I. (2003) Space and transformation, in Malan, C., and McInerney, P. (eds) *Building an African Icon the Northern Cape Provincial Government Complex*, Johannesburg: Meyer Pienaar cc, p.52.
[46] Van den Berg, C. (2003) The artworks integral to the Northern Cape Legislature buildings, in Malan, C., and McInerney, P. (eds) *Building an African Icon the Northern Cape Provincial Government Complex*, Johannesburg: Meyer Pienaar cc, p.86.
[47] Van den Berg, 2012, op. cit.
[48] Noble, 2011, op. cit., p.101
[49] Malan, C. (2003) The architect as artist, in Malan, C., and McInerney, P. (eds) *Building an African Icon the Northern Cape Provincial Government Complex*, Johannesburg: Meyer Pienaar cc, p.102.
[50] Noble, 2011, op. cit.
[51] Van den Berg, 2003, op. cit.
[52] Ibid.
[53] Fisher, R. (2003) The Technologies used in constructing the Northern Cape Legislature, in Malan, C., and McInerney, P. (eds) *Building an African Icon, the Northern Cape Provincial Government Complex*, Johannesburg: Meyer Pienaar cc, p.66.
[54] Ibid.
[55] Louis Ferreira da Silva Architects (2003) Overview of the design, in Malan, C., and McInerney, P. (eds) *Building an African Icon the Northern Cape Provincial Government Complex*, Johannesburg: Meyer Pienaar cc, p.37.
[56] Noble, J. (2009) Constitutional Court, in Joubert, O. (ed.), *10 Years + 100 Buildings, Architecture in a Democratic South Africa*, Cape Town: Bell Roberts, p.116.
[57] Ibid.
[58] Lane, J. (2011, 28 September) Curator at the Constitutional Court, Johannesburg: Interview with author.
[59] [59] Freschi, 2007, op. cit.

[60] Makin, A. (2006) Justice under a tree, in Law-Viljoen, B. (ed.) *Light on a Hill Building the Constitutional Court of South Africa*, David Krut: Johannesburg, p.46.
[61] Lane, 2011, op. cit.
[62] Noble, 2011, op. cit.
[63] Masojada, J. (2012, 8 August) Project architect, OMM Design Workshop, Johannesburg: Interview with author.
[64] Noble, 2011, op. cit., p.149
[65] Masojada, 2012, op. cit.
[66] Freschi, 2007, op. cit.
[67] Noble, 2011, op. cit.
[68] Masojada, 2012, op. cit.
[69] Ibid.
[70] Gaylard, J. (2004) The craft industry in South Africa: A review of ten years of democracy, *African Arts* 37, No 4, Art and freedom: South Africa after apartheid (Winter), pp.26–9.

Bibliography

AMERU (Witwatersrand University) and Culture Art and Jobs (2010, 10 October) The Gauteng creative mapping project, retrieved from: http://srac.gauteng.gov.za.

Cultural Strategy Group (2010, 10 October) The South African craft industry report, retrieved from: http://www.info.gov.za/vie/Download FileAction?id70487.

Designboom (2012, 19 February) Transplastic recent work by the Campana brothers, retrieved from: http://www.designboom.com/contemporary/transplastic.html.

Ferreira da Silva, L. (2011, 25 August) Partner at Luis Ferreira da Silva & Johnston Architects, Johannesburg: Interview with author.

Fisher, R. (2003) The Technologies used in constructing the Northern Cape Legislature, in Malan, C., and McInerney, P. (eds) *Building an African Icon, the Northern Cape Provincial Government Complex*, Johannesburg: Meyer Pienaar cc, p.66.

Freschi, F. (2006) Imagining unity: the construction of an imaginary of 'unity in diversity' in the decorative programme of the Northern Cape Legislature building, *Southern African Humanities* 18(2) December, pp.155–72.

Freschi, F. (2007) Post-apartheid Publics and the Politics of Ornament: Nationalism, Identity, and the Rhetoric of Community in the Decorative Program of the New Constitutional Court, Johannesburg, *Africa Today* 54 (Winter), pp.27–49.

Gaylard, J. (2004) The craft industry in South Africa: A review of ten years of democracy, *African Arts* 37, No 4, Art and freedom: South Africa after apartheid (Winter), pp.26–9.

Kamphuis, H. (2010) Boundary-breaking crafts, *Frame* 73 (March–April), pp.202–7.

Lane, J. (2011, 28 September) Curator at the Constitutional Court, Johannesburg: Interview with author.

Louis Ferreira da Silva Architects (2003) Overview of the design, in Malan, C., and McInerney, P. (eds) *Building an African Icon the Northern Cape Provincial Government Complex*, Johannesburg: Meyer Pienaar cc, p.37.

Low, I. (2003) Space and transformation, in Malan, C., and McInerney, P. (eds) *Building an African Icon the Northern Cape Provincial Government Complex*, Johannesburg: Meyer Pienaar cc, p.52.

Luttich, E. (2012, 2 July) Creative director of the Boitumelo project, Johannesburg: Interview with author.

Makin, A. (2006) Justice under a tree, in Law-Viljoen, B. (ed.) *Light on a Hill Building the Constitutional Court of South Africa*, David Krut: Johannesburg, p.46.

Malan, C. (2003) The architect as artist, in Malan, C., and McInerney, P. (eds) *Building an African Icon the Northern Cape Provincial Government Complex*, Johannesburg: Meyer Pienaar cc, p.102.

Malan, C., and McInerney, P. (eds) (2001) *The making of an African Building, the Mpumalanga Provincial Government Complex*, Johannesburg: Meyer Pienaar Tayob Schnepel Inc.

Marschall, S., and Kearney, B. (2000) *Opportunities for relevance, architecture in the new South Africa*, Pretoria: University of South Africa.

Martin, H. (2010, 4 July) Contemporary South African Furniture Design, retrieved from: http://www.haldanemartin.co.za/zulumama.php.

Masojada, J. (2012, 8 August) Project architect, OMM Design Workshop, Johannesburg: Interview with author.

McInerney, P. (2011, 7 June) Partner at Meyer Pienaar Architects & Urban designers, now Co-Arc International Architects Inc, Johannesburg: Interview with author.

Molewa, E. (2009, 16 November) Archives for Future Generation, retrieved from: http://www.info.gov.za/speeches/2009/09021316451004.htm.

Moroso does Africa. (2009) *Design Indaba Magazine*, Quarter 3, p.7.

Mungoshi, R. (2011, 11 December) Craft Centre opens in Sandton, retrieved from: http://www.joburg.org.za/index.php?option=com_content&task=view&id=37338&Itemid=193.

Noble, J. (2009) Constitutional Court, in Joubert, O. (ed.), *10 Years + 100 Buildings, Architecture in a Democratic South Africa*, Cape Town: Bell Roberts, p.116.

Noble, J. (2011) *African identity in Post-Apartheid Public Architecture: White Skin, Black Masks*, Surrey: Ashgate.

Peters, W. (1991) South Africa Architecture of Symbiosis, in *Architects of South Africa*, Mulgrave: The Images Publishing Group, p.23.

Rowley, S. (ed.) (1997) *Craft and Contemporary theory*, NSW: Allen & Unwin.

Salguiero, V. (2006) Visual culture in Brazil's First Republic (1889–1930): Allegories and elite discourse, *Nations and Nationalism* 12(2), pp.241–60.

Schmahmann, B. (2006) *Mapula Embroidery and Empowerment in the Winterveld*, Parkwood: David Krut Publishing.

Sellschop, S., Goldblatt, W., and Hemp, D. (2002) *Craft South Africa, traditional/transitional/contemporary*, Hyde Park: Pan Macmillan SA.

South African Handmade Collection (2011, 11 December) Retrieved from: http://www.sahc.org.za/ASPX/Public/Home.aspx.

UN Economic and Social Development Division for Sustainable Development (2010, 11 July) Retrieved from: http//:www.in.org/esa/agenda21/.

United Nations Framework Convention on Climate Change (2012, 31 July) Retrieved from: http://unfccc.int/essential_background/items/6031.php.

Vale, L.J. (1992) *Architecture, power and national* identity, New Haven: Yale University Press.

Van den Berg, C. (2003) The artworks integral to the Northern Cape Legislature buildings, in Malan, C., and McInerney, P. (eds) *Building an African Icon the Northern Cape Provincial Government Complex*, Johannesburg: Meyer Pienaar cc, p.86.

Van den Berg, C. (2012, 31 July) Artist, Johannesburg: Interview with author.

Wackernagel, M., and Rees, W. (1996) *Our ecological footprint: reducing human impact on earth*, Gabriola Island: New Society Publishers.

Yacobi, H. (2008) Architecture, Orientalism and identity: The politics of the Israeli built environment, *Israel Studies*, Volume 13, (Number 1), pp.94–118.

Jaime F. GÓMEZ GÓMEZ and
Cintia A. PAEZ RUIZ
University of Guadalajara, México

FOOTPRINTS FROM THE PAST IN THE WORK OF MEXICAN ARCHITECT MANUEL PARRA MERCADO

Di Ruvo and Breytenbach, then, present us with projects that attempt to incorporate traditional interior elements in predominantly modern architectural shells for what we call symbolic and political ends. Much the same can be said of the essay written by Jaime Goméz Goméz and Cintia Paez Ruiz, who examine the work of the post-revolutionary Mexican architect Manuel Parra Mercado in similar terms.

...what Goméz and Paez primarily underline *underline is the deliberate re-use of historic elements, symbols and materials in Parra's works. They call these historical references 'footprints' and stress their antithetical position when compared with the architectural preferences of the government of the time.* ...

These 'footprints' often involved salvaging materials and elements from old sites, buildings that had been left to decay and ruin because they lay outside the then-accepted aesthetic canon... of state-sponsored modernism in the years after the Mexican Revolution.

* * *

'To dwell means to live the traces that past living has left. The traces of dwellings survive, as do the bones of people.'

Ivan Illich

Introduction

The work of the Mexican architect Manuel Parra Mercado is an example of modern architectural design which uses references and pays homage to the architectural traditions of Mexico; it is an architecture that contains *footprints* from the past. It is also, for the most part, new build. Nevertheless, Parra can be defined as an architect of adaptation and re-use: he would re-use materials from older projects and thus physically layer his modern constructions with the footprints of his ancestors; he would also re-use the decorative symbols and construction techniques of his ancestors. Furthermore, he was inspired by traditional ways of living which became fundamental to his architecture and, importantly, to his interiors. It is here that these *footprints* are most clearly evident.

Parra worked during Mexico's post-revolutionary years in the early part of the twentieth century and his work reflects the dual approach to architecture that manifested itself throughout that period – on the one hand staunchly modern and, on the other, threaded through with references to an ancient, pre-colonial past that was celebrated as independent, on both political and social levels. Despite this socio-political context, however, Parra's work remained defiantly idiosyncratic: the expression of the individual force and imagination of a man who, despite the sometimes suffocating political context of state-sponsored modernism around him, trod his own path as a designer and architect.

In explicitly standing out against this political backdrop, it is our suggestion here that Parra's emotive architecture and, above all, his personal interiors can, and perhaps should, be read as political statements. Not in the sense of state propaganda but rather, as a defiant statement against the state and its view of what architecture should be. To understand the context of this interpretation, however, it is necessary to comment briefly on the political and social context that brought the majority of Mexican architecture during Parra's career into line with that of state-inspired socialism; which at that time meant principally that of the Soviet Union.

Context

After three centuries of Spanish rule ended in Mexico in the early years of the nineteenth century, the political instability and interference from foreign powers continued for some time with the French taking over where the Spanish had let off for a brief period from the 1860s.[1] During this period, there were some industrial advances in Mexico but it could be said that Mexico continued to be a pre-industrialised country. This began to change however once independence was regained under the leadership of Porfirio Díaz. The *Porfiriato*[2] oversaw a push towards industrialisation that began to mirror European countries. In a sense, the architecture of the *Porfiriato* could also be said to mirror that of Europe in that, despite constructing new buildings, it clad these buildings in the garments of Neoclassical facades and decorations; albeit in the Mexican case, with a certain number of traditional Mexican motifs as well. As an architectural and interior-design style, it became known as 'nationalism'.

The *Porfiriato* ended with the Mexican Revolution that started in 1910 and which is seen by many as the first socialist-inspired revolution of the twentieth century. Despite a complex beginning, characterised by much internal instability, the new socialist-leaning groupings of the period eventually established themselves as a single political party and Mexico entered what is known as the post-revolutionary period: a period characterised by the implementation of a state-socialist model of government inspired, principally, by the Soviet Union. This period saw the introduction of 'functionalism' as the state's preferred architectural style for all its building projects: schools, hospitals and Parra's own particular specialism, housing.

However, this was seen by the government as not only an effective and cheap way to build but also as serving a symbolic function: it was to represent the new socialist and modern state of post-revolutionary Mexico. Typical in this regard were works such as the social housing projects of Juan O'Gorman and Juan Legarreta. Designed to be efficient and cheap functional solutions, based exclusively on the future inhabitant's most basic needs, these projects used modern materials and technology and were even named according to the philosophy that underlay them: *La Casa Obrera Mínima* (the minimalist worker's house).

The early works of these two architects focused on designing individual houses with the intention of replicating them across several blocks and turning them into social housing solutions on a massive, even industrial, scale. They were ideas that lay dormant, however, until the economic conditions of the 1940s allowed for them to be implemented on this larger scale by Mario Pani. Nevertheless, from day one, they were seen as symbolic of the new government and its intentions.

Nuancing the Symbolism of Modernism in Mexico

Reducing the post-revolutionary government's attitude towards Mexican identity and architecture to an exclusively one-dimensional reading of modernism, however, does not tell the whole story. The aims of the post-revolutionary government were slightly more complex and tied into, albeit in a secondary way, a sense of Mexican identity that also acknowledged the past. A key figure in understanding this was José Vasconcelos who served as Secretary of Education during the presidency of Álvaro Obregón (1921–1924).

Obregón's policies and programs focused on 'taking care of [the country's] citizens', of providing them with education, of distributing land to the peasants and of relieving industrial workers from the oppression of excessively tyrannical bosses. In conjunction with this, Vasconcelos offered the country a new educational system. Vasconcelos was also a philosopher and social critic. He was a humanist and staunch anti-positivist. He viewed Mexico as a complex mix of cultures that was to be celebrated for its diversity. He visualised Mexicans as 'conquerors' of both the spirit and the intellect.

In this context, Vasconcelos promoted these ideas through education and pushed for increased accessibility to education as well as changing the curriculum and placing emphasis on improving educational standards. To this end, he initiated a major building programme for schools, libraries and historical archives. Free text books were given out, a free breakfast programme for children was implemented in schools and the first public book fairs were organised. However, he also saw the fine arts as a basic part of a technical education and wished to promote a rediscovery of Mexican culture, a policy most obvious perhaps in his promotion of historical archives.

For Vasconcelos in particular, the drive to modernism, then, was also linked to the rediscovery of Mexico's pre-Hispanic roots, native culture and the revival of popular arts and customs. Although only limited in scope, this was seen in some of the building programmes of the time. Certain modernist educational buildings, for example, left blank walls on their inexpressive facades onto which murals were painted that would celebrate this tradition. Both David Alfaro Siquieros and Diego Rivera, a friend of Parra's, were involved with this approach to softening modernist architecture with art and historical cultural references. As a manifestation of the integration of the fine arts and modernism as viewed by Vasconcelos, however, it was a 'narrow and distorted' version of 'plastic integration'.[3]

Despite their failings or limitations at introducing traditional features into the overwhelmingly modernist state aesthetic of post-revolutionary Mexico, these buildings were at least an indication of a sensibility latent in Mexico that Parra felt strongly and would develop much more forcefully. It would also manifest itself in the works of Luis Barragán, Ricardo Legorreta and Alberto Arai. Although the work of these designers did not coalesce into an identifiable movement, it would later be defined by the term 'regionalist'. When we examine the work of Manuel Parra, then, we may be looking at the work of an individual, but he was not completely alone: he formed part of an elite group of designers that were swimming against the tide of a Mexican state dedicated to modern functionalist and universal solutions to general problems. For this group and for Parra in particular, the designer's role was to reconnect individuals to an emotive, culturally rich and specific past.

The Individual and the Home

Parra became interested in architecture through the work of two uncles: Baltazar Izaguirre and, later, Antonio Rivas Mercado, an architect of the period well known in Mexico for works such as the *Teatro Juárez*, in the city of Guanajuato, and the national monument of the *Ángel de la Independencia* in Mexico city. He was also the former director of the School of Architecture at *Academia de San Carlos*, Mexico's most prestigious school of fine arts. However, by 1930, when Parra enrolled as an architecture student at *Academia de San Carlos*, modernism was the dominant 'style' of the day and the school was led by the defiant modernist, José Villagrán.

As the head of the Architecture Department at the *Academia*, Villagrán not only promoted modernism in the school's teaching but explicitly aligned it with political ends, thus turning the practice of architecture into an ideological posture. Inevitably,

Figure 1: Steps leading to the main rooms at Casa Diego Rivera 88, San Ángel Inn
Photo: Jaime F. Gómez

this may be seen to have had some effect on Parra; it would be difficult for it not to. Many of his personal friends at the time, such as Juan O'Gorman, were committed to Villagrán's vision and focused on housing, as did Parra. Indeed, in Parra's thesis statement that 'there is no doubt that the problem of housing is and will always be of paramount importance for architecture', one may be able to discern this influence.[4]

However, Parra only ever really paid lip service to modernism as a style and, although certain modernist features are evident in his works, as they are in that of Barragán,

Legorreta and Arai, they did not dominate. In his house for Diego Rivera, for example, the modernist tendency to celebrate smooth plane surfaces is clear (Figure 1); but as we shall see, this was always counterpointed by traditional symbolism and an approach to the house plan and interior décor that was totally anti-modernist in outlook.

Parra's work spanned six decades, from the 1930s to the 1990s, and features many noteworthy residences across the country: in Mexico City, Coyoacán, San Ángel, Guanajuato and Veracruz, to name but a few regions in which he worked. Although his designs echo some aspects of modernism they also feature decorative elements from pre-Hispanic or colonial eras. However, this use of decor did not fall into the category of 'nationalist' design as characterised by the earlier *Porfiriato* and neither did it correspond to the purely decorative tendency of the muralist involvement in the architecture of the day. Whilst in both these cases the intention was to serve the state by creating designs symbolic of a particular national identity, Parra's goal was always more intimate and personal: he wished to provide intimate dwellings for his clients, regardless of their social status or political leanings.

Both Parra's architecture and his interiors were conceived to be humane and designed to fulfil the resident's individual desires, needs and realities. In many cases, they portrayed a sense of humour that was not part of the state's occasional use of cultural references. He was known as 'El Caco' ('The thief') on the basis that he would often 'steal' rubble from demolished colonial buildings and playfully introduce it into his own projects. Not only do these projects reveal his distance from the nationalist and the functionalist schools of Mexico's present and recent past, they reveal him operating in terms that would manifest themselves only years later in Europe and the US: his playful recombination of elements in diverse projects revealing a sort of post-modernist irony.

This tendency was also evident in Parra's work as a film-set designer where he constructed *hacienda* and *cabaret* interiors to represented the conflicts and inequalities between rural and urban Mexico in the 1930s. In 1945, the film director with whom he worked on these sets, Emilio 'El Indio' Fernández, commissioned him to design his house in Coyoacán; a project that would be used as a residence and as a location for shooting films and which would contain all these playful features. However, the project would take years to complete and by then the modern Mexican home had begun to reflect another change in Mexican society: the birth of consumer culture.

In the 1950s and '60s, the Mexican home had begun to incorporate all the conveniences of modern living: refrigerators, washing machines, television sets, garages for the car and such like. Despite the changing society around him, Parra resisted the temptation to allow these features to dominate and tried to 'design them out' by concealing them whenever possible. More significantly, however, he continued to celebrate the traditions of the home and nowhere is that more evident than in the prominence he gave to the kitchen.

Food preparation is an important aspect of every culture and in the Mexican context its *place* in the traditional home was sacrosanct. At the time Parra was working, however,

Figure 2: Kitchen at Casa Fuerte del Indio Fernández
Photo: Jaime F. Gómez

it was under threat with various examples of modernist apartments and houses being designed without a significant kitchen or, indeed, without an individual kitchen at all. One example was the 'Casa obrera mínima'. Although its life was short, this was a project that represented the threat to traditional living patterns coming from various directions of the political spectrum during the period.

In Mexico, a kitchen is a place for 'ritualistic social gathering';[5] a place to prepare food that is seen as reflecting 'the values people attach to preparing food and eating together'.[6] Deeply rooted in the rural tradition, food preparation was a collective feminine activity in Mexican culture which had continued relatively unchanged until the appearance of electric appliances and the social shifts of the twentieth century that saw more women taking up 'professional' positions and leaving the home, formerly the only female place of work. Parra dedicated ample space to the kitchen in his interiors, whether that be in workers' housing or in the residences of upper-class clients. In both cases, they were intended to represent the values attached to this traditional domestic work place.

His best known example was the kitchen built in his project *La Casa Fuerte del Indio Fernández* (1945–1970). As in a rural kitchen, the walls are decorated with common traditional cooking items such as enamel-covered clay pots, spoons, coffee mugs and dishes. Similarly traditional are the wood-framed windows and large blown-glass water bottles that were installed as oculi and the built-in countertops, walls, flooring and furnishings which are richly ornamented with handmade tiles and wood mouldings (Figure 2). Other important features include the hand-crafted wooden cabinets and shelves, a large pantry and the 'hiding places' for modern appliances such as the refrigerator or the gas oven. It was typical of Parra's rejection of the values of modernism and the tendency of this rejection to manifest itself most clearly in the interior.

The Intimate, the Emotive and the Poetic

Despite all of this emphasis on traditional features and his rejection of a modernist aesthetic, Parra's philosophy is perhaps best understood from the standpoint of experience and the perspective of Bachelard, for whom the house was a frame through which to incite imagination. For Bachelard, to inhabit a house is not to inhabit just an inert box: for Bachelard, 'an inhabited space transcends geometric spaces'.[7]

In *The Poetics of Space*, his notions of space and dwelling lead to a series of concepts that are helpful in understanding Parra's work: *corner*, *shell* and *nest*. Although these concepts are simple, each one of them denotes a certain material aspect of the house that take on a particular form in the work of Parra. For Parra, dwelling is not a rational activity; it is evocative and unconscious and is based on 'being at ease'. It is feeling 'at home'. A home, then, becomes a backdrop with scenery for everyday actions with symbols of *shelter* that should permeate throughout.

Although quite early on in his career Parra abandoned the traditional fine arts approach to design and developed a slightly more 'modern' approach to domestic space, as seen in the aesthetic of the Diego Rivera house, he never embraced functionalism. His interiors were always intended to amuse, calm and relax their residents through their aesthetic and, equally importantly, through their spatial layout. Carlos Mijares, a Mexican architect and lecturer at National Autonomous University of México (UNAM), acknowledges this:

> 'His spaces are structured according to different sequences and complex relations so that walking through them inspires a feeling of ease but also of surprise'.[8]

Parra's planning breaks away from a straightforward and conventional building plan that had come to dominant Mexican modernism at the time, a universalist approach that saw one system as applicable to any site. For Parra, in contrast, the site is the starting point, the context into which he always attempted to integrate both the interior and the exterior. His houses always started with a 'welcoming garden' or patio which would draw the visitor into a social area. By avoiding a closed hall, he intended to provide a relaxing small-scale 'promenade', for example, that would be interspersed with seemingly randomly placed rest areas. These promenades incorporated historic *footprints* such as ceramic tiling or carved stone inserts from demolished colonial buildings. They were to be spatially welcoming and aesthetically familiar.

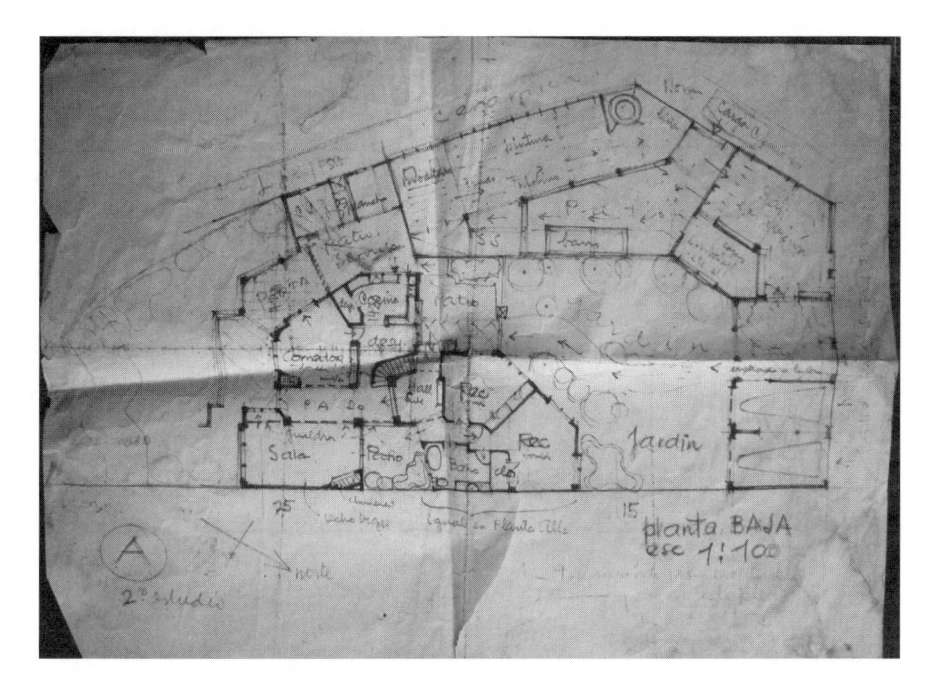

Figure 3: Plan of a house and its site

Aside from amusing dwellers and serving as a comforting and intriguing welcome for the visitor, the garden operated as a source of natural illumination to interior spaces and optimised their thermal conditions by encouraging a flow of air through its interconnected volumes. Beyond this, however, they were also the first element in his more Bachelardian conceptualisation of the house: they were to offer views from the interior and in an attempt to establish a harmonic relationship between the building and the site itself; and in this regard, it was seen as the first set of *corners* offered by the home and its plan (Figure 3).

In Bachelard's terms, a *corner* is a kind of 'half-box: part walls, part door' and in this regard it can be thought of as the dweller's corner in the world.[9] More specifically, inside a given home, it is the chosen space within the house where the dweller feels wrapped-up and attracted by its features and qualities. These properties are supposed to make the resident feel comfortable with him- or herself, allowing him or her to exteriorise general moods and ideas whilst being in a particular physical interior. For Parra, creating these intimate spaces through the intricate combinations of his building elements was a key aspect of his 'individualised' interpretation of the house.

Once inside the building, Parra would carry over the *footprint* patterns found in the social areas into the private and service areas of the house. He always kept in mind the inherent 'meaning' of a given construction element or material and each one was carefully selected on the basis of the history or *footprint* it could provide; what hint of its function or status in the past it could suggest. Instead of using industrial mass-produced building materials, such as steel and concrete, he tended to combine natural elements, craft-produced features and recovered construction materials from demolished or ruined buildings whenever possible. These often came from highly symbolically charged sites such as monasteries and convents from colonial México and were naturally layered as *footprints* any Mexican would understand.

The basic construction materials he used were also often natural and, to an extent, symbolic. He would, whenever possible, use stone cut from the volcanic rock surrounding many sites in Mexico. He also included remnants of raw bricks, ceramic tiles and recycled timber as parts from walls and floors that nobody would see, but which he felt could be 'sensed'. Calling the building structure itself a *shell*, it was seen as the opposite of the modernist crystal box and intended to offer intimacy and privacy to its inhabitants; and to offer some sort of spiritual connection with the history of the site and the history of the place.

In the combination of Parra's tentative acknowledgements of modernism within his overall rejection of it, Benedeto Gravagnuolo identifies something also found in the early work of Adolph Loos. Loos, he says, adopted a number of techniques and ideas from modernism but distanced himself from its separation of elements – both from each other and from their surroundings.[10] Parra too shares Loos' ideas in this regard and integrates elements with each other as well as integrating the building with its context. In this sense, the *shell* does not just represent an opposition to the transparency of high modernism by countering it with opacity; it is a theoretical opposition to modernism's universal *space* that is directly countered with a more rooted notion of *place*.

With regard to our understanding of the concept of space, Josep María Montaner separates two moments or times: pre and post twentieth century. The pre-twentieth-century notion, he suggests, saw space as a volume that was 'identifiable, discontinuous, delimited, specific and static. In short, Cartesian'.[11] Subsequent to the twentieth century, however, he argues that 'the light of the so-called *Modern Movement* seemed to reveal it as free, light, fluid, transparent, abstract, infinite and open'. From Montaner's perspective and that of Parra, both conceptions of *space* have a theoretical, generic and ideal character that they rejected. In contrast to this, they preferred the concept of *place*: something concrete, existential and perhaps undefinable; something more emotive and poetic. It is an idea in some regards based on Heidegger, for whom:

> *'Spaces receive their being from locations, not from 'space'… spaces where life takes place are ought to be places'.*[12]

In the domestic interiors of Parra his intention is precisely this, to turn *space* into *place* through the elements, forms, textures, colours, natural illumination and the symbolic (footprinted) objects he integrates.

This reading is further reinforced by the use of what Parra calls 'markers': non-permanent elements such as furniture used to define spaces or draw a focus to specific areas for a variety of reasons. Manuel Martín established differences between *classical*

Figure 4: Living room at Casa Izaguirre
Photo: Jaime F. Gómez

dwelling and *modern dwelling* by stressing the importance of markers in the former and their corresponding lack of importance in the latter. In line with Parra, he criticises this latter approach for discouraging the inhabitant from leaving their own array of traces and markers; a factor that leads to modernist interiors becoming the scenography of a 'yearning for a harmonious inhabitancy where the civilised man, metropolitan and free, lacks his own origins and culture'.[13]

Markers, then, are statements about Parra's intention to pay homage to the past and, in this regard, repeat his intentions in the use of vernacular permanent features such as hand-crafted ceramic tiles; elements that are often reminiscent of the

Iberian *mudéjar* features from the Talavera and Catalonian regions of Spain that the colonialists had introduced centuries before (Figure 4). Likewise, his frequent use of wooden-structured roofing is reminiscent of this Iberian-peninsula style mixed with regional Mexican construction traditions. All of this, then, ensured that the symbolic values of decontextualised building materials became permanently embedded markers throughout the home and that the sense of the poetic Parra sought to create through his interiors was evident at the level of planning, structure and surfaces.

The historian Enrique X. De Anda argues that Parra's work involves an integration of the house into the landscape or garden, the use of vernacular and crafted techniques, and an understanding of popular culture's plastic potentiality.[14] In this regard, he observed that:

> 'The case of Manuel Parra represents a notable originality with respect to the model of approximation to the Mexican plastic [arts] tradition. Parra understands modern architecture as integrated with materials that possess their own history... Due to the notable environmental quality of his spaces and the great originality of his formal integration, the work of Manuel Parra transcends neo-colonial forms and, in the best cases, is the result of a process of interaction between historical consciousness, cultural identity and the sensitivity towards material expressive potential'.[15]

Influence and Legacy

Whilst De Anda praised Parra's visual association of historical references and spatial organisation, others questioned this position and seriously criticised his form of 'quaint nostalgia'. Architecture critic and historian Israel Katzman disregarded Parra's work as 'pintoresquismo' [*picturesquism*], labelling it as a variation of neo-colonial, neo-pre-Hispanic imitative trends and 'traditionalism'.[16] In Katzman's view, Parra was attracted to the irrationality of the picturesque that was expressed in his use of columns, capitals, windows and other elements from demolished colonial buildings which he saw as being placed at will by a bricklayer. Moreover, Katzman compares Parra to a 'futuristic poet, placing newspaper-cuttings in a bag and then randomly arranging them in a senseless construct he calls poetry; a jumble of words whose meaning is, apparently, full of mystery'.[17]

Adriana Valdés also considered Parra's work an example of historicism and focused her comments entirely on his synthesis of pre-Hispanic, Spanish and Mudejar visual references. In the first case, Katzman ignores the functionality in Parra's planning whilst, in the second, Valdés does not consider his aesthetic compositions as a whole in which light and the landscape's topology both play important roles. In both cases, then, we have criticisms that focus exclusively on the use of decorative motifs by Parra and subsequently miss some his deeper characteristics, meanings and effects.

The fact that Parra's work is about much more then surface decoration and historical motifs became even more evident in the later years of his life when his eyesight began to fail, leaving him eventually completely blind. Despite this, Parra continued to work as an architect and interior designer by developing a design method based on using his hands to model spaces in clay. He also adapted this technique to allow him to give precise instructions to the construction workers on site. In conjunction with this hand modelling, he employed a drawing technique of large, bold strokes and wire models which his hands would explore to understand and develop the voids and enclosures of his building.

He would later identify the organic forms of Danilo Veras, an architecture he had never seen with his eyes but had explored with his hands, as in line with the sensual beauty he sought to create throughout his career.[18] In the view of Javier Seguí, Parra's approach in these later years demonstrates how the eye's visual capacity can be imagined in different ways and that gesticulations, and not just drawing, can also be used as tools for spatial configuration.[19] It also reveals that Parra was far from just a 'visual' artist whose work can be defined in purely aesthetic terms. He was a spatial designer with an intimate understanding of materiality and the multi-sensorial emotive contact we have with the spaces we inhabit. In this regard, his connection with the ideas of Bachelard becomes even clearer. He was clearly an architect of 'poetic space'.

This was certainly obvious to the Mexican architects and designers that would later acknowledge their debt to Parra. The work of Bernal Lascurain Rangel is typical in this regard, his work containing what Alfonso Rodríguez Pulido calls 'Parra's theatricality'.[20]

It is also evident in the work of Enrique Murillo who, having studied under the functionalist doctrine at the National Autonomous University of Mexico, would later acknowledge his regard for the emotive houses and interiors of Parra, which he identified as 'breaking away from the rigidity of the international modernity that dominated Mexican architecture at the time'.[21] For Murillo, Parra's work taught him to value the importance of scenic expressiveness, the use of natural stone as a building material, the building's topological integration with its site and a respect for the vernacular.

For others, Parra's influence would be felt in a very different way, however: as a precursor of the ecological movement. Carlos Mijares Bracho acknowledges Parra as 'a pioneer in the recycling of debris for construction'.[22] With respect to finishes, his work has since been recognised for its use of earthen plaster using lime and prickly pear or *opuntia cactus* slime, whilst his respect for natural and hand-crafted regional materials and techniques in general makes his work echo perfectly with the ideas of Victor Papanek, one of the first recognised advocates of sustainable design, whose work came to prominence in the later years of Parra's life.[23]

In all of these ways, then, it becomes impossible to sustain the one-dimensional criticisms of Parra levelled at him from within the highly politicised domain of Mexican modernism in the post-revolutionary period. These criticisms saw his work as somehow counter-revolutionary: as decadent and whimsical; as eschewing the aims of the revolution and the universal needs of 'the people' in favour of personal and idiosyncratic expressions of individuality and nostalgia. In his lifetime he did very little to counter these charges explicitly. He never lectured on his design methods or theories, preferred to avoid interviews and rejected any kind of public recognition.

However, some time before his death, his friend Victor Manuel Ortiz did manage to persuade him to open up in an interview on a whole range of issues: his childhood influences; the training he received at the Academia; the technique of designing on site; the importance of craftsmen and workers; his love of carpentry and ceramics, and so forth. Shortly afterwards, Ortiz received a postcard, written on his behalf by his wife Leonor, in which he added:

> 'Desde que me di de baja como arquitecto, he trabajado en la clandestinidad y en la penumbra de los bajos fondos de los demoledores. Y así quiero seguir'.
>
> ['Since I gave up being an architect, I have been working in secrecy and in the shade of the demolition underworld. And I want to remain like this'.][24]

Despite this silence, Parra did leave an immense body of built work which, in many ways, speaks for itself. It speaks of a designer whose houses, and in particular their interiors, can and should be understood in Bachelard's terms as *place-corners*; as places that integrate the essences of Mexican culture and life in visual, emotive and intangible terms. The cultural and historical heritage he incorporated into his houses is perhaps most evident in his use craft techniques, especially his penchant for the hand-painted glazed tiles which characterise most of his interiors. However, it is also evident in his use of stones and timbers that once belonged to the pre-Hispanic or colonial past of the country. Furthermore, it is also evident in his refusal to allow the modern, westernised technological developments of the mid twentieth century to dominate the inside of the home.

In all of these ways, Parra insisted on the importance of cultural *footprints* that would help in the creation of the home as a place of rest, of solace and of an emotive connection to the earth and the individual. The aesthetic or constructional techniques he used to create this were fully integrated into a deeper philosophy about the nature of spaces and places and our connection to them. It was connected to his view of place as full of memory and of the home as a container for those memories. It was perhaps this insistence on memory even more than his insistence on the individual that made his houses and his interiors so hard to swallow for the modernists, with their view of the world as always looking forward.

In refusing to accept this persistent and none-stop social dynamic, Parra's idiosyncratic and personal designs take on a very different hue when placed in their full political context. They became a sort of political statement in themselves, a defiant statement that placed the individual above the collective and universalising tendencies of the then-socialist state. These interiors, for so long forgotten or simply ignored, can thus be seen as statements about individual desire and emotion; about individual freedom and individual memories of specific places. They can be seen as defiant footprints that, despite the apparently unstoppable march of modernism, refused to be erased.

Acknowledgements

We would like to thank Adela Fernández, Carmen Parra, Eduardo Izaguirre, Gorki González and Irene Rodríguez for letting us into their houses to explore Parra's environments. The authors would also like to thank Gregg Davis and Wade Alley for reading drafts of this chapter.

Notes

[1] Indirect French rule was through the Habsburg Archduke Ferdinand Maximilian I, a puppet of Napoleon III.
[2] The period of rule of the military leader Porfirio Díaz lasted for approximately 30 years and was known as the *Porfiriato*.
[3] Fraser, V. (2001) *Building the New World: Studies in the Modern Architecture of Latin America 1930–1960*, London: Verso, p.23.
[4] Parra, M. (1936) Tesis profesional de Manuel Parra Mercado, Tesis Licenciatura, UNAM.
[5] Potter, N. (2006) The kitchen as a place to be, *Intimus*, John Wiley and Sons LTD, pp.264–9.
[6] Ibid.
[7] Bachelard, G. (2000) *La poética del espacio*, México, Fondo de Cultura Económica, p.79.
[8] Mijares Bracho, C. (2008, May) A corner revisited, a poet of the everyday, *Artes de México*, Vol. 89, México, May 2008, p.78.
[9] Bachelard, 2000, op. cit., p.171
[10] Gravagnuolo, B. (1972) *Adolf Loos, teoría y obras*, Barcelona, España, NEREA.
[11] Montaner, J.M. (2000) in Solá-Morales et al., *Introducción a la arquitectura: conceptos fundamentales*, Barcelona: Ediciones UPC, p.97.
[12] Ibid.
[13] Martín, M. (2003) La pregunta por el habitar moderno, in Solá-Morales et al., *Teorías de la arquitectura*, Barcelona: Ediciones UPC.
[14] De Anda, E.X. (2006) *Historia de la arquitectura mexicana*, 2nd ed., México, (ed. Gustavo Gili), p.223.
[15] Ibid.
[16] Katzman, I. (1964) *La arquitectura contemporánea mexicana-precedentes y desarrollo*, México, Instituto Nacional de Antropología e Historia, p.85.
[17] Ibid., p.86
[18] The blind architect explored Veras' houses with his hands. He gently touched them by following several trajectories that either made him stretch out or bend down to wander *petting* the ground. See: Seguí de la Riva, J. (2001) El arquitecto ciego, *Encuentros*, No. 1, Madrid, p.11.
[19] Ibid.
[20] Rodríguez Pulido, A. (2011) interview with Cintia Paez.
[21] Winfield Reyes, F., and Mora Perdomo, L. (2010) Dossier – Enrique Murillo: arquitectura y plástica, *La palabra y el hombre, Revista de la Universidad Veracruzana*, Xalapa, no. 11, pp.67–74.

[22] Mijares Bracho, 2008, op. cit., p.78
[23] Papanek, V. (1997) *The Green Imperative: Natural design for the real world*, New York: Thames and Hudson, p.136.
[24] Ortiz, V.M. (1998) Manuel Parra in memoriam, *La Jornada Semanal*, México, 27 de diciembre.

Tonia CARLESS
Oxford Brookes University
School of Architecture

AN ARCHITECTURAL GLEANING

Goméz and Paez, then, frame their arguments about Parra in three ways: the personal, the political and the ecological. In this regard, the ecological is seen as the re-use of found objects and this principal, also identified as a modern trait by Brooker, is the explicit subject of our penultimate text by Tonia Carless. Carless takes on the notion of 'gleaning', the activity of searching through debris to find things that can be re-used and incorporated into anything new – in her case, primarily architectural renovations. ...

She does this by basing her ideas on Agnes Varda's film, The Gleaners and I, *using it to question the nature of capitalism as a consumer-led economy, on the one hand, and to open up the possibility of seeing design as a work of activism, on the other. This is primarily examined through the presentation of design proposals that use the intellectual framework of gleaning and Varda's film as their guide lines...*

Introduction

Les Glaneurs et la Glaneuse [*The Gleaners and I*][1] is a documentary film made in 2000 by the French filmmaker Agnes Varda. It forms the point of departure for a cultural investigation that begins with the famous Jean-Francois Millet painting (1857) of women gathering wheat left over from the harvest (Figure 1). To glean is to take something after it has already been used. Ruth Cruickshank describes it as 'giving something a second life'.[2] It is a process that emerges from contrasting actions: firstly, of discarding and then, secondly, of gathering or collecting up. It is therefore tied up with the notion of dissent; of disagreeing with the dominant notion that something is waste or excess or without value. Gleaning as an act is about contesting whether what is gleaned should have been discarded in the first place.

Figure 1: Jean-Francois Millet, Des Glaneuses, oil painting, 1857

The film follows individuals and groups of people who are on the margins of society and who make an economy out of the process of gleaning. While they are on the fringes, however, they are also able to engage productively with the world through the process of gleaning. In this paper, the concept is applied to architectural research in order to develop a critique of contemporary architectural production and offer an alternative approach to design processes and intentions. The approach to architectural gleaning described here considers the concept of 're-purpose': a concept within which sustainability is embedded in the process of the customisation of materials, space and the city. It goes beyond the materiality of re-use, which is what architecture tends to focus upon, and aligns it with social occupation. Consequently, it is also aligned with a programmatic architectural agenda, rather than the formalist or aesthetic one. The architecture of gleaning, then, is both a spatial and material hacking but also an attitude. It is a cutting into the city and a reappraisal of its ways of living that allows the consideration of the disappearance of boundaries between architect, consumer and user.

The architectural ideas to be discussed here have been examined through the application of an architectural approach that has remade and compressed residual urban spaces, and which also uses a representational method of the 'readymade' (a technique that allows for the architectural recovery of existing drawings). The projects described in the second half of this paper aim to make visible the 'process of making and production' as part of everyday life in the city and also embrace the informal economies of nomadic and transient populations. Both Agnes Varda's film and the architectural projects based upon it, then, take on a critical view of capitalism and urban life. The intention is to use architecture as Varda does film: as a form of cultural critique which raises questions about the effects of globalisation and consumer capitalism. The aim is also to highlight the potential of the architect to be opportunistic and underline the notion that architecture might be an oppositional practice.

This analysis will examine Varda's conceptions of gleaning and describe a possible adaptation of this through architectural and spatial productions. It will consider resources and their use from an understanding described by Baudrillard[3] as 'being an excess of energy rather than a scarcity'. While architecture has embraced many of the ideas of re-use, this text will consider its excess and waste as having its own vital potential. It is based on research that has examined architectural, spatial and the city's detritus as a 'cluster of possibilities'.[4] It is an approach that has emerged from a desire to examine excessive consumption and the excess production of energies apparent in cities where, according to Baudrillard, 'the city feeds on its own hubbub, its own waste, its own carbon dioxide emissions arising from the expenditure of energy, thanks to a sort of miracle of substitution.'[5]

To some extent, the concept is oppositional to the notion of saving resources in architectural production, like those of 'experts who base their calculations solely on the quantitative aspects of an energy system [and who] inevitably, underestimate the peculiar energy source contributed by energy discharge itself.'[6] The work here will examine precisely this energy source, not as a tactic for legitimising the profession of architecture under current ideological and economic stresses but rather as a potential ecology. The works described attempt to draw a parallel and illustrate an 'architectural gleaning' envisioned as a generative process of seeking residues.

They centre on a number of student design projects that were initially carried out at the 1:1 real scale of the human body but which were subsequently translated to the space along Commercial Street in East London – a site on the fringe of the City. They are projects constructed from a reading of Varda's film documentary, in that they select real sites and subject them to processes of extension and conversion through drawing, recording and making exercises; through gleaning both the cultural and physical conditions of the sites. They use a strategy of identifying the architectural researcher as subject, in the same manner that Agnes Varda identifies and places herself in the role of the anthropological subject of her films.

The Gleaners (Les Glaneurs): A People

Varda is one of the world's leading filmmakers and has been making films for over fifty years. She has a 'lifelong commitment to counter cultural activism'[7] and uses the *Gleaners and I* to develop experimental and radical processes such as 'bricolage'. Significantly, it was her first digital film[8] and her method of bricolage is as much about the process of documentary filming as it is the content of her film. Her use of the hand-held digital camera enabled her to get close to her filmic subjects and was ideally suited to the subject of gleaning, as it allows for continuity, immediacy and intimacy. Varda seeks out gleaners in the same way that they seek their forage; she finds extremes of living; she seeks those who exist on 'that which is left over'. 'Her consciousness of such marginal poverty is a characteristic of her most subjective films'.[9]

Through the *Gleaners and I*, we are introduced to gleaning as both a rural and an urban phenomenon. In this sense, it is interesting as, in general, 'gleaning' is most often associated with the rural condition: as the act of gathering up and retrieving leftover crops from fields after the profitable harvest. Its considerable significance to the economy of the rural poor, especially to women, has been highlighted by Peter King, who traces its origins from a biblical reference to its being a charitable practice:[10]

> 'And when ye reap the harvest of your land, thou shalt not make clean riddance of the corners of thy field when thou reapest, neither shalt thou gather any gleaning of thy harvest; thou shalt leave them unto the poor, and to the stranger... (Leviticus 23:22)'[11]

King makes a comparison between the differing status of 'gleaning' in French and British law and states that, from the Middle ages through to the eighteenth century, 'France, unlike England, protected the customary right of gleaners.'[12] Throughout the film, Varda too highlights the legal aspects of gleaning, its origins and associated traditions, always rooting its conception in property status and ownership. Consequently, it becomes inextricably bound up with property and land rights and, by extension, access to the use of space. It can be seen as oppositional to cultivation and accumulation and, indeed, to the concept of ownership itself. Mazierska and Rascaroli argue that 'it is potentially closer to the lifestyle of the nomad as described by Deleuze and Guattari'.[13] They argue that gleaners' lives, both urban and rural, are conceived as being 'smooth in a striated space' and thus, the 'gleaner', as documented by Varda, is seen as a marginal figure and a cultural 'other' whose shifting form is always nomadic and whose changing state or statelessness (the statelessness of the vagrant) are always associated with temporary spatial occupations.

Although primarily a filmmaker, Varda uses her documentary to consider the effects of globalisation through different media: painting, photography and aural accounts of legal documentation and custom are all shown.[14] In the *Gleaners and I*, she refers to the paintings of both Jean-Francios Millet and Jules Breton[15] (both of whom lived in France during a time of significant political, economic and agricultural crises) to draw parallels with contemporary culture. She presents gleaning as a method by which the marginalised may find sustenance, both as physical and psychological nourishment, and reveals how the 'gleaner' seeks out leftovers in attempts to learn, adapt and reap what remains after the harvest. 'It is a mental activity of souvenirs gleaned, of loading up, of salvage and retrieval.'[16]

This is an attitude clearly seen in the early-twentieth-century project *Facteur* (Postman) by Ferdinand Cheval and his Ideal Palace at Hauterives in the French district of La Drome.[17] Cheval was a postman by day and collected stones and shells to construct his own fantastical palace, a process that took over thirty years. Whilst not a gleaner of substances previously used, he was using elements that nature had cast out. He collected stones and tufa in his pockets as he walked his post round across the French countryside and piled them into a wheelbarrow to take home later.

Cheval's work has echoes of the 'artist collector/constructor' who built the towers made of discarded dolls and television sets that we see in Varda's film. There are also echoes of this in the 'house of refrigerators' in Paris, a collection of retrieved refrigerators used to make the walls of an entrance to a dwelling. In all of these cases, we see a form of bricolage:[18] the gathering together of things that may be close at hand but, equally, may be from a diverse area. We also see a form of an embedded frugality, ingenuity and surprise. In each case, we have gleaners: activists stooping to retrieve their hoard, collectors scavenging for miscellaneous elements and artists foraging for unexpected detritus. They are diverse in their preoccupations but comparable in their ethic. The same principal can be applied to architecture.

And I (La Glaneuse): She

The film's title, *Les Glaneurs et la Glaneuse,* when directly translated, refers firstly to 'the gleaners' in the plural as those who are in the film and then to 'the gleaner' (*la glaneuse*, the feminine noun), referring to Varda herself.[19] She identifies the significance of the feminine form of the noun 'gleaner' which does not directly translate into English, saying:

> 'We had to translate it as "The Gleaners and I" which emphasizes in a way the "I". In the French, "glaneuse" refers to an anonymous female gleaner. That little nuance makes it more important than me.'[20]

In the architectural context that is discussed here, the same nuance is significant: the work documented is intended to refer to the wider individual and anonymous architect, on the one hand, and the user/consumer on the other. No significant distinction is made between the two. In applying the notion of gleaning and its philosophy to architectural design, then, this chapter takes the notion of Joseph Beuys that 'everyone is an artist' and interprets it as 'everyone is an architect'.

In addition to facilitating the reconsideration of the architect as a defining individual, however, Varda's film also offers analogies for how we might begin to reconstruct the waste footage of our architectural spaces. The way she does this is through what she describes as the 'dance of the lens cap'. At one point, Varda forgets to switch off the camera and the film keeps rolling: the camera swinging freely at her feet, following the gleaner as she crosses the documentary fields. This clip, inserted into the film, gives us a sense of the possibilities of retrieval. The 'opportunism' of incorporating this footage into the film raises a question about whether the filmmaker has to be an expert; and this is a question we equally ask of architecture which may also be able to benefit from an opportunistic method that is not completely dominated by expertise. Architecture too may be able to embrace 'rushes' or the accidental into its approach to design and construction.

Ruth Hottell describes Varda's cinema as being one of subjective inclusion and, in a sense, it is picked up in the way in which she allows the viewer of the film to do their own gleaning; their own scanning of the screen, its characters and its spaces.[21] More importantly, however, it can also be transposed to questions of 'filmic gleaning': who and what is to be included or rejected by the filmmaker. Varda herself describes the process of making the film as 'always being aware of both the method and the wider regime'. She says: 'I had to piece it together... but without betraying the social issue that I had set out to address – waste and trash: who finds a use for it? How? Can one live on the leftovers of others?'[22] To this end, her film must allow the viewer to 'glean'. She should not determine what is or isn't important.

The architectural projects we will discuss here are intended, in the same manner, to open a discourse on theme and method: to question globalisation, to consider its effects upon socio-economic structures, to research retrieval and reclamation. They thus examine the notion of leftover space and materials but, crucially, do so while simultaneously proposing a collapse of the boundaries between architect and user. Just as Varda leaves space for gleaning in the production and viewing of her film, so too our architectural projects are intended to allow users to appropriate the spaces created and their representations, according to their own ends and desires: to make new forms of social space. They are projects that have considered the possibilities of an architecture that can be, in part, released for its own life and given over to a user or a set of users.

The Labour of Gleaning

Gleaning is a process affected by hand. It implies an engagement with the substance of a material itself and, by implication, is associated with being a slow process – one which might involve minutely intensive labour. Henri Lefebvre described Marx's notions on the labour of production under capitalism, in relation to growth in capitalism and space, saying that:

> 'productive activity (labour) became no longer one with the process of reproduction which perpetuated social life; but in becoming independent of that process, labour fell prey to abstraction, whence abstract social labour – and abstract space.'[23]

Lefebvre's critique of the construction of abstract space is one of the concepts under investigation here. The idea of the labour of production can be seen as another such concept, being significant in terms of how space is organised and, in particular, in terms of the methodologies used in design and construction. It considers the process of commodity reification in capitalism as an expansion of the Marxist ideas proposed by Georg Lukacs, who described the process as being 'determined by the attempt to flee class guilt and, in particular, to efface the traces of production and of other people's labour from the product'.[24] In this context, it is manifest most obviously in the consideration of the issue of authorship. The projects analysed here aim to question notions of originality, open the possibility for manual work to play a part in design and construction, question architect–author control and, in the process, mark design as a process distinct to the now-administrative project of the architect.

Importance is placed here on the question of originality and the figure of the architect as an individual creative figure, which have been explored in various texts over the years, most recently in *Architecture and Authorship* by Anstey, Grillner and Hughes.[25] These are important notions in our context, in that they reopen a dialogue on the concept of 'architectural action' developed by Cedric Price during the late 1960s. This is the idea of a gap between architectural representation, architectural intention, the projection of the building and the building itself. It reopens questions on the relationship between design, the design process and the purpose of architecture found in projects such as Price's *Fun Palace*.[26] The idea of manual work is also important, in that the architectural gleaning projects described here reinstate an emphasis on materials as *spatial* and, potentially, *social* substance, as retrieved materials are re-assembled by both users and designers.

The projects described were intended as vehicles to make visible the 'process of making and production' as potentially a part of everyday life in the city. There is an organic functionality to the gleaning process that makes it engage more immediately with the social condition of occupation. The projects propose the spatial theory of Raymond Ledrut's[27] 'primacy of action' which suggests that, in order for architecture to be anything more than abstract space, it has to be 'a work of life'. It is suggested that this creation of a 'a work of life' can be seen through radical, self-build construction in projects such as the ones envisaged here that find the fragments (material, spatial and cultural) from which to remake the city.

Michel de Certeau's 'practice of everyday life' considers how space is produced through occupation.[28] His notion of 'everyday life' is used here in terms of the need to put into practice subversive strategies which work directly against the structures of power; strategies he describes as being 'never fixed, rarely visible and always constituted through the fleeting and unexpected appropriation of the spaces of established power'.[29] These ideas manifest themselves in this research through projects aimed at working outside the frame of spaces that might be 'recuperated' for tourism and leisure consumption, as 'event' architecture.[30] The design intention in every case was to waste nothing, with everything being reformed: materials, drawings, films, models, information, programs, journeys, paper, portfolios, photographs, plans, sections, buildings, sites, landscapes, highways, railways, everyday life and work. The projects analysed here were intended to offer ways of remaking the city – or at least, remaking fragments of it.

Contemporary architecture has many precedents for this re-use strategy, some purely material but others extending into the social and political domain. One such example is that of Samuel Mockbee and Rural Studio's architectural practice, working in Hale County, Alabama, USA. Active during the 1990s, the work of the studio was in part a system of welfare that embraced many of the concepts of gleaning. Rural Studio's program was one of providing low-income housing and 'an architecture of decency'. Their insistence on 'using inventive building methods and scavenged and unusual materials' distinguishes the studio's approach from that of other low-income housing programs of the same period.[31] Combined with an approach where architects and students designed and built in conjunction with the clients (as a reciprocal process of architectural student education), this meant that the process was slow. Like the process of gleaning, it necessarily accrued over a period of time.

More recently, the work of Wang Shu and Amateur Architecture Studio, in China, has illustrated ideas akin to gleaning and the approach to architecture we advocate here. The projects of Amateur Architecture Studio re-use materials, not merely as an economy of recycling but also as an economy of tradition. The Ningbo Historic Museum in Zhejiang Province has, for example, been built from the materials collected from previously demolished buildings and, according to Shu, the focus is upon architecture that is:

> 'Built spontaneously, illegally and temporarily... [A]mateur architecture challenges professional architecture but is generally considered to be insignificant. Professional architects think of buildings too much as physical objects... They can learn from amateurs in that respect'.[32]

In a country like China, where current change is increasingly rapid, it can also be seen as a practice that attempts to retain some 'histories of production and place'; a phenomenon that inevitably occurs in the architecture of gleaning.

Research Projects

In the projects undertaken with students to develop these ideas, the students were encouraged to 'glean' from the space, to engage directly with found material and to document the site through photography and film. The intention was that they could more immediately engage with the substance of the space and further develop this through representation techniques. One portfolio of work, for example, was constructed as an extension to the found wheels of a shopping trolley; fragments of timber, bolts and string being used to develop an elastic structural model. The portfolio was taken to and from the site as part of the extended gleaning exercise that would allow for the ongoing collection of work and its conversion/use as a discursive model. This process is considered important as part of the understanding of gleaning as a continuous and active process. 'Gleaning means having your hands full; the glaneuse is compelled to work.'[33]

A preliminary project to design an extension and conversion of an existing 'body architecture' (the human body itself) allowed for the use of materials that were able to extend/prolong the life cycle of the existing 'structure'. It also allowed for the

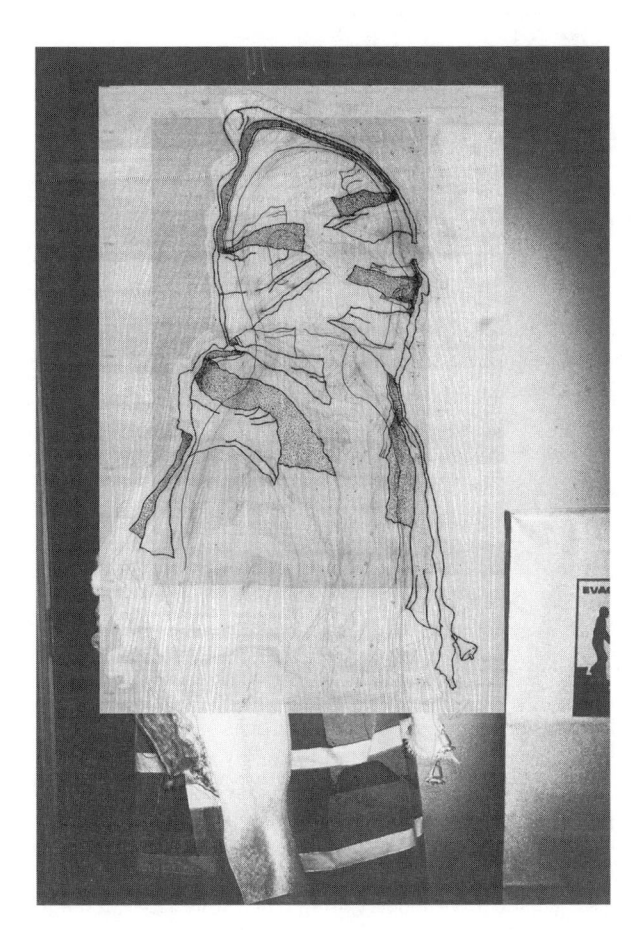

Figure 2: Aural scarf body architecture, collaged drawings, Kah Shuen Lee, 2010

seasonal or functional adjustment of the 'structure' in question and facilitated the use of new technologies to enhance sustainability. The use of the architect/body as 'site' allowed students to work at full/real scale. Furthermore, it allowed for the incorporation of the subject directly into the spatial condition of the project itself (Figure 2). These characteristics may be seen as analogous to Varda's use of herself in the film, particularly in the scene in which she takes up the posture of Jules Breton's *La Glaneuse* pose (with a sheaf of wheat on her shoulder and looking directly into the camera) to 'break down the barriers between filmed subjects and film maker'.[34] The architects here are scavenging for materials and simultaneously recording the process through film and photography and, as a result, the possibility of reading the architect and user as one, or as interconnected and exchangeable, is immediately initiated. It also produces a possible transformation through which 'we become what we glean'.[35]

The idea underlying the 'body architecture program' was that similar remaking strategies might be applicable to the larger social space of the city; we open up the possibility that attention to the smallest existing conditions might generate larger possibilities. This manifest itself in one of the 'body architecture' projects that proposed the unpicking of a garment and the dismantling of other industrial debris into singular component elements; the aim being to completely reconfigure them as a new structural possibility for housing the body in extreme climatic conditions. This was developed into a 'city factory and construction library' which would facilitate the construction of temporary market stalls as modular dwelling frameworks.

The existing market of Petticoat Lane, off Commercial Street in East London, was proposed as a potential space for the subsequent 'city factory and construction library' project. What emerged from the design process that followed (a process that utilised a number of 'gleaning' strategies itself) was a proposal to insert the 'factory and library' behind the existing productive and functioning shops which operated as extensions to the market stalls. The proposed 'factory' would allow for the making, storage and reconfiguration of market stalls that could be distributed along the wider market site and potentially beyond.

The project worked at 'making visible' the process of production within the everyday life of the city but also aimed at developing the most functionally efficient stall-construction system possible to accommodate all of the requirements of the market traders, including increased security and theft-deterrent techniques. Furthermore, the library was to offer an educational facility specifically aimed at aiding the construction processes and increasing the possibilities of self-build retail units. Ultimately, this is aimed at facilitating the extension of the market concept beyond the current users of the space and expanding 'ownership' of the temporary shops. In conception, it had numerous similarities to Walter Segal's self-build initiatives of the 1970s.[36]

The physical architectural intervention all this involved was relatively humble. It involved the use of hoists and cranes, like those of nineteenth-century warehouse storage spaces, or plug-in, exchangeable service devices that have been employed by many contemporary architects to give a flexibility of function. Here the proposal was to use these elements to 'glean' materials from previous market stalls which could be lifted into the new 'factory production space' where they could be re-configured and reassembled before being returned to the city. The architecture envisaged, then, like the *Gleaners and I*, is modest. It is barely visible as an architectural insertion into the street. However, it offers up the conception of 'user' as architect–builder and potential trader of goods and also raises questions that Varda brings up in her film, such as: 'how can one live off the leftovers of others?'[37] Consequently, it can be said that it directs thinking and discourse about 'the social' on various levels: it raises questions of ownership and authorship, on the one hand, and the potential of re-using and reconstituting materials, on the other. It is both social and ecological in outlook and intent.

Another project developed rooftop squatting cities where detritus from the metropolis might begin to form the framework for a 'high-level urban pier', a form of viewing platform that gives public access to new landscapes and terrains above the city streets (Figure 4). This proposal emerged from an engagement with an existing site that had

Figure 3: Non-Commercial House, Commercial Street, London, Tonia Carless, 2010

already been squatted and re-used, as well as being re-named 'Non-Commercial House Free Shop' (Figure 3). It already had its own website that described the site as a 'squatted social centre and free shop with an emphasis on sharing'.[38] A black flag flies defiantly on the roof, graffiti declares the space 'open' and a strip of found tape demarcates its entrance as 'fragile': like the economy upon which it depends. In the case of this project, the question of who finds a use for society's leftovers had already been foregrounded in the space of the building itself.

The second life that had already been gleaned from the site in the form of the squat was used to develop further the concept of architectural gleaning in this project by adding to, rather than replacing, what was already existent. The material gleaning involved in the proposal was most evident on the re-use of urban debris such as tire rubber – an example of an urban and material excess and a potential landfill problem as well. Here, it was used together with scrap timber in the creation of a form of 'pleasure pier' above the city. The rubber gave the practical possibility of a grip to the surface of the structure proposed but also added to 'comfort' through the creation of a soft-surfaced landscape – a technique that made it more like a park.

The proposal involved using Non-Commercial House as the entranceway up to this rooftop city which was envisaged as opening up other 'gleaning' opportunities such

Figure 4: Rooftop squatting city, Commercial Street, London, Charlie Palmer, 2011

as facilitating access to other empty buildings and spaces and aiding in tapping into potential nearby heat sources such as chimneys which could be 'capped' to allow for the extraction of heat. These interventions were all proposals for a functional and material gleaning but, more significantly, they were also a form of social critique: a rejection of the values prescribed under consumer capitalism.

Another program developed for Commercial Street was seen as an 'aural architecture'. In this case, what was gleaned was both the physical substance of the city and its audible and sonic conditions. The proposed function for the project was as a 'menagerie and manufacturing laboratory' for spider silk. The 'body architecture' project from which this design proposal emerged was a 'sonic scarf' made out of hessian cloth (Figure 2). This emitted sound through simple bell attachments and was intended for use in blizzard conditions or 'whiteout visibility conditions' of extreme cold. It was seen as also potentially functioning as a barrier to be used in sand storms and was capable of offering protection under extreme sun-exposure conditions.

The scarf was developed through a layering up of drawings at 1:1 scale, some of which had been 'retrieved' and were repeatedly used in the creation of a type of layered collage. The Hessian cloth used for the body project was gleaned near the site and re-used again for the site model of the larger architectural proposal of the menagerie sand silk lab; only this time other found fragments, materials and drawings were also incorporated into the creative making process. In the architectural model, found cable ties were used to represent reclaimed railway tracks – the main structure of the building

Figure 5: Hessian-and-cable-tie model, retrieved drawings and materials, Kah Shuen Lee, 2011

proposal. The flexibility and tightening collar of the cable ties in their turn fed back into the project by becoming the inspiration and a prototype for a changeable structure finally proposed.

This structure would allow the acoustic properties of the space (the noises of the people, animals and insects inside the menagerie and exterior noises of the city) to

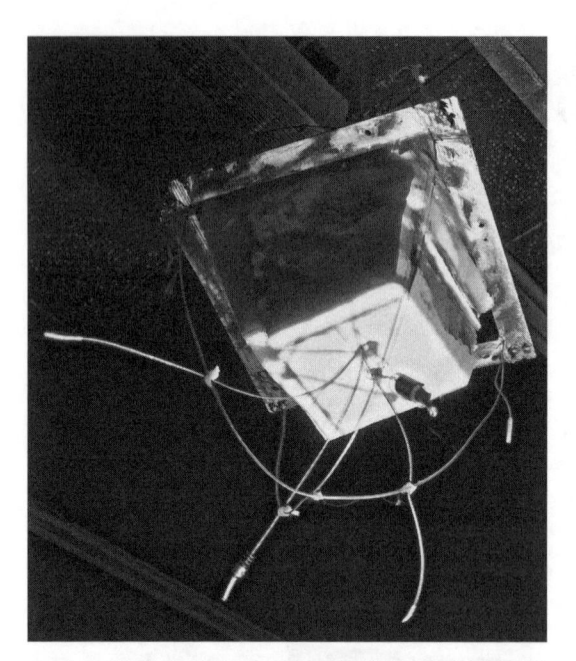

Figure 6: 1:1 model acoustic skin element and interior view of menagerie with vertical aural skin and roof, Kah Shuen Lee, 2011

produce vibration in the building's skin. It was to expand and contract according to the level of absorption required by the particular sound in question (Figure 5). The aim, then, was to use found materials and debris to develop a responsive architectural skin: an acoustic or aural skin.[39] The project also envisaged a giant redwood tree which would function as a structural element by growing in situ and pushing the skin of the structure into new formations as it aged. Nature was to be 'gleaned' in numerous ways.

Beyond the idea of gleaning as re-use, however, this introduction of a natural element such as a tree as a building component suggests a structure with a life span to be measured in hundreds of years – the time required for the full maturation of the tree(s) (Figure 6). This introduces an ecological opposition to the notion of a temporary structure as sustainable, as well as an opposition to the idea that construction and re-use in the city needs to involve 'indestructible' materials with infinite life spans (the opposite to the notion of built-in obsolescence). Here, gleaning takes on the condition of slow and continuous change that contests the designation of the category of waste as a material that has come to the end of its lifecycle.

Shared Practices

The tactic of using found debris in architectural models such as the ones built during this project has often been taken up by students of architecture and interior design as an economy of means. Here, however, it takes on an additional significance: it underlies the whole ethos of the project being presented. Similarly, the gleaned materials proposed for the projects themselves, the reclaimed rail tracks for example, take on another significance beyond that of just the recycling of local materials: they become memory traces, histories that embed themselves in the architectural project that reveal how gleaning can produce its own particular connection with the world.

The gleaning processes applied to the architectural proposals described here all involve picking over and retrieving things that remain. The menagerie project embraced this process through 'listening to the space' over a period of time so as to re-use its sounds and, in this sense (as with the 'market factory – construction library' project and the 'squatted city' project), it allowed the architectural space to evolve as a result of occupation – albeit an occupation of natural elements in this case. The idea that these projects could and should evolve as a result of occupation over time is of course another aspect of the philosophy of gleaning and is evident in each of these projects. In each case, the role of the 'consumer of space' becomes that of the architect: a force or figure that can change the space over time.

Similarly, all these projects share another possible characteristic of gleaning: a diversity of approach and interpretation of the concept and ethic of gleaning itself. In the case of the rooftop squat, it is seen as revolving around the necessity of survival in the city whilst, in the menagerie, it was seen as opening up a new, technologically derived, cultural reading of the city and buildings as material objects. The first project imagined an economy of need coming from the desperation of homelessness and vagrancy in the city whilst the latter emerged from a reworking of the aristocratic menagerie.

Beyond the specifics of each project, however, the nature of the process itself was one that was completely immersed in the concept of gleaning. Developing an exchange across these projects was seen as vital in this regard. Gleaning is, after all, a shared practice that has the potential to operate across class and cultural distinctions. In the case of running these projects, it was thus essential that exchanges between participants, both students and potential clients, were facilitated and encouraged so that ideas on ownership, authorship, control and whose voice is worth listening to could all be challenged.

Returning to the starting point, *The Gleaners and I*, it is possible to identify how Varda demonstrates this fundamental point explicitly. We have already dealt with how she questions notions of authorship through her introduction of the 'accident' and ceding of the act of reading to the viewer. However, through her bricolage technique, she also asks the question of whose voice is worth listening to. The technique allows her to move from one story to the next, each carrying its own socio-cultural critique.[40] Bonner describes it as 'one of Varda's key political strategies'; a strategy through which 'she strives to dismantle the lines that separate poor gleaners from higher classed or recreational gleaners'. In presenting us with these diverse people, Varda shows us that despite 'their different life conditions' there are 'remarkable social connections among them'. Such unusual connections, Bonner suggests, not only show us a diversity of people, they 'question and upend conventions concerning subjects worthy or not of documentation'.[41] Nobody here is given privilege.

This resonates with the words of Amateur Architecture's Wang Shu with regard to a repositioning of what, or rather who, is considered to have value in the architectural context – an issue explicitly dealt with by the projects we have documented in this text. In these projects, there is no regulatory space of hierarchy and control owned by the architectural designer. There is merely a framework for occupation: a ladder to a wider use of the city and a responsive habitat for living. Their intention is to allow for other people (or nature) to develop the projects in the future. In a sense, it is an attitude that makes us connect with the world beyond our own wishes and desires as designers – a connection that energises those normally outside the architectural design and decision process.

That this may be a prerequisite of potential activism is poetically indicated in Varda's film in a scene in which the director and the curator of a small museum in Ville Franche struggle to take a painting out of the 'leftover' archives of the museum stores. The painting by Pierre Edmond Hedouin (1852) is titled *Gleaners Fleeing before the Storm*. As they bring it out into the open and hold it up against the wind, with a real landscape as backdrop, the gleaners in the painting are energised. They no longer stoop humbly as they flee. They are pictured as active participants in their surroundings: critics of the society around them. Although gleaning is a gesture on the margins of survival, it is underlined by Varda as having activist and revolutionary possibilities, as being a critique of waste and a socialist dream.

Notes

[1] Varda, A. (director) (2000) *Les Glaneurs et la Glaneuse* [*The Gleaners and I*] [DVD], France: Zeitgeist.
[2] Cruickshank, R. (2007) The Work of Art in the Age of Global Consumption: Agnes Varda's Les Glaneurs et la Glaneuse, *L'espirit Createur* 47(3): pp.19–32.
[3] Baudrillard, J. (1993) *The Transparency of Evil: Essays on Extreme Phenomena*, Verso, pp.100–5.
[4] See Louis Pons the assemblage artist in *Les Glaneurs et la Glaneuse* (Varda, 2000, op. cit.).
[5] Baudrillard, 1993, op. cit., p.102
[6] Ibid.
[7] Bonner, V. (2009) The Gleaners and 'Us': The Radical Modesty of Agnes Varda Les Glaneurs et la Glaneuse, in Columpar, C., and Mayer, S. (eds) *There She Goes: Feminist Film Making and Beyond*, USA, Detroit: Wayne State University Press, p.124.
[8] European Graduate School Website (1997–2012) Agnes Varda Biography, retrieved from: http://www.egs.edu/faculty/agnes-varda/biography [accessed on 10 July 2012].
[9] Smith, A. (1998) *Agnes Varda*, Manchester University Press, p.83.
[10] King, P. (1992) Legal Change, Customary Right, and Social Conflict in Late 18th century England: The Origins of the Great Gleaning Case of 1788, *Law and History Review* 10(1): pp.1–31.
[11] Hay, D., and Rogers, N. (1997) *Eighteenth Century English society: Shuttles and Swords*, Oxford Paperbacks, OPUS, pp.86–7.
[12] King, 1992, op. cit., p.3
[13] Mazierska, E., and Rascaroli, L. (2006) *Crossing New Europe: Postmodern Travel and The European Road Movie*, London: Wallflower Press, pp.128–9.
[14] In this sense, a parallel can be seen between how Varda presents ideas on the 'capitalization of custom', or of 'turning custom into crime', and the ideas described by the historian E.P. Thompson, who focused on the progression of capitalism in England through *Customs in Common*. (See: Thompson, E.P. (1993) *Customs in Common: Studies in Traditional Popular Culture*, London: Penguin.)
[15] Painting by Jules Breton, *Calling in the Gleaners* (1859, oil on canvas, Musée d'Orsay, Paris).
[16] Varda, 2000, op. cit.
[17] Berger, J. (1991) *Keeping a Rendezvous*, London: Granta Books, p.84.
[18] In Pearsall, J. (ed.) (1998) *The New Oxford Dictionary of English*, Oxford. Clarendon Press, p.225.
[19] Varda, 2000, op. cit.
[20] Ibid.
[21] Hottell, R. (1999) Including ourselves: the role of female spectators in Agnes varda's Le Bonheur and L'une chante, L'autre pas, *Cinema Journal* 38(2): pp.52–72.
[22] Varda, 2000, op. cit.
[23] Lefebvre, H. (1991/1974) *The Production of Space*, Oxford: Blackwell, p.49.

[24] Lukacs, G. (1990) *History and Class Consciousness: Studies in Marxist Dialectics*, Merlin Press, p.264.
[25] Anstey, T., Grillner, K., and Hughes, R. (eds) (2007) *Architecture and Authorship*, London: Black Dog Publishing.
[26] Anstey, T. (2007) Architecture and Rhetoric: Persuasion, Context, Action, in ibid., pp.18–29.
[27] Ledrut, R. (1986) Speech and the Silence of the City, in Gottdiener, M., and Lagopoulos, A. (eds), *The City and the Sign: An Introduction to Urban Semiotics*, New York: Columbia University Press, pp.114–34 and p.125.
[28] Certeau, M. de (1984) *The Practice of Everyday Life*, trans. Steven Rendell, Berkeley: University of California Press.
[29] Ibid., p.93
[30] Debord, G. (1983) *The Society of the Spectacle*, London: Rebel Press.
[31] Oppenheimer Dean, A., and Hursley, T. (2002) *Rural Studio: Samuel Mockbee and sn Architecture of Decency*, New York: Princeton Architectural Press, p.9.
[32] Wang Shu: Local hero [2008]: An Interview with Wang Shu (Amateur Architecture Studio), 28 December 2008, Moving Cities.org, Monitoring the Metropolis, retrieved from: http://movingcities.org/interviews/local-hero-an-interview-with-wang-shu/, [accessed 20 June 2012].
[33] Chrostowska, S.D. (2007) Vis-à-vis The Glaneuse, in *Angelakai, Journal of the Theoretical Humanities* 12(2), Routledge, August, p.130.
[34] Bonner, 2009, op. cit., p.120
[35] Varda, 2000, op. cit.
[36] Walter Segal (1907–1985) was the most significant architectural proponent of self-build in the UK, developing timber-frame methods for rapid and low-cost self-build projects during the 1970s. (See later section of *The Labour of Gleaning* and McKean, J. (1989) *Learning from Segal: Walter Segal's Life, Work and Influence*, Basel and Boston: Birkhauser.)
[37] Varda, 2000, op. cit.
[38] Whitechapel Anarchist Group (January 2010) *Non-Commercial House: Grand Re-Opening!*, retrieved from: http://whitechapelanarchistgroup.wordpress.com/2010/01/14/non-commercial-house-grand-re-opening/ [accessed on 14 July 2012].
[39] This project was more akin to that of the recreational gleaners of Varda's film, where gleaning as an economy is practised for its cultural value, as a recording of the city.
[40] Bonner, 2009, op. cit., p.125
[41] Ibid., p.119

Bibliography

Anstey, T. (2007) Architecture and Rhetoric: Persuasion, Context, Action, in Anstey, T., Grillner, K., and Hughes, R. (eds) *Architecture and Authorship*, London: Black Dog Publishing, pp.18–29.

Anstey, T., Grillner, K., and Hughes, R. (eds) (2007) *Architecture and Authorship*, London: Black Dog Publishing.

Baudrillard, J. (1993) *The Transparency of Evil: Essays on Extreme Phenomena*, Verso, pp.100–5.

Berger, J. (1991) *Keeping a Rendezvous*, London: Granta Books, p.84.

Bonner, V. (2009) The Gleaners and 'Us': The Radical Modesty of Agnes Varda Les Glaneurs et la Glaneuse, in Columpar, C., and Mayer, S. (eds) *There She Goes: Feminist Film Making and Beyond*, USA, Detroit: Wayne State University Press, p.119–25.

Certeau, M. de (1984) *The Practice of Everyday Life*, trans. Steven Rendell, Berkeley: University of California Press, p.93.

Chrostowska, S.D. (2007) Vis-à-vis The Glaneuse, in *Angelakai, Journal of the Theoretical Humanities* 12(2), Routledge, August, p.130.

Cruickshank, R. (2007) The Work of Art in the Age of Global Consumption: Agnes Varda's Les Glaneurs et la Glaneuse, *L'espirit Createur* 47(3): pp.19–32.

Debord, G. (1983) *The Society of the Spectacle*, London: Rebel Press.

European Graduate School Website (1997–2012) Agnes Varda Biography, retrieved from: http://www.egs.edu/faculty/agnes-varda/biography [accessed on 10 July 2012].

Hay, D., and Rogers, N. (1997) *Eighteenth Century English society: Shuttles and Swords*, Oxford Paperbacks, OPUS, pp.86–7.

Hottell, R. (1999) Including ourselves: the role of female spectators in Agnes varda's Le Bonheur and L'une chante, L'autre pas, *Cinema Journal* 38(2): pp.52–72.

King, P. (1992) Legal Change, Customary Right, and Social Conflict in Late 18th century England: The Origins of the Great Gleaning Case of 1788, *Law and History Review* 10(1): pp.1–31.

Ledrut, R. (1986) Speech and the Silence of the City, in Gottdiener, M., and Lagopoulos, A. (eds), *The City and the Sign: An Introduction to Urban Semiotics*, New York: Columbia University Press, pp.114–34 and p.125.

Lefebvre, H. (1991/1974) *The Production of Space*, Oxford: Blackwell, p.49.

Lukacs, G. (1990) *History and Class Consciousness: Studies in Marxist Dialectics*, Merlin Press, p.264.

Mazierska, E., and Rascaroli, L. (2006) *Crossing New Europe: Postmodern Travel and The European Road Movie*, London: Wallflower Press, pp.128–9.

McKean, J. (1989) *Learning from Segal: Walter Segal's Life, Work and Influence*, Basel and Boston: Birkhauser.

Oppenheimer Dean, A., and Hursley, T. (2002) *Rural Studio: Samuel Mockbee and sn Architecture of Decency*, New York: Princeton Architectural Press, p.9.

Smith, A. (1998) *Agnes Varda*, Manchester University Press, p.83.

Thompson, E.P. (1993) *Customs in Common: Studies in Traditional Popular Culture*, London: Penguin.

Varda, A. (director) (2000) *Les Glaneurs et la Glaneuse* [*The Gleaners and I*] [DVD], France: Zeitgeist.

Whitechapel Anarchist Group (January 2010) *Non-Commercial House: Grand Re-Opening!*, retrieved from: http://whitechapelanarchistgroup.wordpress.com/2010/01/14/non-commercial-house-grand-re-opening/ [accessed on 14 July 2012].

Edward HOLLIS
University of Edinburgh

NO LONGER AND NOT YET

In many ways, then, Carless brings us back to some of the ideas marked out early in this volume: the notion of wastespace and adaptive re-use as discussed by our first contributors. In the final chapter of this book, Ed Hollis completes this circle and brings us right back to our first chapter. He reintroduces the ideas of Viollet-le-Duc and John Ruskin with which Plevoets and Van Cleempoel began but also picks up where they left off in another sense. Whereas our first authors suggested the practice of adaptive re-use was in need of a reorientation that would incorporate the interior designer's sensibilities, what they called 'soft values', what Hollis suggests is very different. He suggests that the best option is to do nothing.

In a way, this proposition may be seen as echoing that of John Ruskin and his concern with allowing old buildings to remain in their current state through a careful process of 'conservation'. Hollis's ideas, however, have to be considered in the very specific context within which he works: the debates about the possible re-uses to be given to a very specific building on the outskirts of Glasgow, St Peter's Seminary, designed and built in the 1970s but, by 1987, left as a ruin.

Introduction

The forest of Kilmahew, around twenty miles west of Glasgow, conceals an architectural cautionary tale. In the 1960s, the landscape was radically transformed by a building: St Peter's Seminary was built to house around a hundred Catholic novices. Its plan and section, the work of the architects Gillespie Kidd and Coia, were a rigorous statement of the modernist maxim that form follows function; but within a decade, there were not enough priests to fill it and St Peter's became a form without a function. That was

1987, and since then it has resisted numerous attempts to provide it with a new one: designed as closely as it was to a specific programme, the building remains empty and derelict. It is no longer what it used to be and not yet what it can be. The caution is simple: design a building programmatically and you'll end up with a ruin.

This author has been involved since the Venice Biennale of 2010 with a new proposal for St Peter's led by the Glasgow arts collective NVA. We have no images of what it will look like or when it will be ready. St Peter's isn't going to be restored any time soon. Instead, we propose to leave the building perpetually incomplete – both ruin and building site. It's a model of what all buildings should be: they are, in environmental terms, expensive and we shouldn't be building more of them but exploiting and transforming the ones we already have, again and again. St Peter's was originally designed to teach moral lessons; but now it presents a different ethical challenge. This paper will narrate NVA's proposals and set them in the context of the modernist ethics they question, arguing for a different discourse, of suspension in time – in being no longer and not yet.

1. Space and Light Revisited: The Sad Story of St Peter's Seminary

In 2009, the Scottish director Murray Grigor released a new film. At least, he'd reworked on an old one, premiered at the Royal School of Arts Music and Drama in Glasgow. *Space and Light Revisited* was shown on two screens. Both screens followed one another, shot for shot, around the same building. On the left-hand side, everything was in perfect order. The building was, as the title of the film suggested, a study in space and light. Young men opened doors, walked up and down corridors, ascended and descended stairs, dined in the refectory, cooked in the kitchen, studied in the cells and prayed at the altar.

On the right-hand screen, the building was devoid of people. The charred remains of doors and fragments of smashed windows littered a floor dusted with snow. Corridors had been blasted open to the elements and the stair was no more than a cranked concrete beam, covered in moss. The refectory was cavernous and dark, the kitchen roofless, the cells covered in graffiti and the altar smashed. The two screens were identical in every dimension, save that of time, for the images on the left-hand screen had been shot in 1972, those on the right in 2009. Thirty-seven years separated the functioning modernist machine on the left from the ruin on the right.

The wooded estate of Kilmahew has a long history – in the eighth or ninth centuries a forest hermitage, in the middle ages a feudal estate and in the nineteenth century an arboretum assembled by a shipping dynasty around a mock-baronial mansion. The place had, like many such estates, become impossible to maintain in private hands by the end of World War II. Kilmahew was acquired by the Archdiocese of Glasgow in 1946 and, in 1953, they approached the architects Gillespie Kidd and Coia to convert the baronial mansion into a seminary for around two hundred priests. The design went through several iterations and, by the time it was completed in 1966, St Peter's

Figure 1: St Peter's Seminary in its 'heyday'

Seminary was largely the work of Isi Metzstein and Andy Macmillan; already the *enfants terribles* of the Scottish architectural scene.

Their powerful use of *beton brut*, shallow vaulting and heavy timberwork owes much to the idiosyncrasies of late Le Corbusier, or Frederick Gibberd at Liverpool Cathedral; but the *parti* of the building had more in common with Stirling and Gowan's contemporary experiments in Leicester and Cambridge. Like them, St Peter's was the three-dimensional expression of a functional programme. A single section enclosed, without distinction, a refectory at one end and a chapel at the other. As a later conservation report[1] prepared by John Allan of Avanti Architects in 2008 states: 'buildings were [at that time] conceived primarily as instruments, rather than monuments' and St Peter's was, par excellence, an instrument, a machine, for educating priests.

It was a machine that soon started to malfunction. Even by the time that Grigor filmed *Space and Light*, the seminarians were complaining about the leaks and the cold. But the seminary was also a functional programme that, no sooner had it been clothed in a building, started to wither away. There were never enough trainee priests to fill the building and, by the time it was complete, the church had decided to train priests in parishes and small houses among their congregations, rather than in isolated

Figure 2: The altar of St Peter's, June 2012

phalansteries. In 1980, the Catholic Church closed St Peter's down, and sent the seminarians elsewhere. The place was used as a drug rehabilitation centre for a few years until, in 1986, the building was mothballed. A fence was built around it, the doors were locked and the place abandoned.

St Peter's has fallen remarkably rapidly into ruin. The weather of the west of Scotland has done its work, of course; but so have the locals. The fence the church put about the site is riddled with holes and the building has been comprehensively raided for building materials, used as a canvas for graffiti and a venue for countless parties, usually culminating in some act of other of minor arson. The original baronial house was gutted in one such performance in the mid-1990s and was pulled down by the fire service – it was too dangerous, they said, for anyone to risk visiting it again. Any empty building is, of course, an invitation to its own destruction, particularly any building that is as loathed by its neighbours as completely as St Peter's; and the more it is ruined, the more loathsome it becomes to some. One resident is quoted as saying:

> 'It's an eyesore – a total blot on the land. Nobody but pretentious, self-serving architects would miss it. Let it rot and become a folly to the monumental planning mistakes of the 20th century.'[2]

But the holes in the fence have also permitted entry to other visitors and St Peter's has become, in the process of its ruination, a cult object for artists and architects, locally and internationally. Some graffiti is obscene, sectarian or nihilistic; but others are extraordinary and beautiful. Rock bands occasionally clear the floor of the chapel of its heaps of broken glass to film videos; and students from Glasgow School of Art use the walls of the building to practice on when canvasses and studios became too expensive, or restrictive, for their art.

The elegiac modernist ruin has also provided material for many speculative projects over the years from architecture, art and design students, all of whom find themselves appalled, seduced and provoked by the concrete beast lurking inside its forest fence. Some envisage the complete restoration of the building, others its occupation as a monumental ruin and others still, its complete conversion into something else. And there have been several rather more conventional proposals to bring a new life to the building, notably an attempt by Urban Splash and Gareth Hoskins to turn it into an hotel in 2007. This scheme, like several others, was defeated by the inconvenience of the site, the cost of the proposals and the very specificity of the building itself. Designed as closely as it was around one particular programme, it has proved almost impossible to convert it into anything else.

As the result of this diverse interest in and activity around St Peter's, the building itself has acquired a cultural status that increases in directly inverse proportion to its state of repair. The building was 'A' listed in 1992 and, in 2005, *Prospect* magazine named it the most significant post-war building in Scotland. In 2008, St Peter's joined the World Monuments Watch List of 100 most endangered buildings on the globe and at the same time Avanti Architects prepared a conservation report for Historic Scotland. St Peter's Seminary has become, to invert Avanti's phrase, a monument rather than an instrument; but ruination, as the Catholic Church has learned to its cost, is not a static state. It is, particularly in modern buildings, made of fragile concrete and steel, and riddled with cavities for services, a rapid process. The building has proved uniquely resistant to attempts to 'save it': the remoteness of the site, the restrictive programmatic form of the architecture and the resistant materials of which it is constructed make it difficult to deal with; but leave St Peter's as it is and it will soon disappear.

Thus, what follows in this paper is an examination of a new proposal for St Peter's rooted in the dimension of time, as explored in *Space and Light Revisited*. As John Allan's conservation report states, St Peter's has, between 1986 and 2008, undergone an extraordinary transformation that 'necessitates a double assessment of significance – the significance of St Peter's as built, and the significance of the building in its current state.'[3] The proposal discussed here is based neither on the restoration of the building as it once was, nor the conservation of it as it is now, but on the provocation posed by the journey between those two states and the process of transformation itself.

2. Space and Light Revisited, Revisited: Possible Futures for St Peter's

In November 2011, *Space and Light Revisited* was shown again, this time in a disused church in Venice as the *acqua alta* rose outside. The screening took place as part of Scotland's contribution to the Architecture Biennale of that year, curated by the Glasgow Arts Charity NVA. The name NVA is derived from the acronym 'Nationale Vitae Activa' which means, loosely, 'the right to influence public affairs', and their work is born out of the idea that it is publicly funded. NVA eschew the notion of public art as the provision of static, monumental objects in favour of the organisation of events that provoke public activity.

> 'NVA champion an emerging form of collaborative art practice that aims to galvanise public partners and bridge the gap between political strategy and practical implementation through temporary and permanent works.'[4]

Their best-known work, *The Storr: Unfolding Landscape*, was not, as the images of it might make it seem, a spectacular highland *son et lumiere* but a provocation to explore the mountains of Skye at night. *The Speed of Light*, planned for the 2012 Olympiad, lit up Arthur's Seat in Edinburgh through public participation: the light display was generated by hundreds of volunteer runners jogging around the hill in specially designed light suits and walkers climbing its steep traverses with luminous, singing walking sticks.

And the screening of *Space and Light Revisited* in Venice was no passive night at the movies. When the lights came up, a debate was held. Angus Farquhar, the founder of NVA, was in attendance, with Tilman Latz, the landscape architect responsible for the conversion of the derelict steelworks in Duisberg, Germany, into a park; Hayden Lorimer, the cultural geographer; David Cook, head of the newly refurbished Briggait Arts Centre in Glasgow; Gerrie Van Noord, the artist; Morag Bain of the Lighthouse, Scotland's centre for architecture and design; Adam Scarborough, who runs the Grizedale Arts project in Cumbria; Ian Gilzean from the Scottish Government; Ranald McInnes from Historic Scotland, and several others, including the author of this paper.

These people were gathered together for the different perspectives they might offer on the future of Kilmahew. Some, like Latz, could offer professional perspectives on the conversion of derelict modernist sites. Others, like Cook or Van Noord, were used to working with artists on site-specific projects. Bain, Gilzean and McInnes were present as policy makers and funders, while Scarborough's Grizedale Arts project offers radical models of public engagement with the arts and culture in rural settings, from the establishment of a school for tourists, to the construction of paddy fields in the Lake District. Lorimer's work on the geographies of walking and droving offered a corrective to the natural tendency among the (architect-led) group to concentrate on the building at Kilmahew rather than the landscape as a whole.

While the debate was used to reflect on the film, it also provoked speculation on the future of the building; and since that time, NVA have assembled a proposal for it quite unlike any of the others that have been wrecked against its pebble-dashed concrete. Key to their proposal is that there is no proposal. Nothing complete, anyway. Most of the landscape will be left to run wild. Most of the building will stay ruined, for the moment at least. The project has already, they say, started on site, without a drawing or a designer. It won't be finished for at least another twenty years, if at all. It doesn't sound – or look – much like a proposal.

But the future of Kilmahew speculatively constructed at the Venice Biennale in 2010 represents a carefully considered challenge to the ways in which we deal with existing buildings and, in particular, ruins. In the remainder of this paper, we will show how this alternative future deals with, and questions, some of the key 'building blocks' of our attitudes to the architecture (and the landscapes) of the past. The care of monuments has, since the nineteenth century, existed between two poles of thought: restoration and conservation. The former approach is best articulated by its first great proponent in nineteenth-century France, Viollet-le-Duc:

> 'The term restoration and the thing itself are both modern. To restore a building is not to preserve it, to repair, or to rebuild it; it is reinstate it to a condition of completeness which may never have existed at any given time.'[5]

The restorer supposes that the authenticity of a building lies in its stylistic and aesthetic unity, and that this is an ideal state to which any building may be returned. For example, Viollet-le-Duc worked for many years on the restoration of Notre Dame in Paris. He removed Baroque and Neoclassical additions that he believed to conflict with the purity of the Gothic style of the original building. He also 'completed' many parts that he supposed the medieval masons to have left unfinished.

To imagine a restoration of St Peter's Seminary, then, one must imagine all the graffiti and the overgrowth removed and, at the same time, all the disappeared timber revetment of the structure replaced, so that the building might look exactly as it did in 1986, at the moment of its abandonment by the Catholic Church. This is the approach that the French authorities have taken to the conservation of the Palace of Versailles, for example, which is being restored to its state on the eve of the revolution of October 1789: what the palace is 'for' once the restoration is complete is a question they cannot, or dare not, answer. Quite aside from the cost of the process, palace and seminary were malfunctioning white elephants then, and would be white elephants now.

At the same time as Viollet-le-Duc was writing, conservationists in England, led by John Ruskin, saw restoration as:

> '"a destruction accompanied by the false description of the thing destroyed." For conservationists completeness and authenticity lay in the fact of a building's survival, weathered and worn, in whatever form, from one age of culture to another.'[6]

However, while a building itself might survive, the people and the society that made it do not. Historic buildings stand as epitaphs to their now-obsolete ways of conceiving and making things; and if this is the case, then restoration is a double crime. On the one hand, all sorts of age-old accretions are removed in order to return the building to a spurious modern notion of 'purity'. On the other hand, in order to restore formal unity, gaps in the original execution of the design are filled with modern insertions. These latter cannot be made in the same way or by the same hands as the originals (even the technology that built St Peter's in the late 1960s is already obsolete). They will always be, in the words of Ruskin, 'a false description' even if they do match the original fabric exactly in formal or physical terms. As William Morris, who founded the Society for the Protection of Ancient Buildings in 1877, commented:

> 'Surely it is a curious thing that we are ready to laugh at the idea of the possibility of the Greek workman turning out a Gothic building, or a Gothic workman turning out a Greek one, but we see nothing preposterous in the Victorian workman producing a Gothic one.'[7]

If the historic building is the epitaph of its makers, then nothing might be added or taken away from it without compromising its integrity. The most that might be admitted is unobtrusive repair.

> 'Watch an old building with an anxious care; guard it as best you may, and at any cost, from every influence of dilapidation… bind it together with iron where it loosens; stay it with timber where it declines; do not care about the unsightliness of the aid.'[8]

Conservation is a radical strategy and as such is rarely actually practised since it permits no alteration to what it finds. Viollet-le-Duc said of the principles of conservation:

> 'We understand the rigour of these principles, and we accept them completely: but only when we are dealing with a curious ruin, without a future or an actual use'.[9]

And while this may be appropriate for the ruin or the obsolete shrine, it is an impossible strategy for the vast majority of old buildings. The consequence of 'conserving' St Peter's in the pure form advocated by Ruskin or Morris would be as irrational as restoring it. The building would be stabilised in its current state, as an overgrown ruin surrounded by a fence riddled with holes, perpetually vulnerable to further vandalism, arson and abuse. The nineteenth-century battle between conservation and restoration was fought between ideological extremists; and it was not until late in the century that a third position was evolved, one that allowed architects and historians to contemplate the modern alteration and extension of historic buildings. The first charter regarding the restoration of historic monuments in Italy, from 1883, states that:

> 'Architectural monuments from the past are not only valuable for the study of architecture but contribute as essential documents to explain and illustrate all the facets of the history of various peoples throughout the ages.'[10]

This approach – philological or documentary restoration – sees the authenticity of the historic building not in its aesthetic unity nor in its survival, but in the legibility of the diverse parts of which that survival is composed. For example, the ancient Theatre of Marcellus in Rome, which was converted into a castle in the middle ages and a palace in the Renaissance, has been converted into a block of flats. At the same time, the area around the building has been excavated to expose to the 'reader' all the layers of this complex, collaged, hybrid building.

Postmodernist writers on architecture such as Colin Rowe and Robert Venturi have taken this notion further. They borrow the notion of bricolage and fragmentation from modernist painting and early modernist architecture. Buildings, they suggest, are incomplete assemblies of fragments in the process of perpetual addition and subtraction; and this opens up a new possibility in dealing with old buildings. If they are *already* composites and collages, if their 'purity' is *already* compromised, then there need be no interdict on adding to (or subtracting from) them further, provided that the new 'layer' of alteration is legibly different from its predecessors.

This approach finds its most assured expression in the work of the architect Carlo Scarpa, who carried out radical alterations to the Castelvecchio in Verona and the Palazzo Querini Stampalia in Venice in the 1960s and '70s. His interventions to these ancient buildings comprise excavations, on the one hand, that expose the multiple layers of the existing buildings; and on the other, additions whose asymmetrical form and location, industrial precision and material contrast make it clear to the viewer that they are different, modern superimpositions onto the ancient fabric.

One can imagine, then, a refurbishment of St Peter's in which extraneous historic junk is removed and then the concrete frame, cleaned and exposed, is draped with contemporary interventions that allow the building to perform a new function. This is in fact the strategy that Urban Splash attempted to employ in their 2009 proposal for the building; but it was defeated by something with which Scarpa, working on medieval structures, did not have to deal – the extreme programmatic specificity of a modern building like the seminary, which is so rigid that it makes it almost impossible to envisage new functions for it, without committing serious vandalisms on the structure and ruining whatever vestigial integrity it might still possess. As is implicit in all three of the positions outlined above, history and what to do with its remains are closely bound together: the latter being a concrete metaphor for the former. History is a continuous and multifarious process of change while buildings, on the face of it, are both too fixed and too ephemeral to represent its protean continuities.

Restorationists destroy what is there in order to 'reveal' – in fact create – the intentions of the original designer, which becomes their fetish. History is frozen at the moment of the conception of the building – it is still-born. St Peter's returns to the moment of its abandonment. Conservationists freeze history in the present: the building's life is suspended in coma. This is the result of their fetishisation of the link – seen as sacred and irreproducible – between the intentions of the designer and the building. St Peter's remains an unloved ruin.

The fetishisation of the multiple intentions of the designers of the historic building lead postmodernists to deny it any unity. Each part is separated from the other to aid legibility. History is made discontinuous and the building is eviscerated. St Peter's, in order to be re-used, must sacrifice the functional and spatial integrity that gave it life. It is therefore clear that traditional approaches to architectural restoration/conservation (call it what you will) will not suffice when dealing with a building like St Peter's. Restoration is a sort of still-birth; conservation a mummification; and philological restoration an evisceration. They are all concerned with fixing buildings in time, imposing upon them a static state, an embalming that they never enjoyed 'in life'.

Tilman Latz, reflecting on the debate in Venice, wrote:

> 'Originally the architects of St Peter's were challenged to find a non-dogmatic new architectural form, which created on the one hand a 'sacred place', and on the other hand respected and transformed ecclesiastical traditions of a thousand years of the Roman Catholic Church in Scotland into a conceptual and spatial programme. By cleaning and restoring it, the seminary could possibly tell this story, but it would be devoid of any of its own further history. It would be just another clean museum piece.'[11]

But to conserve the building as it is, even as a mysterious ruin, is also not a sustainable option. While it is no longer habitable in its present state, it is still far from the condition of stump of castle, or ancient temple. Recent as it is, its current state still provokes real loathings and fears (and consequent antisocial behaviour). To refurbish the building completely is, as the Urban Splash experience has already shown, also not a sustainable option – not immediately, anyway. The programmatic specificity of St Peter's precludes any easy conversion from the old use to a new one. The sum of money required to do so is quite simply too large; and the money to be made from the site is too small to reward such a significant investment.

As David Cook, veteran of a long campaign to raise the funds to convert a similarly derelict building in Glasgow into the Briggait Arts Centre, commented:

> 'The very challenges of the building are the things that create the opportunities, in the sense that conservation practice would normally say, 'Let's look for an end use', and once you had found the end use, the ability to develop, the ability to raise money would all pour in. There is a sense of this building waiting for a purpose that is never going to arrive. There is no commercial solution, no practical solution for it, and it will sit and wait forever unless something is done.'[12]

What is needed at St Peter's, then, is time; and NVA believe that doing as little as possible, for the moment, is what will buy it. Angus Farquhar writes: 'I'm glad we can't just go and create some instant fix for St Peter's, because as a result, we can't make the wrong decisions. We have to do this slowly.'[13] NVA's master plan is phased. The first phase involves cutting paths through the woods and making gardens, so that the site is populated with people as a deterrent to vandalism and crime; the second is the stabilisation of the ruin; and the third the occupation of a small part of it, converting the chapel into a meeting hall. Beyond, at some unspecified future date, more of the building might be occupied, but in ways as yet unpredicted. It is a strategy of tiny moves. Latz writes:

> 'Very often business plans then decide about the destiny of such structures in a very short period of time.... I think we need an approach that leads to a practical application in time and in accordance with the public interests. But it is equally important to respect the notion of time that is now accumulated within the site. Consequently it is just as important to take time for interventions, to keep things open and propose structures that can develop further and take new ideas on board.... That's what makes such a project sustainable over time.'[14]

3. Space and Light Revisited, Revisited, Revisited: An Incomplete Proposal for St Peter's

So the incompleteness of NVA's proposals for St Peter's isn't borne out of penny pinching or an excess of respect for the original building; and it's not just a strategy to buy time: it is also a provocation. In his 1949 essay, 'The Future of the Past', John Summerson[15] argues that the pleasure of ruins lies in their suggestiveness – too ruined, and the heap of stone gives no purchase to the imagination. Not ruined enough, and the building restricts its flight.

But the suggestive contemplation of ruins is not just an idle reverie, for every building is, in some sense, a ruin. As Christopher Alexander observed: 'No building is ever perfect. Each building, when it is first built, is an attempt to make a self-maintaining whole configuration. But the predictions are invariably wrong. People use buildings differently from the way they thought they would.' Accordingly, people have to make changes in order to maintain the fit between a structure and the events that take place in it. Each time this happens to a building, 'we assume we are going to transform it, that new wholes will be born, that, indeed, the entire whole which is being repaired will become a different whole as a result.'[16]

This has already happened at St Peter's, whose startling present state is the result of predictions that were invariably wrong. The proposed occupation of St Peter's is (unlike a restoration, conservation or refurbishment) an attempt not to stop this iterative process of transformation, but to perpetuate it, so that the building will always be in flux and incomplete. The incomplete occupation of St Peter's is designed to encourage the proprietors and users of the site to complete their own version of the site, in their minds at first, and then in time, perhaps, on the ground itself. Each new intervention, itself fragmentary, then becomes a new provocation and a new round of intervention can begin.

Buildings and ruins are never whole and this is their very provocation – to reverie, as Summerson suggests; to action, as Alexander proposes; and also to critique. In his studies of British industrial ruins, the geographer Tim Edensor has commented that:

> 'ruins are largely understood – especially by bureaucrats, city promoters and planners

– as offensive to the character and aesthetics of the city. The sooner these scars on the landscape are demolished and swept away, effaced in the name of civic order, the better. They are matter out of place, a continuing rebuke to attempts to render urban space productive, smooth and regular. Imagined as sites of urban disorder, dens into which deviant characters – drug-users, gang-members, vandals and the homeless – are drawn, the imperative is to extinguish their decaying features from the urban backdrop. This website is dedicated to putting forward a different view. The following pages feature photographs and text which attempt to provoke a different assessment of these ruined spaces, and stimulate a critique of certain contemporary social and cultural processes. As spaces by the side of the road, ruins can be explored for effects that talk back to the quest to create an impossibly seamless urban fabric, to the uses to which history and heritage are put, to the extensive over-commodification of places and things, to middle-class aesthetics, and to broader tendencies to fix meanings in the service of power.'[17]

Edensor argues, then, that ruins provide a critique of the city itself – or, at least, of our desire to organise it. It is an idea that finds its source in Richard Sennett's first published book, *The Uses of Disorder*. Writing in the 1960s in the face of mass suburbanisation on the one hand, and youth revolt on the other, Sennett drew parallels between the self-righteous certainties and communities of the teenager and their suburban parents, and saw in both the spectre of, to quote Edensor, 'meanings fixed in the service of power'. 'The myths of community', writes Sennett, 'are self-destructive in that they take a strength developed on the eve of adulthood, and use it to repress other human strengths, like curiosity and the desire to explore.'[18] And they result, he argued, in an approach to society and its habitus, the city, all too familiar in his time:

> *'"Aesthetic and humanistic values and institutions must be in a planned relationship to economic and political values and institutions. Thus all such activities must be designed as a unit both physically and as social structures". ...these are not the words of a mad superman. They are rather a clear statement of the goals of a large and influential segment of the profession that plans modern cities. The ideal is that nothing be out of control'.*[19]

Sennett's response to the planner is to foster disorder in the city: to abolish zoning, local government, central control – in short, to allow the city to be what it is already: chaotic, changing and forever incomplete. It would not, by any means, be easy to live there:

> *'Let us imagine a community free to create its own patterns of life... the outstanding characteristic of the area, for the young people who move into it, would be the high level of tension and unease between the people living there... precisely because the community was on its own, because the people had to deal with each other in order to survive at all, some kind of uneasy truce between these hostile camps, these conflicting interests, would have to be arranged by the people themselves. ...the very diversity of the neighbourhood has built into it the obligation of responsibility.'*[20]

For, at the largest scale, Sennett suggests, diversity, brokenness and constant change are the very drivers that bring us out of adolescence (however old we are) and make us into adults. People, buildings and cities are more than mere machines:

> 'When a machine's parts wear down, which is their "form of experience" in time, the machine cannot operate. But the essence of human development is that growth occurs when old routines break down, when old parts are no longer enough for the needs of the new organism, this same kind of change, in a larger sphere, creates the phenomenon of history in a culture.'[21]

This is an idea about cities but it could also be applied to their microcosm: buildings – and indeed, buildings like St Peter's. The ruin and the partial occupation, then, incomplete, malfunctional (or a-functional), does not just stimulate reverie but demands action and re-action. It invokes freedom – not in the modern sense of choice (although the partial ruin demands that its occupants make choices about its future) but in the sense of liberty and the duties that run concurrently with her rights. In this sense, it is not enough to *be* free – instead, it is required to perform its privileges and duties.

This means that St Peter's as a project can never be finished for, if it is, it will be finished. Morag Bain of the Lighthouse comments:

> 'I am really fascinated by the whole idea that this is about process and that there isn't an end use. The process is the thing that is driving it. Remembering the conversation about how the Church thinks nothing of a hundred years. Thinking of an end use: it might not happen in our lifetime; and that is fine.'[22]

4. The Invisible College

NVA have no idea what their proposal will look like when it is complete. Get it right, and it never will be. They do, however, have a fairly clear idea about how it will happen, for their proposal is not just a matter of architecture. St Peter's was built as a place of sacred reflection and education, but seminaries are not, like monasteries, secluded. Rather, their purpose is to train priests to go out into the world, both locally and further afield. The functional programme planned for the site is intimately connected to the formal programme for the buildings, since it is the former that will drive the latter.

The programme revolves around the idea of an 'invisible college', less an institution than a series of events, in which academics, architects and, crucially, the local people who have spent their lives around the site will investigate its past and, in doing so, model its future. The invisible college, like the site it addresses, is not a fixed entity but a protean body in the process of perpetual evolution. The observations of one summer school provoke the agenda for the next one and, in the process, proposals for the next stage of the fragmentary re-occupation of the building in which it has taken place.

The idea is modelled on the summer schools held in the Old Town of Edinburgh in the late nineteenth century by the cultural geographer and sociologist Patrick Geddes. At the time, the Old Town was a slum. Geddes invited thinkers of international renown to work with local people for a limited period of time. Their task was to conduct what was called a 'regional survey', finding out about living conditions, geography, the weather and the history of the locale.

But they weren't positivistic exercises in data collection. Geddes hoped that, in recording and articulating the place in which they lived, the inhabitants of Edinburgh's Old Town would appreciate its value, understand its problems and, in so doing, begin to find solutions to them. His regional surveys (he went on to carry them out elsewhere – in England, Montpellier and even in India) resulted in significant improvements to areas that had hitherto been slums and, importantly, these improvements weren't imposed from above. Edinburgh's Royal Mile is still dotted with gardens that Geddes encouraged people to make in the drying greens, stairs they were inspired to clean, ancient buildings they shamed the city fathers into preserving.

Farquhar echoes the aspiration:

> 'It's not a process of us becoming tied into a sort of exploitation of individuals who must
>
> pay vast sums of money in order for us to impart wisdom. It should be the inverse of this approach. It is to create places where the subject matter is so interesting and so rich that you would simply use great minds from many different disciplines to allow people to draw what they can from this narrative. Maybe it is about teaching people to grow vegetables; that is as important as understanding the tradition of Ruskin and Scarpa and Le Corbusier and Mackintosh and how their lineage runs through the building.'[23]

Kilmahew still is, as the Old Town of Edinburgh once was, a contested and difficult territory. St Peter's Seminary may be an icon to architects and designers but it is locally loathed and abused. The invisible college is a mechanism designed to heal these wounds and, in so doing, to heal the building itself, step by step, unlocking and articulating the memories it contains.

The invisible college is now well underway. An AHRC grant has been obtained to run three workshops and an application submitted to the ironically named Heritage Lottery Fund for the initial works to the landscape and the building. The first workshops took place in 2012, testing the ground for future activities, and refining the first, fragmentary proposals for the revival of St Peter's Seminary itself.

Two of these workshops have taken place to date, each attended by around fifty diverse guests, from the Australian landscape writer Gini Lee to the Scottish land-rights campaigner Andy Wightman. In each workshop, a walk to the site leads to a series of activities on the ground. In the first workshop, some attendees replanted the old vegetable patch and others excavated a long-lost Japanese garden. In the second workshop, half the guests were given hazard tape and cones, and asked to demarcate and clear areas within the ruined seminary where it would be safe for a child to play. Others were given a spade and invited to excavate patches of earth one-metre square: beneath several decades of turf they found the floor of a Victorian winter garden, an old tennis court and a cobbled lane.

Figure 3: A safe place for a child to play? Workshop 2 at St Peter's Seminary, June 2012

Each of these workshops is carefully designed as a little act of archaeology on the site – a scraping back and revealing that leaves a mark, however tiny, on the building or the landscape. Individually, they are nothing. Incrementally, however, they begin to occupy and ultimately to transform the site from a dangerous, uninhabited *terra incognita* into a place people used to live in, and will again. These activities culminated in the final workshop in September 2012, in which attendees were invited to excavate an object or element from the site – and then to bring it back to a white-painted art gallery in Glasgow, for archaeological display. A building which has suffered decades of neglect and abuse will finally be accorded historic status, even if only for a while, before the junk is returned back behind the fence to the wilderness from whence it came.

Each of these days concludes with keynote addresses – from architects (Tilman Latz), historians (Ed Hollis), geographers (Tim Edensor) and activists (Andy Wightman) – which are designed to set the day's activities in a cultural and theoretical context. However, set as they are in the local village hall and ultimately, it is hoped, in temporary enclosures on the site itself, these concluding thoughts are themselves removed from the context of the studios and lecture halls from whence they came, engaging audiences and bodies of opinion in the wider world. This year's activities are just the first for the invisible college – prototypes for a longer-term testing of the site, not just

Figure 4: Relics of St Peter's bagged, tagged, and placed in the Lighthouse in Glasgow

as a place but as a provocation for thought and action, its medium, its subject and its end result. Plans are already in play to gain further funding to continue the process of conversation between people and place.

5. Conclusion

St Peter's Seminary is unique; but its pasts and futures hold lessons for anyone – and that's everyone – who dwells in and deals with existing buildings.

The building, like so much of our recent inheritance, is just emerging from that period of time when it is no longer what is once was, but not yet what it will become. Medieval castles and Georgian houses were built so long ago that we have forgotten the innumerable cruelties and errors that spawned them. 'Modern' buildings, however much designers might like the way they look, present us with a different sort of problem: no longer instruments, not yet monuments, they provoke unease. But that is not an argument to destroy them. There are too many recent buildings that survive, even if derelict, to make it worth our while or, indeed, environmentally responsible to dispose of them. Their particular forms, rigidly defined by obsolete programmes, also make it financially, functionally, aesthetically and ethically undesirable to restore or conserve them.

This paper has tried to show how traditional methodologies of dealing with such sites are found wanting – St Peter's will not and has not responded kindly to efforts to restore, conserve or intervene into it as a complete building. NVA's approach therefore is to break the problem down and to posit a new model for dealing with ruins – particularly ruins of the modern sort. It is a strategy that is, firstly, realistic: in a period of time without much money, not much needs to be done. Secondly, it attempts to be sensitive: small mistakes are more easily undone than complete ones. Thirdly, it is open ended, allowing the future to alter what it finds as well as the past. And finally, it is challenging: incompleteness, as Sennett has observed, requires response and challenges the visitor not to be a spectator, but a participant.

This proposal flies in face of conventional thinking on this subject and has encountered considerable opposition: mainly from the architectural community, who hold the works of Gillespie Kidd and Coia in high regard and see the dereliction of St Peter's as an act of *damnatio memoriae*; but also from the local community, who would rather the building just disappeared. In seeking funding, NVA must do battle with conventional desires for a beautiful object, delivered on time and on budget – for they cannot and will not deliver one.

As with all buildings, we must learn to accept that St Peter's, Cardross is no longer the instrument it was designed to be nor yet a monument. Once the programme that generated them has disappeared, their form will never, to misquote Louis Sullivan, follow function. Neither are they perfectible, or perfect, and deserving of absolute preservation. Buildings are iterative processes rather than products. They exist in time and never have been, are not, nor ever will be complete. Architecture is an activity, not a thing, no less ephemeral than space or light and always in the process of being revisited.

Notes

[1] Allan, J., Avanti Architects (2008) *St Peter's College, Conservation Report*, Edinburgh: Historic Scotland, p.60.
[2] Corner, P. (posted July 2007) St Peter's Cardross on global endangered sites list, *Urban Realm*, retrieved from: http://www.urbanrealm.com/news/432/St_Peter%E2%80%99s_Cardross_on_global_endangered_sites_list.html [accessed 12 December 2011].
[3] Allan, 2008, op. cit., p.62
[4] http://www.nva.org.uk/about/ [accessed August 2012].
[5] Viollet-le-Duc, *Dictionaire Raisonne VII*, quoted in Jokilehto, J. (1999) *A History of Architectural Conservation*, London: Butterworth Heinemann, p.151.
[6] Ruskin, J., *The Seven Lamps of Architecture: the Lamp of Memory*, quoted in Jokilehto, 1999, op. cit., p.175.
[7] Miele, C. (1996) *William Morris: Building Conservation and the Arts and Crafts Cult of Authenticity, 1877–1939*, p.118.
[8] Ruskin, J., *The Seven Lamps of Architecture: the Lamp of Memory*, quoted in Jokilehto, 1999, op. cit., p.180.

[9] 'Nous comprenons la rigueur de ces principes, nous les acceptons complètement, mais seulement, lorsqu'il s'agira d'une ruine curieuse, sans destination, et sans utilité actuelle.' Viollet-le-Duc and Lassus (1843) *Project de Restauration,* de Mme de Lacombe Paris (trans. by the author).
[10] Boito, C. (1999) *Risoluzione del III Congresso degli ingegneri e architectti Roma 1883,* quoted in Jokilehto, 1999, op. cit., p.201.
[11] Latz, T. (2011) Once Upon a Time, in Van Noord, G. (ed.) *To Have and to Hold: Future of a Contested Landscape,* Edinburgh: Luath Press, p.65.
[12] Cook, D. (2011) Debate Exerts: 'Conservation and Preservation', in Van Noord, 2011, op. cit., p.53.
[13] Farquhar, A. (2011) Debate Exerts: 'Conservation and Preservation', in Van Noord, 2011, op. cit., p.52.
[14] Ibid., p.65
[15] Summerson, J. (1949) *Heavenly Mansions,* London: Butterworth Heinemann.
[16] Alexander, C. (1979) *The Timeless Way of Building,* Oxford University Press, p.479.
[17] http://www.sci-eng.mmu.ac.uk/british_industrial_ruins/ [accessed August 2012].
[18] Sennett, R. (1970) *The Uses of Disorder,* New Haven: Yale University Press, p.43.
[19] Ibid., p.94
[20] Ibid., p.143–4
[21] Ibid., p.98–9
[22] Bain, M. (2011) To Have and to Hold: Future of a Contested Landscape, in Van Noord, 2011, op. cit., p.85.
[23] Farquhar, 2011, op. cit., p.87

Bibliography

Alexander, C. (1979) *The Timeless Way of Building,* Oxford University Press.
Allan, J., Avanti Architects (2008) *St Peter's College, Conservation Report,* Edinburgh: Historic Scotland.
Corner, P. (posted July 2007) St Peter's Cardross on global endangered sites list, *Urban Realm,* retrieved from: http://www.urbanrealm.com/news/432/St_Peter%E2%80%99s_Cardross_on_global_endangered_sites_list.html [accessed 12 December 2011].
Edensor, T. (2012) *British Industrial Ruins,* retrieved from: http://www.sci-eng.mmu.ac.uk/british_industrial_ruins/ [accessed August 2012].
Jokilehto, J. (1999) *A History of Architectural Conservation,* London: Butterworth Heinemann.
Miele, C. (1996) *William Morris: Building Conservation and the Arts and Crafts Cult of Authenticity, 1877–1939.*
Sennett, R. (1970) *The Uses of Disorder,* New Haven: Yale University Press.
Summerson, J. (1949) *Heavenly Mansions,* London: Butterworth Heinemann.
Van Noord, G. (ed.) (2011) *To Have and to Hold: Future of a Contested Landscape,* Edinburgh: Luath Press.
Viollet-le-Duc and Lassus (1843) *Project de Restauration,* Paris: Mme Lacombe, 1845.

Graham CAIRNS

CONCLUSION

The objective of this book has not been to offer an exhaustive overview of the ideas of re-use, adaptation and the renovation of architecture and interiors in a socio-political context. Such a task would require more than one volume and more material than can be gleaned from the type of context from which this book originally stemmed: a two-day conference based on an open-ended interpretation of the theme of *Reinventing Architecture and Interiors*. On the contrary, our objective has been to highlight this perspective of the re-use of existing buildings as one full of potential but which, as yet, has not been fully examined.

The various chapters contained in this volume give an indication of the diversity of views this more focused perspective on the adaptive re-use of architecture is capable of opening up. Amongst the themes that have been recurrent in these particular arguments have been sustainability, the use of waste materials, and the incorporation of particular building elements and features as part of what we may call 'political image'. Also recurrent has been the theme of economic regeneration and the role the creative adaptation of existing buildings can have at local and regional levels.

A further issue that manifested itself on a number of occasions was the argument that seems to have lain at the root of all the design theories to have developed around re-use: that between Viollet-le-Duc and John Ruskin. This debate, with its origins in the nineteenth century, still appears to vex the designers, theorists and authors who today try to find their own balance between its conservation and restoration perspectives. As the first and last chapters underlined, although this debate has moved on, efforts are still being made to come up with a 'theory of renovation', an accepted definition or approach; and furthermore, we still seem some distance from finding one.

Perhaps the terrain of such arguments is best left unfurrowed or, at least, allowed to grow freely; left unrestricted by definitions that tie designers into formal straightjackets or, even worse, tie them into ideological approaches. Under such conditions, it may well be possible for all these ideas to coexist, to inform each other mutually, and to cross contaminate. The idea of redirecting existing approaches to adaptive re-use along the lines of interior design may be able to engage and merge fruitfully with a 'do nothing' policy. Similarly, the use of wastespace may be able to coalesce with a reoriented approach to commercial spaces; and glitzy kitsch may be able to live alongside poetic and political symbols in both institutional and domestic settings.

This range of issues, typologies and approaches has, throughout this book, manifested itself and overlapped numerous times. Indeed, it is an overlapping of such issues that led us to question at the outset the possibility of redefining the different professions that together produce the built environment. If we think beyond the limits of the building shell, for example, the work done by an interior designer may not only cross over with that of the architect, but its consequences may well be noticeable on the urban and regional levels: both physically, when critical mass is achieved through quantity, but also symbolically and economically as particular renovations help regenerate or economically boost given areas.

Thus, after having begun with an open-ended invitation to authors, thinkers, practitioners and teachers to participate in the IE International Conference in 2012, this book has allowed a number of its authors to focus attention on a sub-group of arguments that emerged from it. However, in doing so, we have come to see that such focus often only reveals ever more layers of diversity and interchangeability. It certainly reveals the impossibility of homogeneity in thought, concern and action. Back at our diverse point of departure, then, we offer this volume as just one more of the multitude of efforts necessary to better understand the role re-use plays in the development of our built environment and its relationship with the culture that produces it. That culture, society, milieu, call it what you will, is – as it always is – in flux.

This volume captures a moment of that flux and gives some indication of the concerns, interests and efforts of those involved in adapting the existing building infrastructure of our towns and cities. These people come from two primary fields: education and practice. Others, however, come from the fields of history and conservation. They have all been asked to consider the intricate relationship between the adaptation of buildings and the societies, economies and cultures that lead to their evolution. They have all offered different views, which sometimes overlap and sometimes contradict. They all, however, reveal some insights that, it is hoped, will be of use.

CONTRIBUTOR BIOGRAPHIES

Amanda Breytenbach

Amanda Breytenbach is the Head of the Interior Design Department at the University of Johannesburg. Although she studied architecture as a first professional degree, she has actively taken part in the development and promotion of the interior design discipline since 1999 in South Africa. Over the past 10 years, she has also gained considerable knowledge and experience in the areas of programme curriculation and development; quality assurance; policy development and implementation as well as higher-education management. Currently, her interest and research focus have shifted towards the development and implementation of postgraduate programmes in emergent design disciplines in South Africa, such as the interior design discipline.

Graeme Brooker

Graeme Brooker is a designer, academic and writer based in the UK. He is the Head Of Department of Fashion and Interiors at Middlesex University, London. He has written extensively on the interior and in particular the philosophical and theoretical implications of reworking of existing spaces and buildings. He is the author of nine books on the subject. He is the founder and now Director of I.E. (Interior Educators), the national subject association for interiors in the UK. He is a commissioning editor for the publisher Ashgate and also a member of the editorial advisory board for the magazine *Interiors: Design, Architecture, Culture* (BERG) and the *IDEA* journal in Australia and

New Zealand. His latest books are *Key Interiors Since 1900* (Laurence King, 2013), *From Organisation to Decoration* (with Sally Stone, Routledge, 2013), and *The Handbook of Interior Architecture and Design* (with Lois Weinthal, BERG, 2013).

Graham Cairns

Dr Graham Cairns, UK, has taught at universities in Spain, the UK, the US, Mexico, South Africa and the Gambia. He has worked in architectural studios in London and Hong Kong and, in the 1990s, ran a performing arts company, Hybrid Artworks, with a specialism in video installation and performance art. He is a trustee of Interior Educators UK and is chair of their research group IE(R). He has presented papers at various international conferences and has published articles on architecture, film, interior design and advertising. He has three books on film, advertising and architecture and, in addition to being editor of this volume, is the editor of a forthcoming publication on the role of design and design education in dealing with socio-political issues in a number of countries across the world. Currently, he is editor of the academic journal *Architecture_MPS (ARCHITECTURE_MEDIA_POLITICS_SOCIETY)*.

Dr Tonia Carless

Dr Tonia Carless is an architectural theorist, experimental practitioner and researcher who currently teaches at Oxford Brookes University School of Architecture. Her research covers the areas of 'everyday life' and the production of public spaces, utopias and panoramas. She has been a visiting critic and lecturer at various schools of architecture across the UK and has contributed to a wide range of international conferences. She was author of the papers 'Drawing as Spatial Discourse: Island and Home Analysis of two sets of Architectural Research Drawings' (with Dr Igea Troiani) at the University of Loughborough in 2012 and 'Producing Space: The Confrontation between Abstract Space and Everyday Life' at the Welsh School of Architecture, Cardiff University. Recent publications include: *A New Visibility: The Productive Space of Drawing*, 2011; 'Reclaiming Public Space: A Critical Architecture', 2010; and *Spaces and Flows: An International Journal of Urban and Extra Urban Studies*, 2011.

Monica Di Ruvo

Monica Di Ruvo is an interior design lecturer and head of the interior design department at the Greenside Design Center, a leading college of design in Johannesburg, South Africa. Actively involved in the South African interior-design industry since 1990, Monica also heads an interior-design consultancy, trading as DIA, which has been operating since 1997 and which offers design services to the corporate, retail and hospitality industries in sub-Saharan Africa. As a past winner of the South African Bureau of Standards Design Institute Award (1989), Monica has served on the judging panels of this awards scheme aimed at encouraging entrepreneurship in young designers. She also serves as a judge for the Design Excellence Award that recognises excellence in South African product design. In 1998, she was awarded the Technikon Witwatersrand (now University of Johannesburg) Club 1000 Alumni Young Achiever of the Year Award in recognition of 'an outstanding contribution to the arts and humanities'. She is currently completing a master's degree in interior design at the University of Johannesburg and in her spare time she practices her passion for Italian regional cooking.

Marc Furnival

Marc Furnival is an architect and urban designer with extensive practice experience. His work includes a range of projects varying in scale from small in-fill blocks in existing urban areas to the design of new cities of over 1,000 hectares. He has projects in China, UAE, Fiji, Ireland, South Africa and the UK. He is currently a regeneration consultant working with London Councils to develop housing-renewal-led regeneration. He is a member of the Urban Design Group (UDG) and the Architects Registration Board (ARB), is a regular panel judge for the annual Urban Design book prize (UK) and has recently taken up a role as an MA guest tutor at London Met and the Bartlett, UCL. He is also author of the article 'Out of Scale: Rapid Development in China' that looks at the impact of rapid development on public space, the director of the short film *Loos' and Colomina's* (2011), a social commentary film on the implications of the increasingly mediated view, and runs a blog Id of the Ingenu.

Jaime Francisco Gómez Gómez

Jaime Francisco Gómez Gómez is a professor in Design History and Product Development at the Universidad de Guadalajara, Mexico. He is an industrial-design practitioner and the founding member of Plastival's design department, where he worked as senior designer between 1997 and 2004. He ran the master's degree program in product design and development at his alma mater and has been a visiting professor at the Instituto Tecnológico de Estudios Superiores de Monterrey, Mexico. He has given invited talks on design at events organised for indigenous communities at Veracruz, Oaxaca, Michoacán and Jalisco and has participated in international conferences on design history in Helsinki, Osaka, Brussels, Chicago, London and Tarragona. He is a member of the editorial board of the journal *The Poster* and is currently completing his PhD thesis project at Universidad Politécnica de Cataluña, BarcelonaTech in the field of Materials Sciences and Engineering.

Edward Hollis

Edward Hollis studied architecture at Cambridge and Edinburgh universities. For the subsequent six years, he practised as an architect. He worked first in Sri Lanka, in the practice of Geoffrey Bawa and later in the practice of Richard Murphy. In 1999, he began lecturing in interior architecture at Napier University, Edinburgh. In 2004, he moved to Edinburgh College of Art, where he ran the undergraduate and postgraduate programmes in interior design. Now he is the Director of Research in the School of Design at Edinburgh College of Art. He is currently working on a number of research projects. He is involved with current plans to revive the ruins of Gillespie Kidd and Coia's seminary at Cardross. His first book, *The Secret Lives of Buildings*, a collection of folk tales and stories about mythical buildings, was published in 2009. He is currently writing *The Memory Palace*, a book of lost interiors, due for publication in 2013.

Kirsty Máté

Kirsty Máté is Program Director for Interior Design at the University of Tasmania School of Architecture & Design and is director of Eco Balance – Sustainable Design Consultancy Pty Ltd, Australia. Previously she was Head of Program for Interior Architecture the University of New South Wales and accrued over two decade's experience in sustainable practice. She developed and organised the first Australian sustainable design 'expo', MADE Accountable, in 1995 and has served as the Convenor of the Society for Responsible Design as well as being the Principal Research & Development Officer for the Centre for Design at RMIT, Sydney. Her research areas focus on commercial interior design and sustainability. She has published peer-reviewed papers, presented at various international conferences and has been a chief investigator for an Australian Research Council Linkage Grant. She continues to be a joint sustainability editor for the Australian industry design journal, *InDesign*, and also serves as a judge for various awards including the Banksia Building Design Award, (IDEA) Awards and the Victorian Premiers Design Award. She is currently undertaking a PhD at the University of Tasmania.

Cintia Anastasia Paez Ruiz

Cintia Anastasia Paez Ruiz is a practising interior designer who runs a furniture and design consultancy. She has also worked in the area of commercial display design and interior design. A graduate of the Universidad de Guadalajara, Mexico, she has participated in various academic conferences and workshops including the II Jornada de Motivación a la Investigación, 2005, the VI Semana Internacional del Urbanismo y Medio Ambiente, 2009, Ciudad y Región Urbana en la Perspectiva de Calentamiento Global, 2010, and the International Conference of Design History and Studies in 2010. She completed her master's degree studies at the Universidad de Guadalajara with a study into the theme of her paper in this book: 'El diseño de interiores en la obra del arquitecto mexicano Manuel Parra Mercado (1930–1997)'. This area of specialism is also represented in the presentation of a paper titled 'Constructing utopia through spolia: Manuel Parra Mercado's works', delivered at the thirteenth international conference of the Utopian Studies Society in 2012. She is currently based in Barcelona and recently participated in the academic workshop Arquitectura y Ciudad en el Cine, Barcelona, 1950–2010, at the Universidad Politécnica de Cataluña, BarcelonaTech.

Bie Plevoets

Bie Plevoets teaches at the PHL University College and Hasselt University in Belgium. Her research deals with the tension between heritage- and retail-led redevelopment in historic city centres in Europe. The aim of her work is to develop a tool for (a-priori) evaluations of retail-reuse projects that takes into acount the interests of the various stakeholders involved in such developments. Integrated into this is an examination of the concept of 'soft values' as a theory applicable to the adaptive reuse of buildings. Previously, she studied interior architecture at the PHL University College and completed a master's titled 'The Reuse of Convents: A Social and Architectural Challenge'. She also has a master's in the Conservation of Monuments and Sites from the Raymond Lemaire International Centre for Conservation in Leuven and is currently working towards a doctorate.

Layton Reid

Layton Reid is vice chair of Interior Eductors (IE), course leader of Interior Design Environment Architectures, a chartered designer and a registered and chartered architect. He runs the architectural practice Desitecture Ltd and is a consulter with Touch Media Ltd and APA Architects. He has held visiting professorships in the UK and the US, has been external examiner for some of the UK's leading design courses and has been invited to present at conferences across the world. His work has also been exhibited across Europe, the United States and Asia. His work has won various competitions and awards and he has collaborated with some of the UK's leading design firms on various project and events. He has also been involved with leading exhibitions such as the London International Architecture Biennale, the 100% Design event and the World Architecture Festival in Barcelona. His work has also appeared in a range of publications including *Urbis*, *Domus*, the *Architect's Journal* and the *Guardian*.

Nuala Rooney

Dr Nuala Rooney is a lecturer in interior design at the University of Ulster and director of the Certificate in Higher Education Interior Design course. Previously, she worked at the Hong Kong Polytechnic University during which time she won a Gold Award for a documentary film examining alternative visual research methods. This theme was part of her doctoral studies at Napier University, Edinburgh and her PhD thesis was later published by Hong Kong University Press in 2003. She has been on the executive committee of the Interior Design Association, Hong Kong, and is currently a fellow of the Royal Society of Arts and a member of both Interior Educators (UK) and the Institute of Designers in Ireland (MIDI). She has previously served as external monitor to Auckland Institute of Technology and has been external examiner at Birmingham City University, Dublin Institute of Technology and Griffith College, Dublin. She has presented at design conferences throughout the UK and Hong Kong and has written features on interior design across a wide range of design related journals.

Koenraad Van Cleempoel

Koenraad Van Cleempoel studied Art History in Louvain, Madrid and London. He obtained his PhD degree at the Warburg Institute. Since 2005, he has been engaged in establishing and directing a research unit in interior architecture at Hasselt University/ PHL University College. He has published on the relationship between art and science during the Renaissance, especially in the field of scientific instruments, and currently investigates the theory of interior architecture. He pays particular attention to the adaptive reuse of heritage sites and the phenomenological and hermeneutical method of researching spatial experience.